The Apocalyptic Imagination in Medieval Literature

University of Pennsylvania Press
MIDDLE AGES SERIES
Edited by Edward Peters
Henry Charles Lea Professor
of Medieval History
University of Pennsylvania

A complete listing of the books in this series
appears at the back of this volume

The Apocalyptic Imagination in Medieval Literature

Richard K. Emmerson and Ronald B. Herzman

University of Pennsylvania Press

Philadelphia

The production of this book was aided by support from the Bureau of Faculty Research at Western Washington University and the SUNY Research Foundation.

Library of Congress Cataloging-in-Publication Data

Emmerson, Richard Kenneth.
  The apocalyptic imagination in medieval literature / Richard K. Emmerson and Ronald B. Herzman.
      p.   cm.—(Middle Ages series)
  Includes bibliographical references and index.
  ISBN 0-8122-3122-8
  1. Literature, Medieval—History and criticism.   2. Apocalyptic literature—History and criticism.   3. End of the world in literature.   I. Herzman, Ronald B.   II. Title.   III. Series.
PN671.E47   1992
809'.93382—dc20   92-9400
                                                            CIP

Contents

Illustrations

Preface

THIS BOOK ATTEMPTS to say something intelligible, interesting, and, we hope, true about the Apocalypse, perhaps the most enigmatic book of Christian scripture; about Joachim of Fiore, one of the most elusive, controversial, and important figures in medieval apocalyptic thought; about Bonaventure's *Legenda Maior,* one of the richest texts of medieval hagiography and a key document in the Franciscan tradition; and about three of the most complex and significant vernacular poems of the High Middle Ages, the *Roman de la Rose,* the *Commedia,* and *The Canterbury Tales.* It has certainly occurred to us from time to time that such an enterprise as we have undertaken might well be construed as an act of terminal hubris, dealing as we do with so many seminal texts, any one of which could fruitfully engage the scholarly energies of a lifetime. We are especially grateful, then, to be able to share the blame with an improbably large number of friends and colleagues who have provided assistance and encouragement to us during the period of its composition.

During spring 1985, thanks to Dean Royden Davis, S.J., and Jim Slevin, chair of English, we were able to team-teach a course in medieval apocalyptic literature at Georgetown University. Many of the ideas which became part of this work were first explored with a sharp group of undergraduate and graduate students that semester. Equally important, it was while teaching this course that we first allowed ourselves to think "book," as we began to see how our ideas about the relationships between medieval literature and apocalyptic art and thought fit together. One of the students from that course, Harry Butler, returned to the project six years later when he was drafted into service to help check our translations of medieval Latin.

Our own history of collaboration began much earlier, however. It was during the 1978–79 academic year that we became friends and collaborators as Fellows-in-Residence at the University of Chicago on a grant from the National Endowment for the Humanities. There we learned an enormous amount from David Bevington and our seven colleagues—especially Pamela Sheingorn—about how scholarship can be a collaborative, indeed communal, activity. We hope we were able to put some of what we learned there into practice when we came to NEH to work in the Division of Fellowships and Seminars. During the two years that we worked side by side overseeing the Endowment's seminar programs we had the opportunity to probe and think and explore the ideas that later gave rise to the book. While in Washington we were fortunate to be able to learn from many friends in and out of NEH about the value of scholarship in the humanities.

At least in terms of the completion of this study, life after our joint stint at NEH became more complicated. Herzman returned to full-time teaching at SUNY Geneseo, while Emmerson went first to Walla Walla College, then back to NEH for another three years, and finally to Western Washington University. Our collaboration has thus alternated between a relatively close working relationship and a long-range, even "bi-coastal" one. At every stopping place in our dual pilgrimage many have given us generous help, so that the following list cannot claim to be comprehensive.

At Geneseo, Ronald Herzman gratefully acknowledges Bill Cook, friend and collaborator sine qua non; a supportive and collegial English department; Wes Kennison, a student become teacher; Carol Harter, a president who reads Dante; three undergraduate research assistants, Sherry Tucker Andersen, Eve Salisbury, and Stacey Pogoda Curtis; Marie Henry and Gail English, department secretaries who have been generous in so many ways; Lynn Kennison, who helped keep things in perspective; Ron Pretzer, who provided photographic assistance; participants in NEH School Teachers Seminars in Dante and in Chaucer, who kept their sights and their director's on what was important; and students in Dante, Chaucer, and the Bible.

Richard Emmerson wishes to recognize the crucial support provided for his research by the librarians at Walla Walla College, especially Lee Johnson; the Woodstock Library at Georgetown University; the Folger Shakespeare Library; and the Wilson Library at Western Washington University, especially Dal Symes. He wishes to express special gratitude to Suzanne Lewis and Bernard McGinn, with whom he has collaborated on other projects and from whom he has learned enormously. Finally, he wishes to thank two scholar friends at NEH who provided much encouragement in the midst of bureaucratic duties, Michael Hall and Kathleen Mitchell.

Though much revised and reworked from their original form, portions of Chapters 3, 4, and 5 have appeared previously in *Speculum, Tradi-*

tio, and *Mediaevalia Louvaniensia.* We are grateful to these journals for permission to use the material that appeared there. Sections of the work in progress were also read to thoughtful audiences at the Congress on Medieval Studies, Western Michigan University; at the Center for Medieval and Renaissance Studies, SUNY Binghamton; at the Colloquium on Medieval Eschatology sponsored by the Institut voor Middeleeuwse Studies at Katholieke Universiteit, Leuven; at Geneseo's English Department Colloquium; and at Medieval House at the University of Rochester, whose founder, Russell Peck, has done so much to energize the teaching of Chaucer and medieval literature. Since collaboration in medieval studies is by no means limited simply to the joint authorship of a manuscript but involves a whole set of friends and colleagues with whom one discusses ideas and argues interpretations, we thank several friends and scholars working in various areas of medieval studies for their support and encouragement, including David Fowler, Thomas Heffernan, Peter Klein, Robert Lerner, and Míceál Vaughan. For their bibliographic pointers and very helpful suggestions regarding the manuscript at various stages, we are grateful to several other scholars, including Bill Cook, Ewert Cousins, John Fleming, Albert Haase, OFM, Robert Hollander, William Stephany, and Penn Szittya.

Finally we wish to acknowledge the loving support of our families, without whom we could not have sustained this project and to whom this book is dedicated: Sandra Clayton-Emmerson and Ariel and Alison Emmerson; and Ellen Ferens Herzman and Suzanne and Edward Herzman.

1. The Apocalypse and Joachim of Fiore: Keys to the Medieval Apocalyptic Imagination

At that crucial moment in the *Roman de la Rose* when Faus Semblant and Astenance Contrainte set off in the guise of pilgrims to silence Male Bouche, Astenance Contrainte, disguised as a beguine, is compared to

> le cheval de l'Apochalipse
> qui senefie la gent male,
> d'ypocrisie tainte et pale;
> car cil chevaus seur soi ne porte
> nule coleur, fors pale et morte.

(lines 12,038–42)

> [the horse in the Apocalypse that signified the wicked people, pale and stained with hypocrisy; for that horse bore no color upon himself except a pale, dead one.]

The comparison is rich in significance and typical of much of the biblical language of the poem, especially of its apocalyptic imagery and allusions. As we will show in a later chapter, the net cast by apocalyptic imagery and allusions in the *Roman* is wide enough to deserve careful analysis because it provides insight into the fundamental questions that arise in any interpretation of the poem and that are still very much in dispute. Our interest in this introductory chapter is to show how Jean de Meun's treatment of this imagery is representative of the ways in which in the high Middle Ages theologians, visionaries, and poets interpreted the Apocalypse of John (the Book of Revelation) to discover their place in salvation history, understand the apocalyptic crisis of contemporary society, and condemn with prophetic zeal the abuses of a Church that has placed its own temporal power and material wealth over the spiritual.

Jean de Meun's allusion to the Fourth Horseman of the Apocalypse is typical of the literary use of the apocalyptic tradition. Astenance Contrainte is compared to the pale and deathlike horse that, according to Apocalypse 6:8, arises from Hell at the opening of the fourth seal: "Et ecce equus pallidus, et qui sedebat super eum: nomen illi mors, et infernus sequebatur eum" ["And behold a pale horse, and he that sat upon him, his name was Death, and Hell followed him"]. Jean interprets the Fourth Horseman as a symbol of the hypocrisy that characterizes the evil deceivers, and it is a symbol particularly suitable for the false beguine and her lover, Faus Semblant.[1] As is the case with many of the literary allusions to the Apocalypse, the association of the Fourth Horseman with hypocrisy is based on orthodox scriptural exegesis developed during the twelfth and thirteenth centuries.

This exegesis both expanded and redirected the previously definitive view of Augustine, who understood the last book of the Bible as a symbolic presentation of the conflict of good and evil within the contemporary Christian Church and a prophecy of the Church from the establishment of Christianity to Doomsday. Discussing the thousand-year binding of Satan in the *City of God*, Augustine describes "the whole period embraced by the Apocalypse" as lasting "from the first coming of Christ to the end of the world, which will be Christ's second coming."[2] But from Augustine's viewpoint it is difficult to interpret this concluding book of Scripture, encompassing as it does the present age of uncertainty, that time between the scriptural account of history and the prophecy of eschatology. Many of the prophecies of the Hebrew Bible had been fulfilled in the past and others will be fulfilled in the future, particularly at the end of time. Scripture thus provides a trustworthy account of the past, serves as a model for the history of the two cities, and provides an outline of the six ages of history from Creation to Doomsday.[3] Biblical prophecies carefully studied, moreover, reveal what is to come shortly before the end of the sixth age of history, and Augustine repeatedly cites them in the concluding books of the *City of God* as a guide for our understanding of last-day events.

Until those events occur, however, the prophetic symbols must be interpreted with care and not applied naively to contemporary events. Their spiritual significance should not be limited by a literal interpretation. For Augustine, the key to understanding "the many obscure statements" of the Apocalypse is the realization that John "repeats the same things in many ways, so that he appears to be speaking of different matters, though in fact he is found on examination to be treating of the same subjects in different terms."[4] The emphasis is not so much on specific, historical events but on larger spiritual patterns that reflect the continuing battle between the city of God and the city of man. Augustine is often mistakenly described as "anti-apocalytic," even though he adopts an apocalyptic view of history in his treatment of the seven ages of world history, in his expectation of the appearance of Antichrist in the future, and in his concern with many of the events associated with the end of time.[5] In fact, a careful reading of the concluding books of the *City of God* shows that Augustine was opposed not to apocalyptic lore nor to expectations of the end, but to chiliasm, *literal* interpretations of the apocalyptic numbers, and other naive applications of the esoteric symbols of the Apocalypse to contemporary personages and events. To combat such literalism, for example, he associates the millennium with the time of the Church in this world, opposes interpretations of Gog and Magog as specific nations and peoples, and urges all who wish to predict the number of years between the ascension of Christ and his return to "'Relax your fingers, and give them a rest.'"[6] Augustine is opposed not to apocalypticism as such but to any approach to the Apocalypse that would limit the book's symbolism to a specific or literal interpretation or would see the symbols as revealing a sequential or progressive movement through history.

Most twelfth-century commentators, however, did not share this Augustinian reluctance to interpret specific symbols of the prophecy. Armed with the hindsight of the seven centuries since Augustine, they approached Scripture with a new confidence in history as an effective hermeneutic key. As M.-D. Chenu has shown, "whenever a new awareness of time, of time in the collective conscience, arises, apocalypses discover a new popularity."[7] As early as the eighth century, Bede had emphasized the importance of reading the Apocalypse vision by vision. Recognizing sequential patterns within each vision, Bede specifically interpreted the opening of the seals in historical, if very general, terms:

> In the first seal, accordingly, he beholds the glory of the primitive Church, in the following three the threefold war against it, in the fifth the glory of those who triumph in this war, in the sixth the things which are to come in the time of Antichrist, and that with a brief recapitulation of former events, in the seventh the beginning of eternal rest.[8]

As is evident in the magisterial medieval biblical commentary, the *Glossa ordinaria*, this became the standard exegetical approach to the

Apocalypse by the twelfth century.[9] Theologians now perceived the fulfillment of many aspects of the book's prophecies in specific historical events
and identified the various sequences of sevens in the visions of John with
general patterns of history. For Augustine the entire period of the Church
is represented by the sixth *aetas* of world history, which is undifferentiated
and about which little is known, except that it begins with the Incarnation
of Christ, concludes with the Last Judgment, and is distinct from the seventh or Sabbath age. In contrast, the twelfth-century exegete is able to
differentiate within the sixth age the gradual and periodic progression of
Church history. Augustine's reluctance to measure the present age, furthermore, reflects his opposition to subdividing Christian history into specifically recognizable clusters (such as generations) and to identifying
actual events (with specific dates) that can be related to the prophetic future: "We are now in the sixth epoch, but that cannot be measured by the
number of generations, because it is said, 'It is not for you to know the
dates: the Father has decided those by his own authority.'"[10] On the other
hand, the historical commentator of the twelfth century recognizes in key
figures and developments of Church history the fulfillment of apocalyptic
prophecy.

For example, in his *Dialogues*, the twelfth-century exegete Anselm of
Havelberg interprets the opening of the seven seals (Apoc. 6:1–8:2) as
follows: "Nimirum septem sigilla, quae vidit Joannes, sicut ipse in sua
narrat Apocalypsi, septem sunt status Ecclesiae sibi succedentes ab adventu
Christi usquedum in novissimo omnia consummabuntur, et Deus erit omnia in omnibus" ["Truly the seven seals which John saw as he tells us in
his Revelation are seven successive states of the Church from the coming
of Christ until all things will be consummated at the End and God will be
all in all"].[11] Specifically, the white horse of the first seal represents the
purity of the apostolic church; the red horse of the second seal, the persecution of the pagan emperors; the black horse of the third seal, the teaching of the heretics. The opening of the fourth seal, which reveals the pale
horse ridden by Death, represents the hypocrisy of false Christians:

> Iste nimirum quartus est Ecclesiae status, in quo gravissimum et morti-
> ferum periculum est in falsis fratribus. Nam sicut pallidus color ex albo
> simul et nigro miscetur, nec prorsus album ostendit, sed utrumque
> falso habet; ita nimirum falsi christiani, seu falsi fratres, quorum in-
> numerabilis jam multitudo est, Christum ore publico confitentur, fac-
> tis autem negant.

[This is truly the fourth state of the Church in which the most serious and deadly danger is in false brethren. Just as a pale color is a mixture of white and black and does not show itself a straightforward white but has both colors in a false fashion, so indeed false Christians or false brethren of whom there is now an innumerable multitude, confess Christ publicly but deny him by their deeds.] [12]

Although these first four categories remain somewhat general, all are associated with particular historical periods which were understood to characterize the Church in the past. All, furthermore, were "revealed" sequentially, from the first-century origins of Christianity to the contemporary Church, which many exegetes associated with a time of hypocrisy. The fifth seal breaks this temporal pattern, though. Because according to this scheme the souls of the saints revealed by the opening of the fifth seal represent all those who merit salvation, the fifth seal symbolizes the timeless present of eternity, a transition from the immediate past to the imminent future. The sixth seal then returns to a temporal sequence, representing the imminent future. According to Anselm, the great earthquake that accompanies the opening of the sixth seal signifies the sixth *status* of the Church, "in quo nimirum terraemotus factus est magnus, quae est validissima persecutio, quae futura est temporibus Antichristi" ["in which there will truly be a great earthquake, that is, the very strong persecution which will come in the times of the Antichrist"].[13] As throughout medieval exegesis, in other words, Anselm understands the sixth period of the Church—the last *tempus* in the Augustinian sixth *aetas* of world history—to be the time of Antichrist.[14]

The exegete is now able to set history and prophecy side by side and identify the various sequences of sevens in the Apocalypse with patterns, events, orders, or key figures of Church history. The best known twelfth-century exegete following such an approach is the complex and enigmatic Joachim of Fiore, who even in his lifetime achieved prophetic status.[15] As we will show in our subsequent chapters, his Trinitarian conception of history and visionary pronouncements about the evils of the end were appropriated and radicalized by the Spiritual Franciscans and others claiming to fill a niche in the apocalyptic scheme of history and can be seen as influencing the excesses of both camps in the dispute at the University of Paris, which plays such a prominent role in the *Roman de la Rose*. Nevertheless, Joachim did not break sharply from the twelfth-century exegetical tradition. Although his exegesis ranges widely, juxtaposing disparate passages from throughout Scripture to discover patterns that simultaneously serve as a key to biblical prophecy and contemporary events, his interpretations usually assume conventional patristic hermeneutics, such as the essential concord between the Old and New Testaments and the primary Augustinian division between the two cities. In his *Enchiridion super Apocalypsim*, for example, he elaborates on the cosmic war between good and evil represented by the traditional symbolism:

> Ut enim breviter proferam proelia quae liber iste complectitur, quid esse dicimus Babylonem nisi regnum diaboli, quod est in inferno; et quid esse dicimus istam Hierusalem, nisi regnum Dei, quod est in coelo? Sunt ergo duo reges, unus austri, alius aquilonis, Deus videlicet et diabolus; duae civitates, videlicet Hierusalem et Babylon.[16]

> [For how will I reveal the battles which this book encompasses? What should we say Babylon is if not the kingdom of the devil, which is in Hell? And what shall we say is this Jerusalem, if not the kingdom of God, which is in Heaven. Therefore, there are two kings, one of the south, the other of the north, namely God and the devil; two cities, namely Jerusalem and Babylon.]

Like other visionaries and poets who were fascinated with apocalyptic thought and imagery, however, Joachim is not satisfied merely to recognize the ultimate opposition between the kingdoms of Heaven and Hell; he wishes to discover their human representatives on earth. To do so, he appropriates two series of apocalyptic symbols—one from the Apocalypse, the other from Daniel—to identify the supporters of each of these cities. The armies of Jerusalem are symbolized by the four living creatures of Apocalypse 4:6–7, who announce the four horsemen that come forth during the opening of the first four seals (Apoc. 6:1–8), whereas the opposing combatants are represented by the four beasts of Daniel 7: "Pugnant ergo singulae contra singulam, secundum quod in contrarium oppositae esse videntur. Pugnant specialiter et ad invicem, praeter id quod commune est, leo et leaena, vitulus et ursus, homo et pardus, aquila et bestia quarta"[17] ["Therefore each fights with each, according to which they seem opposed as contraries. They fight specifically and reciprocally, because of what is common to them, the lion and the lioness, the ox and the bear, the man and the leopard, and the eagle and the fourth beast"]. It is here that Joachim goes beyond traditional exegesis, which generally understands the living creatures (the winged lion, ox, man, and eagle) as symbols of the four evangelists and usually identifies Daniel's four beasts (the lioness, bear, leopard, and the unidentified ferocious fourth beast) with the ancient empires of Babylon, Persia, Greece, and Rome.[18]

As is evident in the following table, Joachim both appropriates and expands traditional exegesis, juxtaposing these animal symbols to develop a pattern of Church history that resembles Anselm's interpretation of the opening of the first four seals.[19] Joachim further develops his scheme of Church history in his *Enchiridion super Apocalypsim* by identifying the fifth *tempus* with the continuing conflict between the two Romes: "Romana ecclesia quae est spiritualis Hierusalem" ["the Roman Church which is the spiritual Jerusalem"], and the secular, imperial "Roma quae est altera Babylon" ["Rome which is another Babylon"]. This identification may reflect the contemporary conflict between the papal Church and the Holy Roman Empire, which Joachim usually identified as "nova Babylon." It also brings Church history "ad dies nostros."[20] Like Anselm, he makes the fifth *tempus* a transition between past and future.

The scheme of Joachim of Fiore thus echoes the scheme of Anselm of Havelberg, although it is important to recognize that Joachim's interpre-

Periods of Church History According to Joachim of Fiore and Anselm of Havelberg.

Periods of Church History (tempora)	*First* tempus	*Second* tempus	*Third* tempus	*Fourth* tempus
Joachim's Interpretation				
Creatures vs. Beasts	lion vs. lioness	ox vs. bear	man vs. leopard	eagle vs. terrible beast
Jerusalem vs. Babylon	Apostles vs. Jews	Martyrs vs. Empire	Doctors vs. Arians	Virgins vs. Saracens
Anselm's Interpretation				
Four Horses	white horse	red horse	black horse	pale horse
Status Ecclesiae	purity: Apostles	persecution: Pagans	heresy: Heretics	hypocrisy: False Christians

tation goes further in identifying the representatives of the periods with specific historical groups. For example, whereas Anselm associates the third and fourth horses with heresy and hypocrisy in general, Joachim identifies the third and fourth beasts with specific historical groups, the Arians and Saracens; whereas Anselm views the "ahistorical" present "sub specie aeternitatis"—from the eternal perspective of the souls under the altar—Joachim focuses on the contemporary conflict between Church and Empire. Joachim's interpretation of Apocalypse 12 exemplifies this tendency toward specific historical identifications. This chapter, which is both structurally and thematically central to the Apocalypse, concentrates on the cosmic battle between the forces of good and evil throughout time as symbolized, on the one hand, by the Woman clothed by the sun and, on the other hand, by the Dragon whose tail sweeps a third of the stars from heaven:

> Et signum magnum apparuit in caelo; mulier amicta sole, et luna sub pedibus eius, et in capite eius corona stellarum duodecim. Et in utero habens clamabat parturiens et cruciabatur ut pariat. Et visum est aliud signum in caelo: et ecce draco magnus rufus habens capita septem et cornua decem, et in capitibus eius diademata septem; et cauda eius trahebat tertiam partem stellarum caeli et misit eas in terram; et draco stetit ante mulierem, quae erat paritura, ut, cum peperisset, filium eius devoraret. (Apoc. 12:1–4)

> [And a great sign appeared in heaven: A woman clothed with the sun, and the moon under her feet, and on her head a crown of twelve stars: And being with child, she cried travailing in birth, and was in pain to be delivered. And there was seen another sign in heaven: and behold a great red dragon, having seven heads, and ten horns: and on his heads seven diadems: and his tail drew the third part of the stars of heaven, and cast them to the earth: and the dragon stood before the woman who was ready to be delivered; that, when she should be delivered, he might devour her son.]

In traditional Christian iconography the Woman represents the Church throughout time, whereas the Dragon, who is the "serpens antiquus, qui vocatur Diabolus et Satanas" (Apoc. 12:9) ["old serpent, who is called the devil and Satan"], is a composite image of evil battling the righteous from the primordial fall of the rebel angels to its destruction in the fiery pit at the end of time (Apoc. 20:9).[21] While accepting this traditional framework, Joachim seeks in his *Expositio in Apocalypsim* to discover the particular manifestations of this composite evil in history. His attention is therefore focused on yet another of the many series of apocalyptic sevens, the seven heads of the dragon. Although Joachim's identifications of the seven heads vary depending on the context of his exegesis, they are always individual and usually specific historical persecutors of the Church. The first head of the dragon, for example, represents Herod; the second, Nero; the third, the persecuting Arian emperor Constantius (337–61); and the fourth, either the Persian King Chosroes II (Khusru Parviz, 589–628) or Mohammed. The fifth head is sometimes identified as a king of Babylon—a symbol that, as we have seen above, Joachim often applied to the empire. It may also be identified more specifically as the Holy Roman Emperor, Henry IV (1056–1106).[22] The sixth head represents Saladin, the great Saracen chieftain who died in 1193. Therefore it signifies a contemporary, a figure from Joachim's own time, who was embroiled in the Third Crusade.[23] This contemporary precedes the persecutor represented by the Dragon's seventh head, Antichrist.

These interpretations are made visually explicit in the figure of the seven-headed Dragon (see Figure 1), one of the best-known of Joachim's *Figurae*.[24] Although this *figura* is heavily inscribed with lengthy notes providing elaborate explanations for the Dragon and Antichrist, its visual and immediate message is direct. Above each of the Dragon's first six heads, it explicitly identifies the historical persecutors of the Church: "Herodes. Nero. Constantius. Mahomet. Mesemthus. Salahadinus." Interestingly, despite the fact that Apocalypse 12:3 states that each head of the dragon is crowned, the *figura* crowns only the sixth head of the Dragon, thus implying that the persecutor represented by the sixth head—Saladin—is reigning now and, furthermore, that the Church is in its sixth *tempus*. The gloss inscribed between the necks leading to the fifth and the sixth heads supports this sense of contemporary crisis: "Sexta persecutio inchoata est. VII. sequetur" ["The Sixth Persecution has Begun. The Seventh will Follow"].[25] Joachim evidently understands the coming persecution of Antichrist to be imminent, for the seventh head—which is dramatically larger than the first six—is identified as the Antichrist of traditional apocalyptic expectation: "Hic est septimus rex qui proprie dicitur Antichristus" ["This is the Seventh King, who is properly called Antichrist"].[26]

His scheme, it must be emphasized, is as much scriptural as it is personal, for it is clearly based on his conflation of the seven-headed Dragon

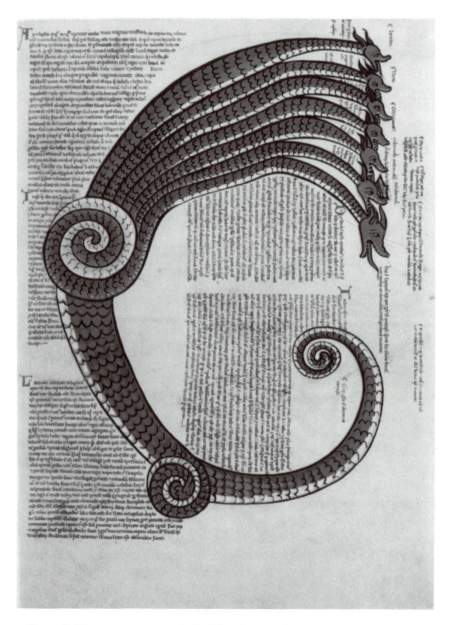

Figure 1. "Draco magnus et rufus" ["The Great Red Dragon"]. *Liber Figurarum*, Corpus Christi College, Oxford, MS 255A, *figura* XIV. (Reproduced by permission of the Librarian, Corpus Christi College, Oxford.)

of Apocalypse 12 with the seven-headed Beast of Apocalypse 17. Thus the gloss on the upper right of the *figura* quotes the words of the angel guide who in Apocalypse 17 explains for the visionary John the chronological sequence of the seven heads: "Reges sunt septem, quinque ceciderunt et unus est et unus nondum venit: et cum venerit, oportet illum breve tempus manere" (Apoc. 17:9–10) ["and they are seven kings: Five are fallen, one is, and the other is not yet come: and when he is come, he must remain a short time"]. In his notes to the *figura*, Joachim comments on the fact that this imminent seventh persecutor will reign for only a short time, conflating Christ's words in Matthew 24:22 with the apocalyptic numbers that establish the traditional length of Antichrist's rule, forty-two months: "Breviabit autem Dominus dies illos propter electos suos ut non excedant numerum mensium XL duorum" ["'The Lord will shorten those days for the sake of his elect,' so that they will not exceed forty-two months"].[27] It is important to note, however, that although Antichrist is the seventh persecutor, he is expected during the sixth period of the Church. The sixth and seventh heads, Joachim notes, are joined together to represent the double persecution of the Church in the sixth period: "Igitur duo extrema capita iuncta sunt simul: quia due istarum tribulationum septimane extreme sub uno sexto tempore consummande sunt" ["Therefore, these two last heads are joined together, because both these tribulations of the final week are destined to be fulfilled under the one sixth time"].[28] Joachim thus accommodates the scheme that outlines seven persecutors of the Church with the traditional outline of the six periods of Church history evident in the exegesis of Anselm of Havelberg and others.

If the sixth head thus represents a tyrannical military persecutor, the seventh represents a deceitful spiritual leader, the traditional Antichrist who, as in the scheme of Anselm of Havelberg, is expected to close the sixth *tempus* of Church history. As has often been noted, Joachim also expects a "final" Antichrist symbolized by the tail of the Dragon and representing the forces of Gog and Magog (Apoc. 20:7) to appear as the last gasp of evil shortly before Christ returns in Judgment: "Inter omnes ergo Antichristos qui apparebunt in mundo duo sunt ceteris deteriores: ille scilicet qui designatus est in capite VII. et ille qui designatus est in cauda" ["Among all the Antichrists who will appear in the world two are worse than the others: the one who is denoted by the seventh head and the one denoted by the tail"].[29]

Robert Lerner and others have argued that the separation of these two Antichrists is one of Joachim's most original contributions to medieval apocalypticism.[30] On the one hand, Augustine—once again spokesman for the traditional view—understood the thousand-year binding of the Dragon (Apoc. 20:2–3) symbolically and, more importantly, ahistorically. To him it represented the age of the Church—that is, the sixth *aetas* of world history—without any further differentiation into periods, during which time the power of Satan would be moderated by the power of the Gospel. The end of the millennium would result in a short period of demonic power, the time of Antichrist's false doctrine and the persecution of the faithful by the Antichristian forces of Gog and Magog. Antichrist and the forces of Gog and Magog would become contemporary allies who as religious and military foes assault the Church immediately before Christ's return in judgment.[31] Joachim, on the other hand, places the millennium at the conclusion of Church history. It becomes the Sabbath *aetas* that follows the sixth *tempus* of the Church, the Sabbath age represented by the opening of the seventh seal following the sixth. Here Joachim, bordering on chiliasm, radically reshapes the contours of medieval apocalypticism.[32]

Although Joachim's distinguishing between these two Antichrists is radically original, the *figura*'s explanation of this distinction nevertheless remains highly traditional. Joachim, in fact, draws on a feature that characterizes the apocalyptic imagination from the fathers on: the portrayal of Antichrist's life and deeds as a parodic inversion of Christ's. This understanding of Antichrist's life assumes that whatever the Bible and salvation history reveal about Christ's character, purposes, and actions is paralleled by a false, inverted, and debased version that in fact reflects Satan's character, purposes, and actions. It is based on the fundamental belief that ever since the failure of his vainglorious challenge in Heaven, Satan has attempted deceitfully to "imitate" God on earth.

As Joachim's *figura* notes, "Nichil enim tam affectat diabolus quam ut per omnia et in omnibus videatur similis Altissimo" ["The devil strives for nothing more than to appear like the Most High in every way possible"].[33] Thus, given the fact that Christ first came to the world as man and has promised to return again as judge, it is not surprising that in the future Satan will first appear as a man—Antichrist—and then again just before Doomsday:

> Ut ergo Christus Iesus venit in signis veris et tamen palliatus et occultus ob similitudinem carnis peccati, ita ut vix a paucis agnosceretur quod ipse esset Christus: ita rex iste septimus venturus est in signis

mendacibus et tamen occultus et palliatus ob similitudinem spiritualis iustitie, adeo ut vix pauci sint qui possint illum agnoscere quod ipse sit Antichristus: propter quod si fieri possit in errorem etiam ducentur electi. Et quia idem Christus Iesus venturus est manifestus in gloria maiestatis, stipatus militia celesti angelorum et hominum, etiam ipse Sathanas apparebit manifestus cum exercitibus hominum impiorum: ut quasi ex terrore militie sue illum se esse mentiatur qui venturus est iudicare vivos et mortuos et seculum per ignem.

[Just as Jesus Christ came with true signs, but cloaked and hidden because of the likeness of sinful human nature so that he was hardly recognized as the Christ by even a few, so too the seventh king will come with false signs and will be hidden and cloaked because of his appearance of spiritual justice, so that only a few will be able to recognize that he is the Antichrist. For this reason even the elect will be led into error if possible. And because the same Christ Jesus will come openly in the glory of his majesty surrounded with a heavenly army of angels and men, so too Satan will appear openly with armies of wicked men, so that on the basis of dread of his forces he may pretend to be him who will come to judge the living and the dead and the world by fire.] [34]

Through this comparison, Joachim implies that Antichrist is the devil incarnate, the demonic inversion of Jesus, God incarnate. Following the tradition developed in Abbot Adso's *Libellus de Antichristo*—the highly influential tenth-century *vita* that consolidated traditional Antichrist lore into a coherent biography of the parodic Christ—Joachim expects Antichrist's life to be a blasphemous parody of the life of Christ. [35]

As the sixth *aetas* of world history began when the divine became incarnate in the life of Jesus Christ, it will end when the demonic becomes "incarnate" in the life of Antichrist. As Joachim notes, the sixth age can be defined as the time "ab adventu primo Domini usque ad ruinam Antichristi." [36] ["from the first advent of the Lord all the way to the ruin of Antichrist"]. Joachim's explanation of the distinctions between the Dragon's seventh head and tail exemplifies his recognition of such parallelism in the history of the Church, at the beginning and end of the sixth age. He supports his explanation by citing two of Christ's most important forerunners, John the Baptist and Elijah: "Ille qui designatus est in capite septimo veniet occultus, sicut Johannes Baptista qui nesciebatur esse Helyas. Ille qui designatus est in cauda veniet manifestus: sicut venturus est manifeste Helyas" ["He who is denoted by the seventh head will come in hidden fashion like John the Baptist, who was not known to be Elijah. He who is denoted by the tail will come in open fashion like Elijah, who will come openly"].[37]

Linking the New Testament John the Baptist with the first Antichrist ("occultus"), and the Old Testament Elijah with the second Antichrist ("manifestus") may seem to be a curious confusion of chronology in its reversal of scriptural order. Yet again, Joachim is here both original and traditional. His originality is evident in his application of Trinitarian theology to his understanding of history, specifically his notion that the double procession of the Holy Spirit from the Father and the Son is reflected in historical patterns. In this scheme, the Holy Spirit and Elijah are closely related. Their relationship is tellingly pictured in the *figura* representing the Trinitarian Circles based on the Tetragrammaton, in which the gloss identifying the Holy Spirit is always accompanied by "Elias."[38]

But the expectation that the Old Testament prophet Elijah, who was taken into Heaven in the fiery chariot (2 Kings 2:11), would return before Doomsday is scriptural: "Ecce ego mittam vobis Eliam prophetam, antequam veniat dies Domini magnus et horribilis" (Mal. 4:5) ["Behold I will send you Elias the prophet, before the coming of the great and dreadful day of the Lord"]. The comparison between John the Baptist and Elijah, furthermore, was first made by Jesus (Matt. 17: 11–13).[39] As John the Baptist preceded Christ's first advent, so Elijah would return in the last days to precede Christ's second advent. Moreover, early in patristic commentary Elijah was identified as one of the Two Witnesses who in the last days will prophesy for 1,260 days and will summon miraculous powers to oppose the enemies of God: "Et si quis voluerit eos nocere, ignis exiet de ore eorum et devorabit inimicos eorum" (Apoc. 11:5) ["And if any man will hurt them, fire shall come out of their mouths, and shall devour their enemies"]. Along with the other witness—in medieval exegesis usually identified as Enoch, who was taken up to heaven by God (Gen. 5:24)— Elijah will be killed by the Beast that rises from the abyss and will then be resurrected (Apoc. 11:7–11). Not surprisingly, to most medieval exegetes this Beast represents Antichrist.[40] These events will transpire just before the seventh angel blows his trumpet, ushering in Christ's second advent and Doomsday (Apoc. 11:15). The apocalyptic imagination revels in such symmetry: just as John the Baptist was murdered by Herod, the persecutor symbolized by the first head of the Dragon, so the Elijah *redivivus* will be murdered by Antichrist, the persecutor symbolized by the seventh head of the Dragon. Joachim simply extends the traditional symmetry, so that Christ's two forerunners parallel the two final Antichrists represented by the Dragon's seventh head and tail.

Here Joachim accepts the patristic notion that just as it is possible and valuable to identify numerous representatives of God and forerunners of Christ throughout salvation history, so it is possible and valuable to identify numerous actual and historical representatives of Satan and forerunners or types of the great Antichrist.[41] In drawing the traditional parallels between Christ and Antichrist, furthermore, the *figura* clearly establishes that the power of Antichrist will derive from his claim to both political and religious leadership: "Ut autem multi reges pii, pontifices vel prophete precesserunt unum Christum, qui fuit rex et pontifex et propheta: ita multi reges impii et pseudoprophete et Antichristi precedunt unum Antichristum qui se esse simulabit regem et pontificem et prophetam" ["Just as many holy kings, priests, and prophets went before the one Christ who was King, priest, and prophet, so likewise many unholy kings, false prophets, and antichrists will go before the one Antichrist who will pretend that he is a king, a priest, and a prophet"].[42] Whether Antichrist is portrayed as a false prophet who seduces kings and thereby gains political support or as a false messianic leader who, victorious in battle, becomes a cruel tyrant, the apocalyptic tradition expects that he will wield both spiritual and political power.[43] Of the several scriptural passages that symbolize this dual manifestation of evil in the last days, Apocalypse 13 is the most important. This chapter not only describes the seven-headed Beast that rises from the sea and receives its power from the Dragon, but also a two-horned false-prophet Beast that rises from the earth:

> Et vidi aliam bestiam ascendentem de terra, et habebat cornua duo similia agni et loquebatur sicut draco. Et postestatem prioris bestiae omnem faciebat in conspectu eius; et fecit terram et habitantes in ea, adorare bestiam primam, cuius curata est plaga mortis. (Apoc. 13 : 11−12)

> [And I saw another beast coming up out of the earth, and he had two horns, like a lamb, and he spoke as a dragon. And he executed all the

power of the former beast in his sight; and he caused the earth, and them that dwell therein, to adore the first beast, whose wound to death was healed.]

Although resembling a lamb, this false-prophet Beast speaks like the Dragon and leads all peoples to adore the sea Beast. As Lerner has noted, "For Joachim these two monsters were complementary manifestations of the one great Antichrist, who was simultaneously king and priest, or, implicitly, the worst imaginable Western emperor and the worst imaginable pope."[44]

The imagery of Apocalypse 13 is one of the clearest examples of how apocalyptic symbolism presents the various manifestations of evil as essentially demonic inversions of good. The seven-headed Dragon, the seven-headed Beast from the sea, and the two-horned false-prophet Beast from the earth are a trinity of evil, a monstrous parody of the Godhead.[45] Although all three creatures are cruel persecutors and deceitful blasphemers, the false-prophet Beast is particularly noted for his supernatural marvels, which form the essence of his deceit and provide the basis of his vicious power:

Et fecit signa magna, ut etiam ignem faceret de caelo descendere in terram in conspectu hominum. Et seduxit habitantes in terra propter signa, quae data sunt illi facere in conspectu bestiae, dicens habitantibus in terra ut faciant imaginem bestiae, quae habet plagam gladii et vixit. (Apoc. 13:13–14)

[And he did great signs, so that he made also fire to come down from heaven unto the earth in the sight of men. And he seduced them that dwell on the earth, for the signs, which were given him to do in the sight of the beast, saying to them that dwell on the earth, that they should make the image of the beast, which had the wound by the sword, and lived.]

Specifically, the apocalyptic imagination feared that the Beast's ability to call fire down from the heavens meant that Antichrist and his disciples will fabricate a pseudo-Pentecost, attempting to manipulate the Holy Spirit in their outrageous claims to be Christ and his disciples. According to Haimo of Auxerre and other medieval exegetes, the false prophet's fire is a *spiritus malignus* that outwardly resembles the *spiritus sanctus* of Pentecost, so that Antichrist's disciples may even speak in tongues.[46]

This interpretation is visually emphasized in the lavishly illuminated Bible Moralisée now in the British Library (MS Harley 1527). It illustrates Apocalypse 13:13 by juxtaposing two roundels that make the significance of these fiery signs explicit (see Figure 2). The first roundel illustrates the literal events described in the text by showing fire falling from a mask in heaven onto a group of men who worship the seven-headed Beast. The two-horned Beast stands in the foreground, looking up to the descending fire. The accompanying roundel then pictures Pentecost, displaying the traditional iconography of this key event in Church history. Flames of fire are dispersed over the heads of the apostles from the mouth of a dove that appears above in the cloudy firmament. The gloss inscribed to the left of the roundel explains that by the Beast from the earth "significantur discipuli antichristi" ["the disciples of Antichrist are signified"] who will be able to call fire down from heaven "sicut descendit super apostolos in die pentecostes"[47] ["as it descended on the apostles on the day of Pentecost"]. This pseudo-Pentecost, another example of Antichrist's ability to work wonders and of his parodic imitation of events connected with Christ, became an important feature of the apocalyptic imagination in the later Middle Ages.

In his presumptuous attempt to manipulate the Holy Spirit and to work other deceitful marvels, Antichrist was often compared to Simon Magus, the heresiarch of the early Church who attempted to purchase the Holy Spirit, soliciting a terrible curse from Simon Peter:

> Cum vidisset autem Simon quia per impositionem manus apostolorum daretur Spiritus sanctus, obtulit eis pecuniam dicens: Date et mihi hanc potestatem, ut cuicumque imposuero manus accipiat Spiritum sanctum. Petrus autem dixit ad eum: Pecunia tua tecum sit in perditionem, quoniam donum Dei existimasti pecunia possideri. (Acts 8:18–20)

> [And when Simon saw, that by the imposition of the hands of the apostles, the Holy Ghost was given, he offered them money, Saying: Give me also this power, that on whomsoever I shall lay my hands, he may receive the Holy Ghost. But Peter said to him: Keep thy money to thyself, to perish with thee, because thou hast thought that the gift of God may be purchased with money.]

This rather cryptic scriptural account became the basis for a lengthy legend recounting the deceitful life of Simon Magus.[48] Because his life was so interwoven with the lives of Paul and especially Peter, Simon Magus, the patriarch of simony, became a common figure in apocalyptic condemnations of Church abuses. The prominence of Simon Magus during the high Middle Ages is no doubt due to both ecclesiastic and hagiographic reasons. On the one hand, simony was pervasive, so that reformers repeatedly addressed this abuse; on the other hand, the story of Simon Magus often was included in the very popular *vita* of Simon Peter, for example, as recounted by Jacobus de Voragine in the *Legenda aurea*. The presence of Simon Magus was therefore felt in a wide range of literature. One lyric from the *Carmina burana*, which speaks as the prophetic "vox clamantis in deserto" ["voice of one crying in the wilderness"] typifies condemnations of Simon's omnipresence in the Church:

Sunt latrones, non latores,
legis dei destructores,
Simon sedet inter eos,
multos facit esse reos.

Simon prefert malos bonis,
Simon totus est in donis,
Simon regnat apud austrum,
Simon frangit omne claustrum.

Simon aufert, Simon donat,
hunc expellit, hunc coronat,
hunc circumdat gravi peste,
illum nuptiali veste.

Si non datur, Simon stridet,
sed, si datur, Simon ridet,
iam se Simon non abscondit,
res permiscet et confundit.

Illi donat diadema,
qui nunc erat anathema:
iste Simon confundatur,
cui tantum posse datur.

[Thus despoiling, not dispensing,
God they flout, His wrath incensing;
Simon Magus 'mongst them thrives,
Many ills that rogue contrives.
Bad men he prefers to good,
Loot is all his livelihood;
Through the South his power extends,
Every convent holds his friends.
Simon steals and Simon bribes,
Some promotes and some proscribes,
Schemes to cause a foe's miscarriage,
Plots a favorite's lucky marriage.
Simon howls unless he wins,
Grease his palm and Simon grins;
Trust him not to travel far
When there's aught to mix or mar.
See, the crown he places now
On a thrice accursed brow.
God confound that Simon Magus
Who is given such power to plague us.][49]

According to the legend, Simon Magus was allied with Nero in opposition to Peter and Paul, claimed to be Christ, attempted to manipulate
the Holy Spirit, and tried to prove himself divine by working unnatural
marvels and ultimately by rising to Heaven. It is thus not surprising that
even in the earliest Christian literature and throughout the Middle Ages,
Simon Magus is compared to Antichrist.[50] In his *Collationes in Hexaemeron*
Bonaventure—who, as we shall see in the following chapter, was himself
influenced by Joachim's apocalyptic exegesis—refers to several of the features that associate Simon Magus and Antichrist. The context of his comparison is provided by his discussion of the various ways in which Christ
and Antichrist reflect what Bonaventure calls the twelve principal mysteries contained in Scripture, an exegesis which reflects the traditional parallelism drawn between the true and false Christ. Specifically, in his
discussion of the eleventh mystery, which deals with the gifts of the Holy
Spirit, the Seraphic Doctor states that Antichrist is symbolized by Simon
the Magician:

In mysterio undecimo, scilicet diffusionis charismatum, signatur per
Simonem magum, qui voluit emere Spiritum sanctum et in altum

ascendit et postea cecidit, qui daemones invocabit. Erit enim menda-
cissimus, et veniat in signis et prodigiis mendacibus.

[In the eleventh mystery, the diffusion of charismatic gifts, he is symbolized by Simon the Magician, who wanted to buy the Holy Spirit,
who rose up to great heights and then fell, who called upon evil spirits. For he will be the worst liar: he will come with deceitful signs and
prodigies.][51]

As we shall see in later chapters, Bonaventure is here simply developing a
long and established medieval tradition, which highlighted Simon Magus
as being one of the arch-opponents of Christ and his Church and the most
pernicious forerunner of Antichrist. As Chaucer's Parson states, the sin of
Simon Magus is "the gretteste synne that may be, after the synne of Lucifer and Antecrist."[52]

Throughout the Middle Ages, for the medieval poet no less than the
exegete, the thought of the one deceiver often suggested the deeds of
the other. Thus, in explaining the deceit of the Antichrist symbolized by
the seventh head of the Dragon, Joachim's *figura* cites the example of
Simon Magus:

In tempore quoque illo consurget septimum caput draconis: rex scilicet ille qui dicitur Antichristus et multitudo pseudo-prophetarum
cum eo. Surget autem, ut putamus, ab Occidente et veniet in adiuto-
rium illius regis qui erit caput paganorum et faciet signa magna coram
ipso et exercitu eius sicut Simon magus fecit in conspectu Neronis: et
erit tribulatio magna qualis non fuit ab initio: ita ut si fieri possit in
errorem inducantur etiam electi.

[In that time also the seventh head of the dragon will arise, namely,
that king who is called Antichrist, and a multitude of false prophets
with him. We think that he will arise from the West and will come to
the aid of that king who will be the head of the pagans. He will
perform great signs before him and his army, just as Simon Magus
did in the sight of Nero. "There will be great tribulation, such as has
not been from the beginning, in order to deceive, if possible, even the
elect."][53]

The comparison is dependent upon Antichrist's ability to perform great
marvels and rests on the premise that just as the false spiritual leader

Simon Magus aided Nero's persecution of the apostles by performing marvels that he claimed were accomplished through the power of the Holy Spirit, so Antichrist will aid the *caput paganorum* in his assault on the Church.[54] The persecutors of the early Church and of the last days, furthermore, are linked by a shared symbolism, the two beasts of Apocalypse 13. To Joachim, the Beast that rises from the sea is a great king like Nero, "quasi imperator totius orbis" ["like the emperor of the whole world"], whereas the false-prophet Beast is a great prelate like Simon Magus, "quasi vniuersalis pontifex in toto orbe terrarum" ["like the universal priest of the whole world"], and therefore like Antichrist.[55]

It is surely true that Joachim adds a new dimension to medieval expectations of Antichrist by distinguishing between the Antichrist who closes the sixth period of Church history (the "Antichristus occultus" ["hidden Antichrist"], symbolized by the seventh head of the Dragon) and the Antichrist who closes the seventh—Sabbath—period (the "Antichristus manifestus" ["open Antichrist"], or Gog, symbolized by the tail of the Dragon). Nevertheless, as we have seen, in describing Antichrist's essential character, defining his role in Satan's attempt to pervert divine providence, and comparing him with his evil forerunners and contrasting him with his righteous counterparts in Church history, Joachim appropriates much that is traditional in medieval apocalypticism. What is truly original is his ability to focus this tradition on a single image, in this case the *figura* of the seven-headed Dragon. He ranges easily and widely throughout the tradition, calling on exegetical interpretations and apocryphal lore both to visualize and explain the meaning of this demonic image.

Although we have investigated at some length the extensive gloss that frames the margins of this *figura* and fills the significantly ample space between the seven heads and the tail of the Dragon, the concentrated power of Joachim's vision of evil and understanding of Antichrist derives from his ability to funnel these varying expectations into a single visual image. In so doing, Joachim creatively shapes the inherited symbolism, often for startlingly new effect. He is thus both traditional and original, very much like the prophetic author of the Apocalypse with whom he has been not unfavorably compared.[56] Joachim also anticipates the ways in which the most imaginative thinkers and poets of the high Middle Ages manipulate apocalyptic imagery. We refer here of course to those who are the subjects of our subsequent chapters: to Bonaventure and to Jean de Meun, to Dante and to Chaucer, as well as to a host of poets mentioned in passing whose apocalypticism also deserves further study, poets as diverse as Jacopone da Todi and Petrarch.

Joachim's exegesis is based on his sophisticated application of the notion of concords between the Old and New Testaments and his equally sophisticated Trinitarian philosophy of history.[57] It is not clear how well his method was understood by later theologians and polemicists, who generally remember Joachim more as a prophet of Antichrist than as a systematic exegete and theologian and who judge Joachim more in terms of the excesses of his followers than of a careful perusal of his own work.[58] A study of the hermeneutic principles implied in his *figura* of the seven-headed Dragon does, however, highlight certain characteristics that typify what we are calling the apocalyptic imagination and which are evident in the thirteenth- and fourteenth-century works that are the subjects of later chapters of this study. All of these works draw on apocalyptic imagery to make sense of the present. We are not suggesting that these later works necessarily were influenced by Joachim directly or even indirectly, although clearly Joachimist thought is evident in Bonaventure's exegesis, the mendicant debates reflected in the *Roman de la Rose*, and in Dante's *Paradiso*.[59] Nevertheless, this is emphatically not a study of a Joachimist literary tradition. For one thing, even if Joachimist influence were present—even in someone like Chaucer, who seems conspicuously non-Joachimist—what these later authors share with Joachim is an imaginative manipulation of the tradition, rather than interpretations of specific images or a philosophy of history. Instead, we have concentrated on Joachim's *figura* of the seven-headed Dragon here in order to highlight certain common principles that inform the manipulation of apocalyptic imagery in religious and poetic narratives written after the twelfth century.

Taking our cue from Augustine's explanation of the *Rules* of Tyconius, we will understand these principles to be "keys" by which "the obscurities of the Divine Scriptures might be opened," specifically the obscurities of the enigmatic and patterned symbolism that informs the apocalyptic imagination.[60] Like Joachim's exegesis, these keys are cast from the traditional mold by which apocalyptic imagery was understood since the fathers, while being shaped by more recent developments that place apocalyptic symbolism in a historical context and manipulate it to understand, reform, and even prophetically denounce the present.

The most important key that unlocks the mystery of apocalyptic symbolism is exemplified by the two ways in which Joachim's *figura* visually links the seven heads of the Dragon. First, they are joined by means of their respective necks through the body of the Dragon, which represents the generalized body of evil that exists through all time and is universal. As the "serpens antiquus, qui vocatur Diabolus et Satanas, qui seducit universum orbem" (Apoc. 12:9) ["old serpent, who is called the devil and Satan, who seduceth the whole world"], it is the source of their demonic power. By so linking the heads, Joachim's *figura* draws on a tradition that can be traced back to Tyconius in the fourth century and that characterizes patristic and monastic exegesis, which interprets even the details of apocalyptic symbolism in universal, timeless, allegorical terms. "The Battle Against the Antichrist," one of the lauds of the great Franciscan poet-prophet Jacopone da Todi, exemplifies the continuity of the allegorical reading of apocalyptic imagery. Writing about a century after Joachim's *Figurae*, Jacopone describes the present as suffering from the release of the Dragon after its thousand-year imprisonment and as witnessing the cosmic signs expected to precede the final attack of Antichrist:

> The moon is black, the sun darkened, stars fall out of the heavens,
> The ancient serpent has broken out of captivity,
> And the world follows in his train.[61]

Rather than detecting these signs in actual natural phenomena, however, Jacopone spiritualizes them, explaining that the sun is Christ, who seems absent from the world; the moon is the Church of Christ, whose former "radiance is blotted black"; and "The stars that have fallen out of heaven / Are the religious orders, fallen on evil days."

Joachim's *figura* pictures the heads of the Dragon as being linked in a second way as well, however. They are connected by virtue of being juxtaposed, one head biting the next, each individual leading to the next, which suggests one historical persecutor following another. Here the *figura* reflects the growing historical concerns of the twelfth century, which is interested in the sequential manifestation of specific apocalyptic symbolism in time. What is new, of course, is this equation of symbolic creatures and numbers with historical individuals and events, but the new historicizing approach to apocalyptic symbolism did not replace the earlier allegorizing approach. As is evident in the *Glossa ordinaria* and in late medieval illuminated manuscripts, the two approaches were equally popular, each providing the basis for particular insights into the biblical text.[62] After the twelfth century the medieval apocalyptic imagination generally balances the awareness of the universal nature of the conflict between good and evil with a recognition of its individual representatives in church history. The first interpretive key, therefore, provides a complex understanding of eschatology and apocalyptic symbolism in terms that link the cosmic, universal, and allegorical, on the one hand, to the personal, individual, and historical on the other hand.

A second interpretive key evident in Joachim's *figura* that informs many later literary and artistic manifestations of the apocalyptic imagination is the recognition that in this cosmic conflict the agents of evil—whether supernatural beings such as Satan and his demonic cohorts, or human tyrants and heretics such as Nero and Simon Magus—act in ways that make them essentially inversions of the agents of good. The historical citizens of the City of God and the City of Man, therefore, parallel each other in time; the apocalyptic tradition understands the latter to be an inversion of the former, an imitation in outward form for opposing inner reasons. As we have seen, the true and false manipulation of the Spirit as represented symbolically by fire exemplifies this inverted parallelism especially well. As Christ promised (Acts 1:5) and sent the Holy Spirit (Acts 2:1–4) in the flames of Pentecost, Satan supported Simon Magus in his attempt to purchase the Holy Spirit and his claims to manipulate its gifts. As Enoch and Elijah, Christ's representatives in the last days, will come to convert the Jews and those deceived by Antichrist, miraculously spewing fire on their enemies, Antichrist—Satan's most vicious representative on earth—will call fire down from Heaven, staging a pseudo-Pentecost. This principle is evident as well throughout the Apocalypse, especially in its pairing of symbols. The glorious vision of the victorious Lamb on Mount Zion whose redeemed followers have divine names written on their foreheads (Apoc. 14:1) follows immediately after the brutal scenes picturing the two-horned lamblike Beast whose reprobate followers are branded on their foreheads with the mark of the Beast (Apoc. 13:17–18). Similarly, the radiant New Jerusalem—whose vision concludes the Apocalypse—comes down from Heaven (Apoc. 21:10), becoming the city for redeemed citizens who will live eternal lives. It replaces the vicious Babylon, ultimately destroyed (Apoc. 18:2), whose citizens are damned to Hell.

The pure Woman clothed in the sun (Apoc. 12:1) and her filthy inversion, the Whore of Babylon (Apoc. 17:5), are another such pair particularly worth investigating because each has dealings with a seven-headed monster, although with strikingly different results. As we noted earlier, Joachim alludes to this chapter in his *figura* to find biblical precedent for his interpretation of the Dragon's seven heads and specifically to argue ominously that the sixth persecution (Saladin's) has begun and that the seventh (Antichrist's) will soon follow. The association in Apocalypse 17 between the seven-headed Beast and the Whore of Babylon is, further-more, another way in which the forces of evil in the last days are under-stood to be political and spiritual as well as demonic inversions of the forces of good.

Paralleling the imagery of chapter 12, chapter 17 describes both a mon-strous seven-headed creature and a woman. Like the apocalyptic Woman portrayed earlier—who is described as pregnant (Apoc. 12:2)—the woman of Apocalypse 17 is also a sexual being. Both women are alike, furthermore, in that ultimately each is attacked by the seven-headed mon-ster (cf. Apoc. 12:13 and 17:16). Here the comparison ends, however, for the bloody Whore of Babylon is clearly the treacherous and demonic in-version of the persecuted and chaste Woman of Apocalypse 12:

> Et vidi mulierem sedentem super bestiam coccineam, plenam nomi-nibus blasphemiae, habentem capita septem et cornua decem. Et mu-lier erat circumdata purpura et coccino et inaurata auro et lapide pretioso et margaritis, habens poculum aureum in manu sua plenum abominatione et immunditia fornicationis eius; et in fronte eius no-men scriptum mysterium, "Babylon magna, mater fornicationum et abominationum terrae." Et vidi mulierem ebriam de sanguine sanc-torum et de sanguine martyrum Iesu; et miratus sum, cum vidissem illam, admiratione magna.
>
> (Apoc. 17:3–6)

> [And I saw a woman sitting upon a scarlet-coloured beast, full of names of blasphemy, having seven heads and ten horns. And the woman was clothed round about with purple and scarlet, and gilt with gold, and precious stones and pearls, having a golden cup in her hand, full of the abomination and filthiness of her fornication. And on her forehead a name was written: A mystery; Babylon the great, the mother of the fornications, and the abominations of the earth. And I saw the woman drunk with the blood of the saints, and with the blood of the martyrs of Jesus. And I wondered, when I had seen her, with great amazement.]

As the Woman about to give birth traditionally represents *Ecclesia*, the fecund true Church, so in medieval exegesis the Whore of Babylon represents *Synagoga*, the false, spiritually barren church. Iconographically, the two are opposites: the Whore is a deceitful and powerful mockery of the Woman, but, like Babylon itself, temporal and ultimately to be destroyed; whereas the Woman, like the New Jerusalem, is eternal.

This interpretation is evident, for example, in the *Hortus Deliciarum*, an encyclopedia probably compiled by Herrad of Hohenbourg, a contemporary of Joachim of Fiore. It devotes two full-page miniatures to the Whore of Babylon, the first representing her mounted on the Beast, the second her drunken fall, mourned by her followers who are identified as "universitas malorum" ["the totality of evil"]. Following these two illustrations of Apocalypse 17, the encyclopedia then reverses the order of Scripture and portrays the Apocalyptic Woman of chapter 12, inscribed "Mulier hec est ecclesia que sole amicta et luna sub pedibus ejus" ["This woman who is clothed with the sun and with the moon under her feet is the Church"]. Although the monsters representing Antichrist and Satan are present in the illustration, she commands the center of attention and is definitely portrayed as victorious. Just as the miniature of the Whore on the Beast is followed by a depiction of her followers' "rewards," the miniature of the Woman is similarly linked to a following miniature, a representation of the souls of the blessed in Abraham's Bosom.[63] In its organization as well as its iconography and text, this late twelfth-century encyclopedia concludes with a vision of the promised reward of the righteous.

The *Hortus Deliciarum* miniatures assume that the various symbols of the Apocalypse are closely related to one another. The apocalyptic imagination similarly expects that the many human manifestations of these symbols, although appearing at various times throughout history, are inextricably linked. This third key to the apocalyptic imagination, therefore, is evident in the numerous parallels medieval writers perceive between the careers of a wide range of biblical and historical figures. These parallels, which are understood as linking these figures one to another, include similar virtues and sins motivating their lives, analogous relationships with third parties, and comparable actions that characterize their otherwise distinct careers. Among the citizens of the City of God, martyrdom is the most common credential. Thus Joachim explains in his *Enchiridion super Apocalypsim* that the martyrs of the last days will suffer the same persecution that characterized the establishment of the Church:

Erit autem istud in consummatione sexti temporis, in quo sancti Dei occidendi sunt sicut Dominus Jesus a gentibus Judaeis impiissimis tradentibus eum occisus est, et ante ipsum Joannes Baptista, aut certe sicut Petrus et Paulus, qui altercante cum eis Simone in conspectu Neronis ab ejus apparitoribus martyrizati sunt.[64]

[This will take place in the consummation of the sixth period (*tempus*), when God's holy ones are to be killed, just as the Lord Jesus was killed by the gentiles when the impious Jews handed him over; just as John the Baptist before him, and certainly just as Peter and Paul, who were martyred by Nero's servants when Simon was contending with them in his sight.]

Although dying at various times and at the hands of different persecutors—Herod, Nero, Antichrist—each follows Christ's example and each is his witness (Greek *mártys*).

The citizens of Babylon are similarly linked by such parallels, as is evident in the comparisons that theologians, poets, and artists draw between Simon Magus and Antichrist. A miniature in the Gulbenkian Apocalypse, the fascinating thirteenth-century illuminated manuscript now in Lisbon that probably belonged to Pope Clement IX, illustrates such comparisons (see Figure 3).[65] Although a very crowded composition, it is highly symmetrical, visually suggesting how the apocalyptic imagination portrays the careers of the two deceivers as resembling one another. The two figures are juxtaposed in the center, each identified by a gloss inscribed above the miniature's border. Simon Magus, who is winged and hooded, stands on the left facing Antichrist. His head, however, is turned over his right shoulder toward two groups of men whose backs are placed against the left margin of the miniature. One group, standing, represents those converted by the magician's false doctrine, which is symbolized by the book that Simon holds in his left hand. The other group, naked and rising from tombs, represents those whom Simon Magus apparently resurrects from the dead. Over their heads he holds a scroll stating "ex morte resurgire" ["arise from the dead"]. Antichrist is seated beside him, crowned, and holding in his right hand a scepter. His left hand similarly holds a scroll, inscribed "potestatem habeo suscitare mortuos" ["I have the power of resurrecting the dead"]. It floats above two groups of men who, like those on the left, frame the much larger deceivers who command the miniature's center. Once again, the standing group represents those converted to the false prophet, whereas below them the naked rising from the tomb represent those resurrected by Antichrist.

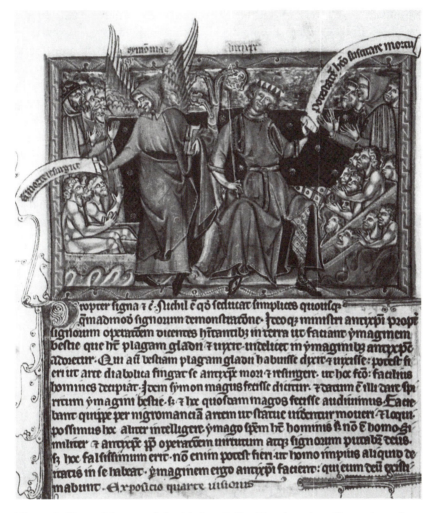

Figure 3. Simon Magus and Antichrist. *Gulbenkian Apocalypse* illustration of Apoc. 13:14–15. Lisbon, Museu Calouste Gulbenkian MS L.A. 139, fol. 39ᵛ. (Reproduced by permission, Calouste Gulbenkian Foundation Museum.)

The miniature thus highlights the deceit of Simon Magus and Antichrist as evident in their false doctrine and terrifying miracles. This emphasis is appropriate, because the scene illustrates Apocalypse 13:14, which warns against the great signs performed by the two-horned Beast from the earth. But it suggests other parallels as well, which show how the artist was influenced by the rich apocalyptic tradition that links the two deceivers. That Simon Magus is winged, for example, alludes to his abortive attempt to imitate Christ by rising—with the aid of demons—into heaven, a feat that Antichrist will similarly attempt unsuccessfully during the last days. As Suzanne Lewis has noted, furthermore, the figure of the seated Antichrist may have been adapted from illustrations that portray Simon Magus standing before an enthroned Nero.[66] If so, then the Gulbenkian miniature suggests yet another link between Simon Magus and Antichrist, whose scepter and cruel reputation as persecutor recalls the iconography representing Nero's tyrannical characteristics. Nero is the common denominator of both Simon Magus and Antichrist.

The apocalyptic imagination applies the keys of inversion and linkage through parallel actions to expand the insight provided by the first key that relates the universal to the personal, the cosmic to the historical. Thus it is able to identify specific human historical manifestations of the cosmic conflict between good and evil. Yet another, fourth, key evident in Joachim's *figura*—the understanding of the symbolic numerical patterns of the Apocalypse in historical terms—is then used to organize the apocalyptic vision of history. The modern reader needs to be reminded of the importance of number symbolism for premodern cultures: rather than being simple abstract signs, numbers were, as Bernard McGinn has phrased it, "not only forms within which to organize everyday reality, but they were also ways in which man came into contact with essential dimensions of transcendent reality. Numbers not only described, they in some sense revealed, the really real."[67] The importance of number symbolism as a basis of organizing and analyzing everything—from sins to the psyche, from imaginary geography to the angelic hierarchies, from elaborate poems to towering cathedrals—is evident throughout medieval culture, philosophy, and theology.

Sometimes the medieval explication of numbers can seem arbitrary and forced, motivated by the need to detect meaning in random phenomena, coincidental patterns, and so forth. Thus Peter John Olivi in his commentary on the Rule of St. Francis detects a pattern based on the number six which relates an event in the life of Francis to the prophetic mission of the Franciscans. Olivi argues that just as Francis sought to convert the Saracens in the sixth year after his conversion, so will pagans and Jews be converted to Christianity in the period of the Church represented by the opening of the sixth seal.[68] The argument, however, is based on a simple premise, which, as we will see, Bonaventure inscribes in his *Legenda Maior*: the life of Francis is analogous to the life of the Church. Depending on our modern sense of the interpreter's work, we may find such a premise to be naive or even self-serving. We must not forget, however, that to so interpret numbers is to extend logically the medieval sense of the universal divine plan, to detect providence at work in historical experience and especially in the lives of prominent members of the City of God. It is also to follow scriptural precedent.

The apocalyptic imagination was particularly fascinated by the numerous patterns of sevens found throughout the Apocalypse: the seven letters to the churches, the opening of the seven seals, the blowing of the seven trumpets, the pouring out of the seven vials, as well as the seven heads of the Dragon (Apoc. 12), Beast from the sea (Apoc. 13), and the Beast ridden by the Whore of Babylon (Apoc. 17). As we noted at the beginning of this study, the sequential nature of numerical patterns encouraged the historicizing interpretation of the Apocalypse by Anselm of Havelberg and other twelfth-century exegetes, particularly since the number seven was already associated with historical periodization through Augustine's theory of the seven *aetates* of world history. The numerical patterns also allowed exegetes to emphasize certain crucial moments and actors in history and thus ultimately to draw on the past to understand the present and speculate about the future. In his *figura* of the seven-headed Dragon, for example, Joachim emphasizes the close relationship between the events of the Church's second *tempus*—that time symbolized by the red horse of Apocalypse 6:4 and represented by the persecution of Nero—and its sixth *tempus*, now witnessing Saladin's persecution and soon to experience Antichrist's deceits. The *figura* stresses this relationship by inscribing only the glosses identifying the second, sixth, and seventh heads in red ink. As a result, Nero, Saladin, and Antichrist are not only typologically linked but visually emphasized, suggesting that Joachim's contemporary world is reliving both the political tyranny and the spiritual deceit faced by the early Church. As we shall see in the following chapters, Joachim was not alone in this belief.

Although Joachim's exegesis is clearly a continuation and development of twelfth-century Apocalypse exegesis, as Bernard McGinn explains, it breaks new ground and results in a very un-Augustinian reading of the Apocalypse: "Unlike earlier commentators, who at times had seen a reference to the ages of the Church in parts of the book, Joachim sees the *entire book* as presenting a historical message, and not one that is generic and vague, but rather a revelation that can be tied down to specific persons, events, and dates. In this Joachim stands in resolute, if silent, opposition to Augustine."[69] Although not necessarily unorthodox, Joachim's tying down of the Apocalypse "to specific persons, events, and dates" is certainly potentially explosive, not to say dangerous. It is this approach that allows and even encourages later authors to read the Apocalypse specifically and polemically. Now one can identify the apocalyptic villains not only with past persecutors of the Church (e.g., Herod, Nero) and specific groups (e.g., Arians, Saracens), but also with contemporary "persecutors," political or spiritual representatives of Antichrist. This approach was appropriated by all parties during the many ecclesiastical and imperial controversies of the thirteenth century. Thus Gregory IX could identify Frederick II as the seven-headed Beast of Apocalypse 13, and Frederick's partisans could in turn decipher the number of the Beast—666—in *Innocencius papa*, a reference to Innocent IV.[70]

If such polemics are often viewed by twentieth-century readers with bewilderment or even condescension, it is because the polemicists seem to have wrenched the biblical symbolism out of context and viciously misappropriated it for political reasons and personal advantage. Clearly, in the heat of the moment, hasty expediency could take the place of thoughtful exegesis. It is also true, nevertheless, that many medieval authors believed that the prophecies of the Apocalypse and other visionary works were being fulfilled in the present, that the scriptural warnings were given so that Christians could prepare for the persecution that doctrine taught was imminent, and that it was imperative that they speak out with prophetic fervor condemning contemporary evils. In other words, they took apocalyptic symbolism seriously and applied it seriously, as is evident even in the writings of that most representative of early humanist poets, Petrarch. In a letter to Francesco Nelli, Petrarch specifically draws on the symbolism of Apocalypse 17 to condemn the Avignon Papacy, the "Babylon situated on the banks of the fierce Rhône, the famous, rather, the infamous prostitute who fornicates with the kings of the earth!"[71] Even this highly charged and bitter attack, however, reflects the principles of interpretation that we have cited as representative of the medieval apocalyptic imagination. The letter, for example, distinguishes both the universal categories of good and evil—symbolized by Jerusalem and Babylon—and highly individualized representatives of each city, including a lecherous cardinal and a poor young girl. It repeatedly emphasizes how the perverted "Babylonian whore" has inverted the good. Noting that "Some things are never learned better than through their contraries," Petrarch ironically recommends Avignon: "Do you wish to know the beauty of God, see how obscene his enemies are. You do not have to search far; they dwell in Babylon." The poet, furthermore, explictly comments on the historical continuity of evil, linking the present chaos with the heresiarch: "I do not speak of the heritage of Simon and of that type of heresy which is not the least—the sale of the gifts of the Holy Spirit." The besetting sin of simony, so rampant in the Avignonese church, is thus placed in its historical and apocalyptic context. Finally, Petrarch hints ominously that the papacy has been taken over by Antichrist, the devil incarnate known for his deceitful marvels: "For truly you are become the habitation, or rather, the kingdom of demons who—allowed the human form—rule in you by their artifices."

The apocalyptic imagination, which cannot be overlooked in an obviously polemical letter, can easily be dismissed if not actually missed in what are among the most complex narratives of the Middle Ages. Petrarch's apocalypticism, responding to the corruption of the Avignon papacy in the fourteenth century, explicitly informs his evaluation of the contemporary Church and its need for imminent *renovatio*. A century earlier in his *Legenda Maior* Bonaventure similarly stressed the importance of *renovatio*, and especially the role of Francis as a prophetic reformer who rebuilds the collapsing Church. Although his apocalypticism is less strident than Petrarch's—let alone Joachim's—as we shall see in the next chapter, the apocalyptic imagination nevertheless informs the structure of his narrative, his conception of history, and his understanding of the unique role Francis is to play during the last days of Church history. At approximately the same time, Jean de Meun's visionary and allegorical romance takes a surprising turn toward contemporary social criticism. This criticism is informed throughout by a sophisticated and subtle use of the apocalyptic imagination, drawing on imagery that Jean extracted from a highly polemical local controversy and applied to a broader critique of contemporary society. Our third chapter shows how a knowledge of the poem's apocalyptic structure provides clues for a reading of the *Roman de la Rose*.

The last two chapters examine the two greatest poems of the fourteenth century, the *Commedia* and the *Canterbury Tales*. It has often been noted that Dante's great epic is suffused with apocalyptic language and imagery, although the significance of this recognition has not been explored systematically. The apocalyptic dimension of Chaucer's poem, on the other hand, has been all but ignored. Yet through the eschatological perspective provided by its pilgrimage frame and by means of the parodic inversions evident throughout the tales, the *Canterbury Tales* is suffused with apocalyptic resonances. In sharing the apocalyptic imagination, Dante and Chaucer also reflect what we have called the first key opening apocalyptic symbolism: they emphasize how the particular is informed by the universal and how the cosmic is manifested in history. They share this key with Bonaventure, who understands the details of Francis's life as reflecting the larger patterns of apocalyptic history, and with Jean de Meun, who interprets the specific issues in the mendicant debate within the larger context of the problems facing French society and Church history.

Before turning to the chapters that analyze these texts, we must directly face the fact that these are not the texts that one would ordinarily discuss to exemplify the apocalyptic imagination. We are not, for example, analyzing in depth numerous sermons ranging from those of Ælfric to Bernardino of Siena and many poems ranging from Old English lyrics to the *Lauds* of Jacopone da Todi and the *Canzone* of Petrarch. Nor do we study in depth such works as the *Ludus de Antichristo, Jour du Jugement, Tournoiement de l'Antecrist* of Huon de Méry, *Piers Plowman, Pearl,* or the Chester Cycle Antichrist plays. These works certainly deserve careful attention, and even though they have in fact been examined from apocalyptic perspectives, such analysis is far from complete. But to limit analysis to these works is to recognize the influence of apocalypticism in medieval culture only when an author cites an obviously apocalyptic figure such as Antichrist or when a literary work quotes extensively from the Apocalypse.[72] If there is a polemical thrust to our work, it is that the apocalyptic imagination is more widespread, more subtle, and more significant than has previously been understood.[73] It is for this reason that we have selected texts that are central to Latin hagiography and Old French allegory, as well as the two great comedies of the fourteenth century, Chaucer's human comedy no less than Dante's divine.

The four major medieval narratives that we will analyze in the following chapters develop the first key of the apocalyptic imagination that is evident in Joachim's *figura*. They take the traditional allegorical symbols of good and evil and apply them to specific historical situations to make sense of the present and reflect on the imminent future. And, as we shall see, all four narratives similarly develop the other three keys of the apocalyptic imagination as well. They show, for example, that the agents of evil are essentially inversions of the agents of good and that this cast of characters is extricably linked throughout history. Finally, these works make use of number symbolism and other apocalyptic patterns not only to shape the narratives, but also to develop significant themes and to inform specific events, scenes, and characters.

2. The *Legenda Maior*: Bonaventure's Apocalyptic Francis

It would be hard to find a work that calls attention to an apocalyptic agenda more clearly or more immediately than Bonaventure's Life of St. Francis, the *Legenda Maior*, a work commissioned in 1260, completed in 1263, and made the official biography of the order in 1266.[1] Bonaventure places the entire work in an apocalyptic context by beginning with an apocalyptically charged reference to the last times:

> Apparuit gratia Dei Salvatoris nostri diebus istis novissimis in servo suo Francisco omnibus vere humilibus et sanctae paupertatis amicis. (p. 3)

> [In these last days
> the grace of our saviour has appeared
> in his servant Francis
> to all who are truly humble and lovers of holy poverty.]
>
> (p. 179)

By alluding to 2 Timothy 3:1, "Hoc autem scito, quod in novissimis diebus instabunt tempora periculosa" ["Know also this, that, in the last days, shall come dangerous times"], Bonaventure plays on the ambiguity of "diebus istis novissimis," which can be and was taken to mean both the most recent time and the time directly before the end.[2] Thus Bonaventure establishes at the outset that Francis has a particular and crucial place in the history of the Church as well as in the history of the order. Much of the *Legenda* is concerned with exploring the implications of the historical and—as we shall see—the apocalyptic role of Francis.

This concern with history—which, as we argued in the first chapter, typifies the apocalyptic imagination—is inseparable from Bonaventure's apocalyptic vision. Moreover, the apocalyptic dimension brought to the attention of the reader in the opening lines of the *Legenda Maior* is immediately enhanced by a reference at the end of the same opening paragraph to a striking image from the Apocalypse of John:

> Ideoque alterius amici Sponsi, Apostoli et Evangelistae Ioannis vaticinatione veridica sub similitudine Angeli ascendentis ab ortu solis signumque Dei vivi habentis adstruitur non immerito designatus. Sub apertione namque sexti sigilli vidi, ait Ioannes in Apocalypsi, alterum Angelum ascendentem ab ortu solis, habentem signum Dei vivi. (p. 4)

> [And so not without reason
> is he considered to be symbolized by the angel
> who ascends from the sunrise
> bearing the seal of the living God,
> in the true prophecy
> of that other friend of the Bridegroom,
> John the Apostle and Evangelist.
> For "when the sixth seal was opened,"
> John says in the Apocalypse,
> "I saw another Angel,
> ascending from the rising of the sun,
> having the seal of the living God."]

(p. 181)

By equating Francis and the Angel of the sixth seal at the very beginning of his *Legenda*, Bonaventure clearly gives Francis a very important place indeed in the history of salvation.[3] These charged references speak to the entire *Legenda*, coming as they do in a prologue whose obvious purpose is to explain the theological meaning of the work. Drawing on what we have called the fourth key to the apocalyptic imagination, Bonaventure appropriates a symbolic numerical pattern to organize the structure of his narrative and uncover the crucial significance of the life of Francis. The allusion to the seven seals forces the reader to consider the fact that the numerical patterns so prominent within the work will not be without apocalyptic significance: in important ways the *Legenda Maior* imitates the very structure of the Apocalypse.

This image of Francis as the Angel of the sixth seal and its apocalyptic resonances are subsequently connected to the most significant event in the life of the saint, his reception of the stigmata—the wounds of Christ—on Mount La Verna two years before his death:

> verum etiam irrefragabili veritatis testificatione confirmat signaculum similitudinis Dei viventis, Christi videlicet crucifixi, quod in corpore ipsius fuit impressum, non per naturae virtutem vel ingenium artis, sed potius per admirandam potentiam Spiritus Dei vivi. (p. 5)

> [But even more is this confirmed
> with the irrefutable testimony of truth
> by the seal of the likeness of the living God,
> namely of Christ crucified,
> which was imprinted on his body
> not by natural forces or human skill
> but by the wondrous power
> of the Spirit of the living God.]

(p. 182)

Thus this all-important event too becomes for Bonaventure something that can only be understood fully in apocalyptic terms. As we shall see in the body of the *Legenda*, the several refences to Francis as the Angel of the sixth seal suggest that Bonaventure considered the stigmata—Francis's seal of the living God—to be a sign of the end of time.

Francis's significance as the Angel of the sixth seal cannot be understood simply by looking at these various references in the *Legenda*, important as these are. To understand them fully, we must first consider some of the other contexts which help explain their meaning. The most basic of these, of course, is the Apocalypse itself. There, the reference to the Angel of the sixth seal comes at a climactic point within a series of plagues which are let loose by the opening of the seven seals of a heavenly book. As is often the case in the multiple patterns of seven which are structurally so significant in the Apocalypse, that pattern is subdivided into a pattern of six and one, with a significant break between the sixth and the seventh of the pattern.[4] In this case the significant break is a scene which is inserted after the sixth plague/sixth seal. Four angels stand at the four corners of the earth and create a great silence by holding back the four winds. It is at this moment that the visionary sees another angel: "Et vidi alterum angelum ascendentem ab ortu solis, habentem signum Dei vivi" (Apoc. 7:2) ["And I saw another angel ascending from the rising of the sun, having the sign of the living God"]. This angel commands the plagues to cease "quoadusque signemus servos Dei nostri in frontibus eorum" (Apoc. 7:3) ["till we sign the servants of our God in their foreheads"]. Those sealed, we are told in the next verse, number 144,000. Thus the Angel of the sixth seal, as John Fleming has aptly phrased it, is a herald of things to come, "the contemplative navigator of that brief period remaining in the sixth age before the sabbath rest begins."[5] By identifying Francis as the Angel of the sixth seal, Bonaventure not only highlights the prophetic character of Francis, but also gives him a key role in the events that unfold during the sixth *tempus* of Church history which concludes the sixth *aetas* of world history. Bonaventure thus places Francis—and therefore the Franciscan order and contemporary Christianity—directly in the time immediately preceding Doomsday as outlined in the historical interpretations of Apocalypse 6:1–8:2 developed by Anselm of Havelberg and other medieval exegetes.[6]

As we noted in Chapter 1, traditional Augustinian exegesis understood the last book of Scripture as encompassing all of Church history, so that contemporary exegesis of the Apocalypse could provide Bonaventure with the basic keys of interpretation to unlock the apocalyptic significance of Church history.[7] But Bonaventure applied these apocalyptic keys to the Franciscan order as well, because in the thirteenth century sympathizers and enemies alike appropriated the language and symbolism characteristic of the apocalyptic imagination to debate the role of Francis in Church and world history. To resolve that debate, Bonaventure had to bring to it a deeper understanding of the apocalyptic tradition than displayed by earlier polemicists. We will examine the extent of Bonaventure's understanding of the Apocalypse after tracing the events and arguments that embroiled the order in apocalyptic polemics.

Ironically, Bonaventure is often thought of as a non-apocalyptic thinker. Perhaps this is because part of the purpose of the *Legenda* was to reject the radical claims made for Francis by the extreme Spiritual wing of the order, claims that were buttressed by a radical and often heretical apocalypticism. In particular the *Liber introductorius in evangelium aeternum* of Gerard of Borgo San Donnino made extravagant claims for the special role of St. Francis and the Franciscan rigorists based on the apocalyptic promise of the eternal gospel:

> Et vidi alterum angelum volantem per medium caeli, habentem evangelium aeternum, ut evangelizaret sedentibus super terram et super

omnem gentem et tribum et linguam et populum; dicens magna
voce: Timete Dominum et date illi honorem, quia venit hora iudicii
eius; et adorate eum qui fecit caelum et terram, mare et fontes
aquarum. (Apoc. 14 : 6−7)

[And I saw another angel flying through the midst of heaven, having
the eternal gospel, to preach unto them that sit upon the earth, and
over every nation, and tribe, and tongue, and people: Saying with a
loud voice: Fear the Lord, and give him honour, because the hour of
his judgment is come; and adore ye him, that made heaven and earth,
the sea, and the fountains of waters.]

Gerard's radical apocalyptic claims seemed to blur any real distinction between Francis and Christ. The *Liber introductorius* became, not surprisingly, something of a scandal to the order, and was connected with the
very reasons why Bonaventure became Minister General in 1257. John of
Parma, his predecessor, was asked to resign in part because he was thought
to be overly sympathetic to Gerard and his views. Thus in both his custo-
dianship of the order and in his writings, Bonaventure was responsible for
presenting a more responsible view of Francis, and this view has often
been assumed, almost as a reflex, to be "non-apocalyptic."

The *Liber introductorius* not only had a scandalous effect within the
order, but outside it as well. Since there were many who for a variety of
reasons were looking for an opportunity to discredit the Franciscan order,
Gerard's heretical excesses provided them with a welcome opportunity. In
particular, a secular master at the University of Paris, Guillaume de Saint-
Amour, published a treatise in 1254 that manipulated the imagery of
Apocalypse 13, 2 Timothy, and other apocalyptic passages in the New Testament to discredit Gerard, the Spirituals, and even more importantly,
mendicancy itself. Guillaume's most important work, *De periculis novissimorum temporum*, began a long and significant tradition of anti-fraternal
writing which continued throughout the Middle Ages, and which, as we
shall see in the next chapter, particularly influenced the *Roman de la Rose*.[8]
But its more immediate effects concern us here, for in the drama caused
by this external scandal, Bonaventure played a significant role. One result
of Guillaume's denunciation of the mendicant way of life was to heat up
considerably an already existing quarrel between the seculars and the mendicants at the University of Paris. In the attempt of the mendicants to
acquit themselves, they called upon their greatest thinkers, in particular

Thomas Aquinas and Bonaventure. Bonaventure's contribution to the debate, his *Defense of the Mendicants*, is a brilliant theoretical defense of the ideals of Gospel poverty, perhaps the most important academic defense of poverty and the order ever written.[9]

His participation in the apocalyptically charged quarrel between the secular and mendicant masters at the University of Paris shows that Bonaventure was clearly aware not only of the apocalyptic significance of his opening to the *Legenda*, but also of its polemical dimension. In fact, he begins the *Legenda*, as we have seen, with the very scriptural citation (2 Tim. 3:1) that forms the title of Guillaume de Saint-Amour's attack. Unlike the *Defense of the Mendicants*, however, the purpose of his life of Francis is neither academic nor polemical. It is pastoral, attempting to proclaim to the largest possible audience the meaning of Francis's life. For Bonaventure, the apocalyptic imagination—the extensive use he makes of a rich and resonant tradition—is one of the important means at his disposal for achieving this purpose. As such it is important to remind ourselves that the apocalyptic imagination can be perfectly orthodox, which it clearly is as manifested in the *Legenda*. Bonaventure avoids the extravagant claims of the radical apocalypticism of a Gerard of Borgo San Donnino and the equally extravagant claims of the polemical apocalypticism of Guillaume. In rejecting the polemical appropriation of the apocalyptic imagination, Bonaventure—like Augustine before him—nevertheless avails himself of its energies in subtle and sophisticated ways. To understand how he develops these apocalytic themes, we must first say something about the peculiar history of the *Legenda Maior*.

Bonaventure's *Legenda Maior* should be a fundamental text for studies not only of Bonaventure and Francis but also of medieval culture. The importance of the saint's life as a genre has been increasingly—even if sometimes grudgingly—acknowledged, both as a means of understanding medieval society and as one of the significant artistic achievements of that society. If any example of the genre can make a claim to preeminence, it is the *Legenda*, both because of the saint who is its subject and the saint who is its author. Francis of Assisi is the best-known saint of the Middle Ages, and the popularity he has retained in our own time is a true reflection of the popularity and importance that he had during his own. Bonaventure of Bagnorea, the aptly-named second founder of the Franciscan order, is one of the seminal thinkers of the Middle Ages, a systematic theologian and philosopher of undisputed genius. The combination is formidable, and it is with just praise that John Fleming characterizes the *Legenda* as "preeminent among Franciscan literary sources" and as "a work that enjoyed an authoritative monopology in the Late Middle Ages and that was further powerfully recommended by the comprehensiveness of its contents, the lucidity of its style, and the brilliance of its organization."[10]

Unfortunately, although the *Legenda Maior* has been studied by those interested in the Franciscan order and the history of spirituality, modern scholarship has not always shared the medieval appreciation of the *Legenda*.[11] Scholars in search of the "historical Francis" often blame it for replacing the "real" Francis with an artificial and unnecessarily theologized portrait. Thus John Moorman's standard history of the order argues that the earlier lives by Thomas of Celano are much more authentically "Franciscan."[12] The search for the historical Francis has assumed that chronology is of the utmost importance. Because *I Celano* dates from only a few years after the death of Francis, it is considered a more trustworthy document than *II Celano*, written almost a generation later, and certainly more trustworthy than the *Legenda Maior*, written later still and depending on many of the incidents reported in Celano's two lives.[13] As E. Randolph Daniel rightly notes, "Since the publication of Paul Sabatier's *Vie de Saint François*, the recovery of Thomas of Celano's *Vita secunda* and the various *legendae* in the Leonine tradition, the *Legenda Maior* has been evaluated unfavorably as an attempt to unify the Order by glossing over or omitting controversial elements in the earlier lives. This judgment, based principally on arguments *ex silentio*, is unfair."[14] Only recently have scholarly studies suggested that this is an inadequate assessment of Bonaventure's brilliant work.[15]

Franciscan studies entered a new phase with the publication of Kajetan Esser's critical edition of the works of Francis.[16] This major scholarly achievement allows us to recognize the extent to which *all* the early lives—when compared to the writings of Francis—are carefully theologized accounts. If we shift the question from "What are the facts about Francis?" to "What is the meaning of Francis's life?" we discover that each life provides a somewhat different answer for a different audience. The inevitable comparison with the Gospels may be useful here. Rather than assume, in the search for "the historical Jesus," that the earliest Gospel is by definition the most accurate, one needs to view each of the Gospels as a complementary reflection on the meaning of the life of Jesus. Thus John's Gospel, because it was written later, can add much to one's understanding that was not present in the earlier accounts precisely because it has reflected on the earlier accounts. The *Legenda Maior* is the Joannine account in Franciscan hagiography.

The purpose of *I Celano* was to proclaim triumphantly the meaning of the life of Francis throughout Christendom at the time of his canonization, only two years after his death. If it is, as is sometimes claimed, the most important document in the tradition of Franciscan hagiography, it is not because it tells us who Francis "really" was, but because it raises all the important questions that subsequently serve as the basis for discourse about Francis. It shows that the meaning of his life was in no way simple or univocal. A generation later, events within the order proved that the meaning of the life of Francis was still a matter of dispute, for his followers could not agree on what it meant to follow his literal reenactment of the Gospel. Written during a time of crisis, *II Celano* did not so much seek to proclaim the meaning of his life to the entire Church as to reform the order. It asked those who were already explicitly and organizationally followers of Francis a new set of questions: "If Francis were here now, what would he say to us? How would he deal with the problems created by institutionalization and by the necessity of remaining true to his commitment to poverty?" By asking these questions, Celano implicitly recognized that the original circumstances had changed and that proclamation was no longer separable from reformation.

For Bonaventure the problem of reformation was even more acute, because the order now truly was a major force within the Church. The Council of Narbonne, reacting to the continuing strife between those who would later come to be known as the Spirituals and the Conventuals—between those who fought all changes from Francis's original simplicity and poverty and the majority who saw the need to accept some modifications because of the growing institutionalization of the order—commissioned Bonaventure to write a definitive life of Francis and ordered the earlier lives destroyed. In his work as well as his own life, Bonaventure was a peacemaker. The *Legenda Maior* attempted to reconcile both sides in the conflict generated by the rapid institutionalization of the order by balancing what was best in their claims and ideals. Focusing on this purpose, Bonaventure's critics have dismissed the *Legenda* as little more than a deft piece of political propaganda, an obligatory tour de force by a minister general required to be a peacemaker.[17] A less superficial reading of the *Legenda*, however, suggests that Bonaventure believed that his task as peacemaker could only be accomplished by first reflecting deeply on the meaning of Francis for all Christendom and on his place in the scheme of history. In the Middle Ages Bonaventure's reflections on the meaning of history were second only to Augustine's in depth and complexity, and like the bishop of Hippo, the Franciscan minister general understood history as including the apocalyptic perspective. By appropriating apocalyptic themes, Bonaventure carefully placed Francis within salvation history, and it is precisely because it interprets its subject within the scheme of Christian history that the *Legenda Maior* remains the definitive life of Francis.

If in the past scholars searching for "the historical Francis" have devalued the *Legenda Maior* because it seemed too artificially theologized, scholars focusing on the thought of Bonaventure have devalued it because within his corpus it seemed tangential, only of interest for what it reveals about the author's "second career" as minister general. As a saint's life it was not seen as a vehicle for serious theological reflection; it thus was not worthy to be considered along with Bonaventure's magisterial theological and philosophical works. Once again, a less superficial examination of the *Legenda* is helpful and necessary, this time to reveal its close connection with several of Bonaventure's theological works, particularly with those emphasizing Christology, mysticism, and the meaning of salvation history. For example, the Francis of the *Legenda*, conformed to Christ through a carefully articulated theological program, is directly connected to the mystical Christology of such works as the *Itinerarium mentis in Deum* and the *Collationes in Hexaemeron*.[18] Similarly, its concern with the place of Francis in salvation history means that the *Legenda Maior* is highly relevant to any comprehensive discussion of Bonaventure's thought, which—unlike that of other scholastics, and especially in contrast to Thomas's thought—emphasized the *ordo historiae*.[19] The *Collationes*, which Bernard McGinn calls the "most original theology of *history* that the period of high Scholasticism has left us," articulates Bonaventure's philosophy of history explicitly.[20] But the *Legenda* does so implicitly, and the figure of Francis can be fully understood only within the same philosophy of history. The *Collationes* and the *Legenda* provide a kind of commentary on each other.

The mutually illuminating concerns of the *Collationes* and the *Legenda* are evident in their identification of Francis as the Angel of the sixth seal. Joseph Ratzinger, whose standard study of Bonaventure's theology of history unfortunately gives only passing attention to the *Legenda*, notes that the *Collationes* identifies Francis as the Angel five times.[21] The most explicit of these is in the sixteenth collation (16:16):

Et necesse fuit, ut in hoc tempre veniret unus ordo, scilicet habitus propheticus, similis ordini Iesu Christi, cuius caput esset Angelus, ascendens ab ortu solis habens signum Dei vivi, et conformis Christo.—Et dixit, quod iam venerat.

[For it was necessary that in this time there come a single order, that is, a prophetical disposition similar to the order of Jesus Christ, and of which the head would be an angel ascending from the rising sun, having the seal of the living God, and conforming to Christ. And he said that he had already come.][22]

As McGinn has rightly observed, "references to the angel of the sixth seal leave no doubt that Bonaventure believed he had already come in the person of Francis."[23] It is somewhere between astonishing and unbelievable that the English translator of the *Collationes* states in his note to this passage that "If Bonaventure is referring to the angel of the Apocalypse, it is hard to understand what he means."[24] The only conceivable way to fail to understand what he means is by being utterly ignorant of, among other things, the *Legenda Maior*. That this should be true of the English translator of five volumes of Bonaventure is as strong a proof as is needed of the neglect of the *Legenda* in the very places where one ought to be able to take its presence for granted.

Without doubt, then, the identification of the Angel of the sixth seal with Francis is fundamental to Bonaventure. Like the Angel, Francis not only bears the seal of the living God himself, but he also seals others:

Nolite nocere terra et mari neque arboribus, quoadusque signemus servos Dei nostri in frontibus eorum. Et audivi numerum signatorum centum quadragintaquattuor milia signati ex omni tribu filiorum Israel. (Apoc. 7:3–4)

[Hurt not the earth, nor the sea, nor the trees, till we sign the servants of our God in their foreheads. And I heard the number of them that were signed, a hundred forty-four thousand were signed: of every tribe of the children of Israel.]

The notion of "sealing" or "signing," however, in the thirteenth century was interpreted in two distinctly different ways leading to radically opposing results—one exclusive, the other inclusive. On the one hand, those who came to be called Spiritual Franciscans understood the "sealed" and therefore saved remnant to be a small and exclusive group, namely themselves. Bonaventure, on the other hand, rejected the notion that the remnant were an already chosen specific group. For Bonaventure, the remnant is rather an inclusive group whose identification is conditional: those who follow Francis and do penance will become the sealed remnant. The identification of Francis as the Angel of the sixth seal thus becomes an invitation for others. Whereas the Spirituals oppose themselves to everyone else, Bonaventure would have us all be incorporated with Francis as the penitent remnant. Avoiding the extravagant claims of the Spirituals, Bonaventure clearly draws upon the apocalyptic imagination not as a tool for polemic attack but to define and clarify an orthodox position by placing it within a larger framework. By connecting Francis with the Angel of the sixth seal, he creates a justification for striving to imitate the saint's life that lasts beyond Francis's own lifetime. This justification is one of the major themes of the *Legenda*: Francis provides a model for those wishing to follow the cross of Christ, just as the cross of Christ provides the touchstone for those wishing to imitate Francis.

The passage in the prologue that identifies Francis as the Angel of the sixth seal explicitly states that the sign that marks the remnant is the same sign that seals Francis:

Ad quod quidem fideliter sentiendum et pie, non solum inducit officium quod habuit, vocandi ad fletum et planctum, calvitium et cingulum sacci signandique Thau super frontes virorum gementium et dolentium signo poenitentialis crucis et habitus cruci conformis. (pp. 4–5)

[We are led to hold this firmly and devoutly
because of his ministry
to call men to weep and mourn,
to shave their heads, and to put on sackcloth,
and to mark with a Tau
the foreheads of men who moan and grieve,
signing them with the cross of penance
and clothing them with his habit,
which is in the form of a cross.]

(p. 182)

The Tau, an alternative form of the cross, is a dense and highly charged symbol that is both Franciscan and scriptural, more specifically apocalyptic. It is Franciscan in that it was Francis's own sign, his own mark. For instance, during the retreat to La Verna in which he received the stigmata, Francis signed the blessing for Brother Leo with the Tau. This authentic autograph, one of the most precious Franciscan relics, is simply the best known example of Francis's "habitual use of the *tau* sign." [25]

The scriptural resonances of the Tau clarify its special meaning for Francis and its precise apocalyptic associations in Bonaventure's prologue. It links two of the most important apocalyptic books of the Bible, Ezekiel and the Apocalypse, by identifying the remnant during both a past and a future time of tribulation. Just as the remnant in the last days are to be marked on the forehead, so the Tau was the saving seal that identified the remnant during the Old Testament time of tribulation connected with the Babylonian captivity:

> et [Dominus] vocavit virum, qui indutus erat lineis et atramentarium scriptoris habebat in lumbis suis, et dixit Dominus ad eum: Transi per mediam civitatem, in medio Ierusalem, et signa thau super frontes virorum gementium et dolentium super cunctis abominationibus quae fiunt in medio eius. Et illis dixit, audiente me: Transite per civitatem sequentes eum et percutite, non parcat oculus vester neque misereamini: senem, adulescentulum et virginem, parvulum et mulieres, interficite usque ad internecionem; omnem autem super quem videritis thau, ne occidatis, et a sanctuario meo incipite. (Ez. 9:3–6)

> [and he called to the man that was clothed with linen, and had a writer's inkhorn at his loins. And the Lord said to him: Go through the midst of the city, through the midst of Jerusalem: and mark Thau upon the foreheads of the men that sigh, and mourn for all the abominations that are committed in the midst thereof. And to the others he said in my hearing: Go ye after him through the city, and strike: let not your eyes spare, nor be ye moved with pity. Utterly destroy old and young, maidens, children and women: but upon whomsoever you shall see Thau, kill him not, and begin ye at my sanctuary.]

Ratzinger notes that "already in antiquity" Apocalypse 7:2 was associated with this passage in Ezekiel.[26] Given the significance of the Tau to Francis, therefore, it was possible to identify Francis both with the man in the linen garment and the Angel of the sixth seal. As John Fleming comments, "The Angel of the sixth seal is an obvious New Testament reflex of the man in linen and Bonaventure, who was sure that Francis was the former, naturally therefore identified him with the latter."[27] The density of the image points in yet another apocalyptic direction, moreover. Because the writing of the Tau on the foreheads of those to be saved in Ezekiel was quite naturally associated with the saving mark made by the blood of the lamb at the passover, the Tau could be connected with the blood of the lamb of the new passover described in the Apocalypse and thus with the crucifixion. For Francis as Angel of the sixth seal, therefore, the Tau and the seal of the living God are in fact the same thing: the cross of Christ crucified. Francis is sealed with the cross, bearing the wounds of Christ on his own body. Through this seal he marks others, by teaching them the way of the cross in their own lives.

In 1215, Innocent III had opened the Fourth Lateran Council with a homily based on the text of Ezekiel 9:4 in which the signing with the Tau became a symbol for spiritual renewal in the Church. Francis, thought to have been present at this event, became a figure of renewal who carried out Innocent's program both literally and spiritually.[28] Bonaventure continues the work of renewal by making Francis's life an apocalyptic sign to be read by those who come after Francis. In his prologue Bonaventure articulates the meaning of Francis's life, which is then embodied in the narrative of Francis, the subject of the body of the text. Just as the seals are connected with openings and readings in the Apocalypse, the stigmata as seal in the *Legenda* is connected with reading also: it authenticates Francis as a book to be read. Bonaventure calls our attention to the paradox that what is most unique to Francis allows him to be considered simultaneously within a general framework of history. Because, as we noted in Chapter 1, it is characteristic of apocalypticism to link the particular to the general, by giving Francis an apocalyptic role, Bonaventure can preserve what is unique to Francis and at the same time incorporate his life into a more universal framework than provided by any of the earlier lives.

The exegetical interpretation of the Angel of the sixth seal also provides important background for understanding Bonaventure's appropriation of the symbol. As we noted in Chapter 1, the best known exegete who identified the various patterns of sevens in the Apocalypse with patterns, events, states, and key figures of church history is the controversial twelfth-century Calabrian Abbot, Joachim of Fiore. Joachim is a significant figure in this context because his Trinitarian conception of history and his visionary pronouncements about the evils of the end inspired both camps in the dispute between the regulars and the mendicants at the University of Paris. They were especially powerful in the work of Gerard of Borgo San Donnino, whose *Liber Introductorius* was, in fact, an introduction to an edition of Joachim's work. Joachim, as E. Randolph Daniel comments, was "intensely interested in the sixth seal and its opening."[29]

He writes about the angel of the sixth seal in his *Liber de Concordia Noui ac Veteris Testamenti*, a work that, as its title suggests, attempts to discern parallels between historical events in the Old Testament and the New. In Book Three of the *Concordia*, Joachim sees the parallel in terms of two historical persecutions of Israel recorded in the Old Testament, those during the time of Judith and Esther. In this same passage, the opening of the sixth seal is also equated with another time of crisis, the time of the prophets Ezekiel and Daniel: "Sub magnis illis uiris qui prophetauerunt in Babilone postquam desolata est ciuitas Iherusalem, Ezechiel scilicet et Daniel, sextum signaculum prediximus inchoasse" ["We have predicted that the sixth seal had begun under those great men who prophesied in Babylon after the city of Jerusalem was destroyed, namely Ezekiel and Daniel"].[30] These two prophets, whose visionary experiences greatly influenced the imagery of the Apocalypse and the medieval apocalyptic imagination, serve as appropriate models for the Angel of the sixth seal.

Bonaventure could well have known this interpretation directly, for as Daniel points out, "while it cannot be proven that Bonaventure read the *Liber de Concordia*, it is clear that the *Concordia* was available to him in Paris."[31] Joachim's identification of the opening of the sixth seal with the time of imminent persecution also fits the agenda of the Spirituals, of course. Their polemical strategy connected the time of persecution associated with the last days to their present "persecution," and they cited this connection to prove the justice of their cause. It is this direct and too specific identification that Bonaventure is both calling to mind and rejecting by his own reference to Francis as Angel of the sixth seal. Bonaventure—whether he knew of Joachim's interpretation directly or only as filtered through the claims of the rigorists within the Franciscan order—is concerned about the state of the Church as a whole, which is collapsing both from within and without as it suffers from the troubles of the last days. He understands Francis, as Angel of the sixth seal, as coming during this time of crisis as a figure of *renovatio*. Bonaventure explores the implications of this apocalyptic image used by the Franciscan rigorists, therefore, not for their specific and radical purposes, but to place Francis within a general and orthodox eschatological framework. He identifies Francis with the Angel of the sixth seal in a threefold manner: Francis bears the mark of the living God, he brings about the *renovatio* signified by the half hour of silence (Apoc. 8:10), and he prepares the Church as a herald of Christ's second coming.

By identifying Francis as the Angel of the sixth seal, therefore, Bonaventure places Francis within the universal scheme of salvation history, at the moment of crisis before the end of time. He not only symbolically relates him to the prophets Daniel and Ezekiel, but he also relates Francis typologically to other Old Testament figures, specifically Moses and Elijah. Like Moses, who miraculously drew water from the desert rock (Deut. 32:13), Francis through prayer produced a stream of water for the poor man (p. 63/p. 248). Like Moses, he came down from the mountain after seeing God, although the image he brought is not depicted "on tablets of stone" (p. 109/p. 307). Like Elijah, the greatest of the Old Testament prophets, he foresaw future events, "as if he were another Elisha, who had acquired the twofold spirit of Elijah" (p. 92/p. 285). Like Elijah, who—as we noted in our first chapter—is expected to precede the Messiah and restore all (Mal. 4:5–6; Matt. 17:11), Francis is a forerunner of Christ. Because Moses is the wellspring of the law and the "prophet" of the passover, and because Elijah is the wellspring of the prophets, the *Legenda* presents Francis as both lawgiver and prophet by making these typological connections. This association, moreover, suggests another of Bonaventure's primary purposes in the prologue, to present in outline what will become the major theme of the text itself: the identification of Francis with Christ. The Sermon on the Mount presents Christ very specifically as the fulfillment of Moses and Elijah, so that by making a similar Gospel-like association, Bonaventure is able to further identify Francis with Christ. The reception of the stigmata is "merely" the culmination of that process. No small part of Bonaventure's achievement is his ability to bring together a multiplicity of structural, narrative, and iconographic details to reinforce that identification.

But Moses and Elijah are not simply figures to whom Francis must be compared typologically to bring about this identification. The imagery of the *Legenda* suggests that they are also figures with whom he is meant to be identified eschatologically. Francis, for example, is described in prophetic terms as calling men to put on "cingulum sacci" (p. 5) ["to put on sackcloth" (p. 181)]. This dress, traditionally identifying a prophet, is worn by two of the most important figures of the apocalyptic imagination, the Two Witnesses: "Et dabo duobus testibus meis, et prophetabunt diebus mille ducentis sexaginta amicti saccis" (Apoc. 11:3) ["And I will give unto my two witnesses, and they shall prophesy a thousand two hundred sixty days, clothed in sackcloth"]. According to most medieval exegetes, the Two Witnesses are expected to appear at the end of time to oppose Antichrist. In traditional interpretations they are usually identified as Enoch (Gen. 5:24) and Elijah (2 Kings 2:11), the patriarch and the prophet who did not die but were taken into heaven to await the final eschatological battle.[32]

Bonaventure draws on this tradition in the *Collationes*, for example, where he explains that in the fifth time of the New Testament, which corresponds with the apocalyptic eleventh hour, Enoch and Elijah will come to restore all things, although the Beast of Apocalypse 11:7 will conquer them. He then explains ominously:

> Unde necesse est, ut prius ruant, et fiat ruina et postea restauratio; tanta erit tribulatio, ut in errorem inducantur, si fieri potest, etiam electi.

> [It is necessary that they fail, so that there be first a ruin and then a restoration; and there will be so great a tribulation . . . as to lead astray, if possible, even the elect]. [33]

It is thus not surprising that Bonaventure links Francis with both Enoch and Elijah near the conclusion of the *Legenda*:

> Erat re vera condignum, ut quem Deus in vita sibi placentem et dilectum effectum in paradisum per contemplationis gratiam transtulerat ut Henoch, et ad caelum in curru igneo per caritatis zelum rapuerat ut Eliam, eius iam vernantis inter flores illos caelicos plantationis aeternae ossa illa felicia de loco suo pullulatione mirifica redolerent. (p. 124)

> [It was truly appropriate
> that he who was pleasing to God and beloved by him
> in this life;
> who, like Enoch,
> had been borne into paradise
> by the grace of contemplation,
> and carried off to heaven,
> like Elijah in a fiery chariot;
> now that his soul is blossoming
> in eternal springtime
> among heavenly flowers
> it was, indeed, truly appropriate
> that his blessed bones too
> should sprout with fragrant miracles
> in their own place of rest.]

(p. 326)

The comparison truly is appropriate, for like the apocalyptic witnesses who convert many from Antichrist to true Christianity through their miraculous power (Apoc. 11:5–6), Francis's life and miracles are instrumental in directing the new *renovatio* during these final times of tribulation.[34]

Generally, though, in the *Legenda* Bonaventure follows an alternate tradition, also very powerful, that identifies the Two Witnesses with Moses and Elijah. This tradition finds support in the coupling of Moses and Elijah with Christ in the Transfiguration (Matt. 17:1–8), to which Bonaventure alludes in his discussion of the stigmata (pp. 105–6/p. 303)—as we shall presently show in more detail.[35] The connections are evident throughout Francis's life. Bonaventure repeatedly identifies Francis as the "herald of Christ," as is evident in his first prophetic words when ambushed by robbers in a forest (p. 17/p. 195), his warnings to the Christian forces at Damietta (pp. 89-90/p. 282), and the prophetic power of his preaching:

> Cum his et aliis multis miraculorum prodigiis praeco Christi praedicans coruscaret, attendebatur his quae dicebantur ab eo, ac si Angelus Domini loqueretur. (p. 105)

> [Since the herald of Christ
> in his preaching
> brilliantly shone with these and with many other miracles,
> people paid attention to what he said
> as if an angel of the lord was speaking."]

(p. 301)

Thus the prologue's association of Francis with Moses and Elijah, like its identification of Francis with the Angel of the sixth seal, resonates with apocalyptic significance.

The apocalyptic imagination is concerned with the history of the Church and the necessity of learning to interpret the signs that make that history intelligible. Bonaventure urges the reader to interpret the life of Francis in an analogous way. Just as in the Apocalypse the opening of the seven seals provides the key to understanding Church history, so the seven visionary or miraculous appearances of the Cross either to or involving Francis serve as the keys to the meaning of his life. He is thus portrayed as an apocalyptic text to be read, an idea central to the structure of the *Legenda* that is first introduced in the prologue where the Tau is identified with the cross and the stigmata is identified with the seal of the living God. It is developed in the narrative when the stigmata and the Angel of the sixth seal are associated in chapter 13, which relates the reception of the stigmata; and in chapter 4, which describes the founding of the order. Since the stigmata is the bull that confirms the rule, Francis is himself the rule, a document to be read authored by God. As we are told in the prologue, the seal is imprinted on Francis by the wondrous power of the living God (p. 5/p. 182).

The prologue to the *Legenda Maior* is not only a sophisticated introduction to the theological meaning of Francis's life, it is also a revealing statement of Bonaventure's method. One of Bonaventure's concerns is to establish his own credentials, which he does in part by describing his personal connection with Francis:

> Utpote qui per ipsius invocationem et merita in puerili aetate, sicut recenti memoria teneo, a mortis faucibus erutus, si praeconia laudis eius tacuero, timeo sceleris argui ut ingratus. (p. 5)

> [For when I was a boy, as I still vividly remember, I was snatched from the jaws of death by his invocation and merits. So if I remained silent and did not sing his praises, I fear that I would be rightly accused of the crime of ingratitude.] (p. 182)

Bonaventure presents himself as compelled by his experience to speak of Francis, an obligation distinct from the more formal one imposed on him by the Council of Narbonne and clearly meant to be seen as complementary to it.

Bonaventure then establishes a claim to authority based on the authenticity of his sources, relating how he personally visited "locum originis, conversationis et transitus viri sancti" (p. 6) ["the sites of the birth, life and death of this holy man" (p. 183)] and interviewed those companions of Francis who were still alive. Finally, in an intriguing comment, he explains how he has decided to put these sources together:

> Nec semper historiam secundum ordinem temporis texui, propter confusionem vitandam, sed potius ordinem servare studui magis aptae iuncturae, secundum quod eodem peracta tempore diversis materiis, vel diversis patrata temporibus eidem materiae congruere videbantur. (p. 6)

[To avoid confusion I did not always weave the story together in chronological order. Rather, I strove to maintain a more thematic order, relating to the same theme events that happened at different times, and to different themes events that happened at the same time, as seemed appropriate.] (p. 183)

Chronological accuracy, however, is generally not considered a way of generating confusion; Bonaventure is simply reinforcing the primacy of the theological emphases that he has already articulated in the prologue. While being loyal to his sources, he will emphasize not their chronology but their broader significance, and thereby suggest the general meaning of the particular event.

But a careful reader will also notice that Bonaventure seems to be at best half truthful in stating that he is not using a chronological method. A closer look at the outline of the *Legenda Maior* with which Bonaventure concludes his prologue shows that he does not reject chronology altogether. Rather he divides the fifteen chapters into two major divisions, one arranged thematically, the other chronologically. The central thematic chapters (5–12), which Bonaventure describes as an exposition of the many virtues of Francis (p. 38/p. 217), present the events of his life grouped together by means of their relationship to each other, so that, for example, all the stories connected with his poverty are brought together (chapter 7) as are all the stories connected with his humility and his obedience (chapter 6). There are eight such chapters, an appropriate number to encompass the manifold virtues of Francis, for the number eight is associated with eternity and timelessness. As Augustine explains at the conclusion of the *City of God*, in the ages of world history the "eighth" both follows and supplants history at the end of time: "The important thing is that the seventh will be our Sabbath, whose end will not be an evening, but the Lord's Day, an eighth day, as it were, which is to last for ever, a day consecrated by the resurrection of Christ, foreshadowing the eternal rest not only of the spirit but of the body also."[36] Drawing on the traditional symbolism of the number eight, these central chapters would imply that Francis's virtues are relevant for all time.

We have suggested that Bonaventure presents Francis as an apocalyptic text to be read, and it is thus not surprising that his outline for the *Legenda* follows in important ways the contours of the Apocalypse, particularly drawing on the fourth key to the apocalyptic imagination, number symbolism. Because the eight thematic chapters are embedded within the chronological chapters (1–4 and 13–15), the chronological-thematic distinction actually creates a tripartite structure for the *Legenda*. Bonaventure acknowledges this structure by referring to the "initium . . . progressus et consummatio" (p. 6) ["beginning, progress, and end" (p. 183)] of Francis's life. The *Legenda* begins with the chronological story of the early life of Francis, and then shifts to a thematic arrangement at the point in his life when he wins the support of the institutional Church for the establishment of the order. Finally, the *Legenda* returns to chronology to narrate the last two years of his life, from the time of the stigmatization to his death and his canonization. The chronological chapters are thus appropriately seven, the number usually associated with chronology and the passing of history in the traditional schemes of the ages of the world, the periods of Church history, and the apocalyptic movement from time to eternity. In these seven chapters, then, Bonaventure relates those key historical moments that are unique to the life of Francis. The four chapters (1–4) preceding the thematic chapters describe his early life, conversion, and the establishment of the order, whereas the three chapters (13–15) following the eight central chapters narrate his stigmatization, death, and canonization. Thus here too Francis's life is presented according to the pattern of seven, even as the visions of the cross to Francis are presented according to the same numerical pattern. Here too, Bonaventure tells us, Francis's life needs to be read apocalyptically.

We have noted before that the apocalyptic imagination tries to make sense of history by drawing upon number symbolism, so that it is not surprising to see such symbolic structures at work in the *Legenda*. In fact, the four-three distinction resulting from the *Legenda*'s division of Francis's life into four preliminary chronological chapters, followed by a central thematic section, and concluding with three chronological chapters is clearly connected to an important apocalyptic numerical pattern that finds its model in the Apocalypse. The book's several patterns of seven frequently are divided into groupings of four and three, as, for example, in the opening of the seals (Apoc. 4–7), the sounding of the trumpets (Apoc. 8–11), and the appearance of the central visions (Apoc. 12–14).[37] The *Legenda*'s four-three division thus becomes another way of recalling the apocalyptic resonances of Francis's life.

As we noted in Chapter 1 and will explain further in Chapter 3, in twelfth- and thirteenth-century interpretations of the Apocalypse, the first three seals are associated with the triumphant origins and persecutions of the early Church, whereas the opening of the fourth seal is associated with hypocrisy and therefore with the present condition of the Church. A four-three scheme is seen, for example, in the *Dialogues* of Anselm of Havel-berg, who interprets the opening of the fourth seal of Apocalypse 6:8—which reveals the pale horse ridden by death—as representing the hypocrisy of false Christians.[38] Following this pattern, then, the four chap-ters relating the life of Francis up to the founding of the order and its approval by the Church parallel symbolically the history of the Church up to the present, from its apostolic beginnings and victories over material powers and heretics to the establishment of a universal institutional Church. The present condition of hypocrisy and lukewarmness, evident in the lives of most contemporaries, further explains Bonaventure's emphasis upon Francis's role as apocalyptic reformer and forerunner of Christ in "these last days," who exhorted his followers, like Christ, to go forth and prepare the world to hear the words of Christ at Doomsday:

> Nonnumquam fratres ad petendum eleemosynam hortans, verbis ute-batur huiusmodi: "Ite," inquit, "quoniam hac novissima hora fratres Minores commodati sunt mundo, ut electi in eis impleant, unde a Iudice commendentur, illud audientes suavissimum verbum: Quam-diu fecistis uni ex his fratribus meis minimis, mihi fecistis." (pp. 60–61)

> [Sometimes he would exhort the friars to beg for alms with words such as these: "Go forth because in this last hour the Friars Minor have been given to the world that through them the elect might have the opportunity to fulfill what will be commmended by the Judge as they hear those most sweet words: 'As long as you have done it to one of these, the least of my brothers, you did it to me.'" (Matt. 25:40)] (p. 245)

The eight thematic chapters (5–12) that are grouped together and placed in the midst of the seven historical chapters at this point thus cor-respond to the actions of Francis in the apocalyptically significant present. Just as in the schemes based upon exegesis of the opening of the seven seals, which place a timeless interval after the first four *tempora* of church history and before the events of the last days, these eight thematic chapters represent timeless actions. This timelessness, furthermore, is implied not only by their symbolic number but also by their being framed between two discussions of the stigmata. As we have seen, these chapters are introduced at the end of chapter 4 when Bonaventure emphasizes that the real seal of Francis's life is the seal of God, achieved by Francis in his stigmatization (p. 38/p. 217). Significantly, the account of the stigmatization then immediately follows the eight chapters on his timeless virtues (pp. 105–14/pp. 303–14). These eight chapters detail the role of Francis as prophet and instigator of the *renovatio*, for they describe his prophetic words, his visionary experiences in which the hidden secrets of heaven are revealed, and his being lifted up in ecstatic contemplation (p. 83/p. 273) in a manner resembling John's rapture in the Apocalypse:

> Post haec vidi, et ecce ostium apertum in caelo et vox prima, quam audivi, tanquam tubae loquentis mecum, dicens: Ascende huc, et ostendam tibi quae oportet fieri post haec. Et statim fui in spiritu. (Apoc. 4:1–2)

> [After these things I looked, and behold a door was opened in heaven, and the first voice which I heard, as it were, of a trumpet speaking with me, said: Come up hither, and I will shew thee the things which must be done hereafter. And immediately I was in the spirit.]

Furthermore, they reveal Francis to be the present forerunner of the imminent future, preparing the Church for Christ's second advent. It is for this reason that Bonaventure begins the *Legenda* by comparing Francis to John the Baptist, the herald of Christ's first advent:

> secundum imitatoriam quoque similitudinem Praecursoris destinatus a Deo, ut viam parans in deserto altissimae paupertatis, tam exemplo quam verbo poenitentiam praedicaret. (p. 4)

> [Like John the Baptist
> he was appointed by God to prepare in the desert
> a way of the highest poverty
> and to preach repentance by word and example.]

(p. 180)

Francis's life, therefore, is a model of conduct—a book to be read in the present—for all those who, living "in these last days," are readers of

Bonaventure's work and find in Francis the pattern for imitation at the end of time.

In the four-three division that characterizes the numerical patterns of the Apocalypse, the first four are usually understood as preparatory, whereas the final three are climactic.[39] As we have seen, traditional exegesis of the opening of the six seals identifies the first four as a movement through the historical periods of the Church from the apostolic age to the hypocritical present. The opening of the fifth seal, which portrays the bloody souls under the altar (Apoc. 6:9–11), symbolizes all those martyrs who have been killed for the word of God throughout time. This seal represents a transition from past to future and is closely related to the timeless sacrifice of Christ who, according to Anselm of Havelberg, is symbolized by the altar. The opening of the sixth seal reveals the Angel bearing the seal of the living God and represents the imminent end, those events immediately preceding Doomsday and eternity. These eschatological events beyond history are then symbolized by the seventh seal. Thus in the apocalyptic opening of the seals, a six-one pattern that distinguishes events within history (the first six *tempora*) from those beyond time (the seventh period of Church history and seventh age of the world) is superimposed upon the four-three pattern of past preparation and present climax.

This superimposed pattern is evident as well in the apocalyptically structured *Legenda Maior*. The first four chapters (1–4) lead chronologically through Francis's life to the stigmata, which is then related in full in chapter 13. Coming after the eight thematic chapters (ch. 5–12), it is the fifth chapter devoted to the chronology of Francis's life. Following the pattern provided by the opening of the seals, this fifth chronological chapter portrays Francis, like the bloody souls seen during the opening of the fifth seal, as a Christ figure, marked with the seal of blood.

The sixth chronological chapter (14) then details the prophetic role of Francis at the end of time and his actions now that, like the Angel of the sixth seal, he has been marked with the sign of the living God (Apoc. 7:2). As he approaches death, he is portrayed in stark contrast to the sinners of the sixth seal who, fearing death and the judgment of God, seek to hide from the Lord:

Et reges terrae et principes et tribuni et divites et fortes et omnis servus et liber absconderunt se in speluncis et in petris montium, et dicunt montibus et petris: "Cadite super nos" et abscondite nos a facie sedentis super thronum et ab ira Agni; quoniam venit dies magnus irae ipsorum, et quis poterit stare? (Apoc. 6:15–17)

[And the kings of the earth, and the princes, and tribunes, and the rich, and the strong, and every bondman, and every freeman, hid themselves in the dens and in the rocks of mountains: And they say to the mountains and the rocks: Fall upon us, and hide us from the face of him that sitteth upon the throne, and from the wrath of the Lamb: For the great day of their wrath is come, and who shall be able to stand?]

Instead, Francis, his life having been "squared like a stone to be fitted into the construction of the heavenly Jerusalem," lies naked and faces the Lord:

Decubans sic in terra, saccina veste deposita, faciem solito more levavit in caelum, et intendens illi gloriae totus, manu sinistra dextri lateris vulnus, ne videretur, obtexit. Et ait ad fratres: "Ego quod meum est feci; quod vestrum est Christus edoceat." (p. 117)

[Lying like this on the ground stripped of his garments of sackcloth, he lifted his face to heaven in his accustomed way and gave his whole attention to its glory, covering the wound in his right side with his left hand lest it be seen. And he said to his friars: "I have done my duty (3 Kings 19:20); may Christ teach you (Eph. 4:21) yours."] (p. 317)

This sixth chronological chapter concludes with the death of Francis, which ends his participation in history.

Finally, the seventh chronological chapter (15) moves the narrative of Francis beyond time into the Sabbath age, placing him in eternity through his canonization. Thus through the incorporation of an apocalyptically significant structure in the *Legenda*, Bonaventure is paradoxically remaining true to his statement of method even when he seems not to be—perhaps especially when he seems not to be. Particularly in those chapters that are presented chronologically, significance is to be found not in chronology for its own sake, but in chronology as it conforms to an apocalyptic number pattern.

Thus the prologue provides a concise overview for the *Legenda*, presenting a carefully articulated theology of Francis's life and suggesting its apocalyptic patterns. The body of the text then presents the events of Francis's life, which are to be understood within the theological and apocalyptic frame established in the prologue. It is thus not surprising that specific events in the life of Francis are imbued with apocalyptic significance, and that these are often associated with visions of the cross. Altogether there are seven appearances of the cross during the life of Francis, six plus the culminating appearance of the stigmata. The numerical pattern of six plus one is, as we have argued, replete with apocalyptic significance, doubly so in that it is connected with Francis as both the Angel of the sixth seal and as the prophet who signs with the Tau. It should not be surprising, then, that the individual appearances of the cross have apocalyptic significance for Francis as well. The sixth one, for example, is a crucifixion scene in which Francis himself appears to the friars in the form of one crucified (p. 36/p. 215), whereas the seventh—the stigmata—is appropriately described in sabbatical terms:

> Ecce, iam septem apparitionibus crucis Christi in te et circa te secundum ordinem temporum mirabiliter exhibitis et monstratis, quasi sex gradibus ad istam septimam, in qua finaliter requiesceres, pervenisti. (p. 114)

> [Behold
> these seven visions of the cross of Christ,
> miraculously shown and manifested
> to you or about you
> at different stages of your life.
> The first were like steps
> leading to the seventh
> in which you have found your final rest.]

(p. 314)

Furthermore, the pattern of four plus three, which repeatedly reoccurs in the number symbolism that characterizes the apocalyptic imagination, is also evident in the appearances of the cross. They are patterned not only so as to reach their culmination in the reception of the stigmata, but also to distinguish the preparatory from the climactic appearances. These seven appearances reflect a movement toward deeper meaning as they develop from literal to spiritual and from the early external signs of the cross to the later internalized visions, in which Francis and the cross become one.

His first vision of the cross takes place shortly after Francis, following the model of Saint Martin, has clothed with his own garments a poor but noble knight:

Nocte vero sequenti, cum se sopori dedisset, palatium speciosum et magnum cum militaribus armis crucis Christi signaculo insignitis clementia sibi divina monstravit, ut misericordiam pro summi Regis amore pauperi exhibitam militi praeostenderet incomparabili compensandam esse mercede. (p. 10)

[The following night, when he had fallen asleep, God in his goodness showed him a large and splendid palace full of military weapons emblazoned with the insignia of Christ's cross. Thus God vividly indicated that the compassion he had exhibited toward the poor knight for love of the supreme King would be repaid with an incomparable reward. (p. 187)]

This vision, which connects the saint to the ideals of knighthood, Francis mistakenly interprets to mean that he will gain worldly prosperity. His natural response is to seek the glory of knighthood in the service of a count in Apulia. Francis, Bonaventure comments, had not yet learned how to understand his visions:

cum nondum haberet exercitatum animum ad divina perscrutanda mysteria nesciretque per visibilium species transire ad contuendam invisibilium veritatem. (p. 10)

[for he had no experience in interpreting divine mysteries nor did he know how to pass through visible images to grasp the invisible truth beyond.] (pp. 187–88)

Just as in the course of his journey Francis will learn to spiritualize knighthood, so he will learn *per visibilium* to reach *invisibilium veritatem*. Thus his response to his second vision, in which the crucified Christ appears to him at prayer, is also to render service, but to lepers rather than to a count (p. 12/pp. 189–90). This second vision evokes a pattern of affective devotion that remains throughout his life.

The third vision of the cross is set within one of the most powerful narratives in the *Legenda Maior*, the story of the restoration of the three churches by Francis (chapter 2). Along with his renunciation of his earthly father (pp. 16–17/pp. 193–94) and his decision to live with lepers (pp. 17–18/pp. 195–96), his restoration of the churches is one of the key actions he takes immediately after his conversion. The story begins with the command given to Francis from the cross at San Damiano, his third vision of the cross:

> Cumque lacrymosis oculis intenderet in dominicam crucem, vocem de ipsa cruce dilapsam ad eum corporeis audivit auribus, ter dicentem: "Francisce, vade et repara domum meam, quae, ut cernis, tota destruitur!" (p. 14)

> [While his tear-stained eyes were gazing at the Lord's cross, he heard with his bodily ears a voice coming from the cross, telling him three times: "Francis, go and repair my house which, as you see, is falling completely into ruin."] (p. 191)

His response is a microcosm of the *Legenda* as a whole, for in learning to read the message of the cross more deeply, Francis moves from a literal to a spiritual understanding of his mission. Bonaventure presents both Francis's response to that command and his own significant commentary on that response, which asks the reader to interpret this third vision of the cross prophetically:

> Tremefactus Franciscus, cum esset in ecclesia solus, stupet ad tam mirandae vocis auditum, cordeque percipiens divini virtutem eloquii, mentis alienatur excessu. In se tandem reversus, ad obediendum se parat, totum se recolligit ad mandatum de materiali ecclesia reparanda, licet principalior intentio verbi ad eam ferretur, quam Christus suo sanguine acquisivit, sicut eum Spiritus sanctus edocuit, et ipse postmodum fratribus revelavit. (p. 14)

> [Trembling with fear, Francis was amazed at the sound of this astonishing voice, since he was alone in the church; and as he received in his heart the power of the divine words, he fell into a state of ecstasy. Returning finally to his senses, he prepared to obey, gathering himself together to carry out the command of repairing the church materially, although the principal intention of the words referred to that Church which Christ purchased with his own blood (Acts 20:28), as the Holy Spirit taught him and as he himself later disclosed to the friars.] (pp. 191–92)

Bonaventure now describes in some detail the specific way in which Francis goes about the literal business of repairing the churches. Since

Francis heard the voice three times, his response is to find three churches to repair. In showing how Francis learns his mission inch-by-inch, getting the money, loading up the stones, dealing with the abuse of those who fail to understand his purpose, Bonaventure is indeed presenting a microcosm of Francis's mission, and the subsequent mission of the order.

At the conclusion of chapter 2, Bonaventure sets these literal events in an explicitly apocalyptic context by explaining that they inaugurate the *renovatio* of the Church. After describing how Francis repaired the Portiuncula, the third church after San Damiano and St. Peter, Bonaventure notes that this church is where Francis first instituted the Order of Friars Minor. Inspired "per divinae revelationis" [by "divine revelation"], his physical repair of the three churches not only revealed that he was learning "a sensibilibus ad intelligibilia, a minoribus ad maiora ordinato progressu conscenderet" ["to ascend in an orderly progression / from the sensible realm to the intelligible, / from the lesser to the greater"] but also prophetically symbolized his *renovatio* of *ecclesia*:

> Nam instar reparatae triplicis fabricae ipsius sancti viri ducatu, secundum datam ab eo formam, regulam et doctrinam Christi triformiter renovanda erat Ecclesia trinaque triumphatura militia salvandorum, sicut et nunc cernimus esse completum. (pp. 19–20)

> [For like the three buildings he repaired,
> so Christ's church—
> with its threefold victorious army
> of those who are to be saved—
> was to be renewed under his leadership
> in three ways:
> by the structure, rule and teaching
> which he would provide.
> And now we see
> that this prophecy has been fulfilled.]

(pp. 197–98)

The *renovatio* of *ecclesia* is explicitly identified with the three orders that Francis establishes—Friars, Clares and the Third Order—as well as with "the structure, rule and teaching" which is Francis, himself a document signed by the seal of the living God. The idea of Francis as a figure of *renovatio* exercises a powerful control in the *Legenda Maior*.

These orders could thus be identified with the *viri spirituales*, the new spiritual men whom earlier Joachim of Fiore had expected to be among "the most potent of the champions of good at the time of the Antichrist."[40] The expectation of a *renovatio* led by these *viri spirituales* was appropriated by radical Franciscans in later polemics and became, for example, one of the keystones of Gerard of Borgo San Donnino's Joachite eschatology. Gerard, as we have noted earlier, failed to distinguish sufficiently between the eschatological roles of Francis and Christ. But when Bonaventure highlights the apocalyptic significance of Francis, he avoids the dangerous, heretical, or indeed blasphemous associations of Gerard. In the *Legenda* Francis is the *vir spiritualis* responsible for the *renovatio* of the Church due to his obedience to divine commands which initially have as their object the homey and ordinary task of repairing broken-down church buildings. Bonaventure thus domesticates the Joachite eschatology of Gerard and the Spirituals by keeping faith with the literal accounts of Francis's life while infusing these accounts with apocalyptic significance. E. Randolph Daniel has already noted that the expectation of a *renovatio* to occur at the end of the sixth age is not necessarily Joachite or unorthodox, because it was already part of orthodox Augustinian belief: "Franciscan eschatology was Augustinian both in its concept of a sixth age and its emphasis on *renovatio*. That perfection which Christ and his apostles taught and lived is to be renewed amidst the increasing evil of the last times by St. Francis and his brothers so that both Christians and non-Christians may see this model and by preaching imitate it themselves."[41] Yet it is not even necessary to choose between Augustine and Joachim as source for Bonaventure, since he was fully aware and saw the essential agreement of both traditions on this matter.

The fourth appearance of the cross similarly resonates with apocalyptic significance. Although the obvious connection has not been made by editors or previous studies of the *Legenda*, the vision of the priest Sylvester clearly reflects imagery drawn from the apocalyptic imagination. In the dream, which Bonaventure identifies as "a Domino . . . visio non tacenda" (p. 22) ["a vision by the Lord which should not be passed over in silence" (p. 201)], a huge dragon encircles and threatens to destroy all of Assisi. The city is saved when a golden cross, "cuius summitas caelos tangebat, cuiusque brachia protensa in latum, usque ad mundi fines videbantur extendi" (p. 23) ["whose top touched heaven and whose arms stretched far and wide and seemed to extend to the ends of the world" (pp. 201–2)], emerges from Francis's mouth. The apocalyptic resonances of this "divinum . . . oraculum" (p. 23) ["divine revelation" (p. 202)]—the fourth of the seven appearances of the cross—are manifold. The dragon, of course, resembles the great red Dragon of Apocalypse 12, the fallen angel that threatens the Woman by spewing water to sweep her away in the flood. The Woman, who traditionally is identified as *Ecclesia* and in the marriage imagery of Apocalypse is associated with the bride of the bridegroom, is saved when the earth opens its mouth to swallow the water (Apoc. 12:16). In Sylvester's dream the cross coming from the mouth of Francis that saves the city by driving away the dragon links him with the earth that opens its mouth to save the Woman. But the cross also links him with Christ's crucifixion and with the sword extending from the mouths of the Son of Man (Apoc. 1:16) and the bridegroom who defeats the powers of evil in the final apocalyptic battle (Apoc. 19:15).

Finally, Francis, who is inspired by Sylvester's vision "ad hostis antiqui fugandam versutiam et crucis Christi gloriam praedicandam" (p. 23) ["to put to flight our ancient enemy with his cunning and to preach the glory of the cross of Christ" (p. 202)], is associated with St. Michael, who defeats the Dragon in Apocalypse 12:7–9. This association is particularly apt as well as powerful, because Bonaventure stresses that Francis "Beato autem Michaeli Archangelo ... speciali erat amore devotior" (p. 76) ["was devoted with a special love to blessed Michael the Archangel" (p. 264)] and reminds the reader that "angelicus vir Franciscus" (p. 109) ["Francis the angelic man" (p. 307)] received the stigmata while fasting in honor of St. Michael. This fourth appearance of the cross thus serves as a nucleus of apocalyptic imagery that Bonaventure develops to emphasize Francis's eschatological role. It further radiates throughout the *Legenda*, lending meaning to other passages where Francis is called "Sponsi amicus" (p. 74) ["the friend of the Bridegroom" (p. 262)] or where a friar in vision is told that Francis will take the splendid heavenly throne vacated by one of the fallen angels (pp. 51-52/p. 234).

The four early chronological chapters of the *Legenda* include other references to the apocalyptic significance of Francis's life as well. In addition to relating Sylvester's dream, the third chapter deals with the broad outlines of the institutionalization of the order, starting with Francis's desire to live in strict conformity with "spiritum evangelicae veritatis" (p. 20) ["the spirit of the truth of the Gospel" (p. 199)] and moving to the reception of Francis and the approval of his order by Innocent III (pp. 25-28/pp. 204–6). This process is continued in chapter four, which ends with the approval of the rule of 1223 by Honorius III (pp. 36-37/p. 216). But even while detailing this growing institutionalization, Bonaventure emphasizes the spirit rather than the letter of the rule—its internal rather than external significance. He describes, for example, how Francis and his followers lived in a hut near Assisi:

> Vacabant enim ibidem divinis precibus incessanter, mentaliter potius quam vocaliter studio intendentes orationis devotae, pro eo quod nondum ecclesiasticos libros habebant, in quibus possent horas canonicas decantare. Loco tamen illorum librum crucis Christi continuatis aspectibus diebus ac noctibus revolvebant, exemplo patris et eloquio eruditi, qui iugiter faciebat eis de Christi cruce sermonem. (p. 29)

> [They spent their time there praying incessantly, devoting themselves to mental rather than vocal prayer because they did not yet have liturgical books from which to chant the canonical hours. In place they had the book of Christ's cross which they studied continually day and night, taught by the example and words of their father who spoke to them constantly about the cross of Christ.] (p. 208)

That Christ's cross is a book to be read suggests that the book of the universe, of salvation history, can be read whether or not written texts are available.

Similarly, Francis as book can be read whether or not he is present in person, a lesson the first Franciscans learned as well. Once when Francis had left the hut to preach in Assisi, "currus igneus mirandi splendoris, per ostium domus intrans, huc atque illuc per domicilium tertio se convertit, supra quem globus lucidus residebat, qui solis habens spectum, noctem clarere fecit" (p. 30) ["a fiery chariot of wonderful brilliance entered through the door of the house and turned here and there three times through the house. A globe of light rested above it which shone like the sun and lit up the night" (p. 209)]. Through this brilliant light the brothers realized that Francis, "sanctum patrem absentem corpore, praesentem spiritu tali 'transfiguratum' effigie" (p. 30) ["their holy father, who was absent physically, was present in spirit (1 Cor. 5:3), transfigured in this image" (p. 209)].

Significantly, Bonaventure then compares Francis to his most important Old Testament type, the apocalyptically charged figure of Elijah:

Supernis irradiatum fulgoribus et ardoribus inflammatum superna-
turali virtute in curru splendente simul et igneo sibi demonstrari a
Domino, ut tamquam veri Israelitae post illum incederent, qui vivo-
rum spiritualium, ut alter Elias, factus fuerat a Deo currus et auriga.
Credendum sane, quod ille horum simplicium aperuit oculos ad
preces Francisci, ut viderent magnalia Dei, qui oculos quondam ape-
ruerat pueri ad videndum montem plenum equorum et igneorum cur-
rum in circuitu Elisei. (pp. 30–31)

[And they realized that by supernatural power the Lord had shown
him to them in this glowing chariot of fire (4 Kings 2:11), radiant
with heavenly splendor and inflamed with burning ardor so that they
might follow him like true Israelites (John 1:47). Like a second Elijah, God had made him a chariot and charioteer for spiritual men (4
Kings 2:12). Certainly we can believe that God opened the eyes (John
9:32) of these simple men at the prayers of Francis so that they might
see the wonders of God (Acts 2:11; Ecclus. 18:5) just as he had once
opened the eyes of the servant of Elisha so that he could see the
mountain full of horses and chariots of fire round about the prophet
(4 Kings 6:17).] (p. 209)

These early Franciscans, in other words, are likened to Elisha, the first
follower of Elijah, the Old Testament prophet who provides a model for
Francis's apocalyptic role. It is now that Francis becomes "evangelicus
praeco" ["a herald of the Gospel"] as he, "annuntians regnum Dei" ["proclaiming the kingdom of God"], appears to be "homo alterius saeculi"
(p. 31) ["a man of another world" (p. 210)].

In the midst of detailing the institutionalization of the order, the
fourth chapter also relates the fifth and sixth appearances of the cross. The
fifth appearance took place when a worldly poet visited Francis, who at
the time was preaching in a monastery at San Severino. The poet saw
Francis in vision when "facta manu Domini super se" ["the hand of the
Lord came upon him (Ezech. 1:3)"]:

vidit eumdem crucis Christi praedicatorem Franciscum duobus trans-
versis ensibus valde fulgentibus in modum crucis signatum, quorum
unus a capite ad pedes, alius a manu in manum per pectus transver-
saliter tendebatur. (p. 34)

[and he saw Francis, the preacher of Christ's cross, signed with a cross, in the form of two flashing swords, one of which stretched from his head to his feet, the other crossed his chest from one hand to the other."] (p. 214)

Converted as a result of his vision and renamed Brother Pacificus, the poet was sent to France as the first provincial minister, another example of how the institutionalization of the order is related to the visions of the cross. Bonaventure also notes the apocalyptic significance of this visionary conversion as well. He explains that Brother Pacificus received a second vision in which he saw "magnum Thau in fronte Francisci . . . , quod colorum varietate distinctum, faciem ipsius miro venustabat ornatu" (p. 35) ["a great Tau on Francis's forehead, which shone in a variety of colors and caused his face to glow with wonderful beauty" (p. 214)].

The sixth appearance of the cross took place in Arles, again during a sermon. When St. Anthony of Padua was preaching on the inscription of the cross (John 19:19), a friar Monaldus received a vision in which Francis appears in the form of a cross:

> quidam frater probatae virtutis, Monaldus nomine, ad ostium capituli divina commonitione respiciens, vidit corporeis oculis beatum Franciscum in aëre sublevatum, extensis velut in cruce manibus, benedicentem fratres. Tanta vero et tam insolita fratres omnes consolatione spiritus repletos se fuisse senserunt, ut de vera sancti patris praesentia certum eis intra se Spiritus testimonium perhiberet. (p. 36)

> [A certain friar of proven virtue, Monaldus by name, was moved by divine inspiration to look toward the door of the chapter and saw with his bodily eyes blessed Francis lifted up in midair, his arms extended as though on a cross, and blessing the friars. All the friars felt themselves filled with such unusual inner consolation that it was clear the Spirit was giving them certain testimony (John 1:7) that their holy father had been really present.] (p. 215)

The appearances of the cross have progressed in a clear pattern from exterior to interior, from Francis's misunderstood dream of the cross emblazoned on military weapons to Mondaldus's perception of Francis and the cross as one and the same. At the same time these appearances continue to recall scriptural and hagiographic models that suggest Francis's role as prophet, reformer, angelic defender, and saint. For example, St. Martin is associated both with the first dream, which took place after Francis clothed the poor knight, and with the sixth, in which Bonaventure compares Francis to Ambrose who miraculously appeared at the burial of St. Martin (p. 36/p. 215).

The fourth chapter ends by describing the seventh appearance of the cross, the most significant apocalyptic event in the life of Francis, his reception of the stigmata. Significantly, it is linked to the major concerns of chapters 3 and 4, the development of the rule and the growing institutionalization of the order. After describing the confirmation of the rule by Honorius III in 1223, Bonaventure provides the following sophisticated gloss on the meaning of the rule and of the life of Francis:

> Ad cuius observantiam fratres ferventer inducens, dicebat se nihil ibi posuisse secundum industriam propriam, sed omnia sic scribi fecisse, sicut sibi fuerant divinitus revelata. Quod ut certius constaret testimonio Dei paucis admodum evolutis diebus, impressa sunt ei stigmata Domini Iesu digito Dei vivi tamquam bulla summi Pontificis Christi ad confirmationem omnimodam regulae et commendationem auctoris, sicut post suarum enarrationem virtutum suo loco inferius describetur. (pp. 37–38)

> [Fervently exhorting the friars
> to observe this rule,
> Francis used to say
> that nothing of what he had placed there
> came from his own efforts
> but that he dictated everything
> just as it had been revealed by God.
> To confirm this with greater certainty
> by God's own testimony,
> when only a few days had passed,
> the stigmata of Our Lord Jesus
> were imprinted upon him
> by the finger of the living God,
> as the bull or seal
> of Christ, the Supreme Pontiff,
> for the complete confirmation of the rule
> and approval of its author,
> as will be described below,
> after our exposition of his virtues.]

(p. 217)

The same linking of Francis as the Angel of the sixth seal who bears the seal of the living God and Francis as the recipient of the seal of the stigmata is implied here, this time through an expansion of the brilliant image by which Francis himself becomes a document to be read. The wounds of the stigmata have the likeness of a literal seal in that the blood-colored wounds on the body of Francis resemble wax seals on a document. Thus moving yet once more from the literal to the spiritual, the wounds are to be understood as the authenticating seals that their author, Christ, put on his document, Francis. Just as the Angel of the sixth seal carries a message to be read, Francis is now a document to be read. Equally important, Francis is now a document to be read by his followers in the same way that Bonaventure described the cross of Christ as a book read by Francis's earliest followers at the beginning of his mission.[42] The real rule of the order, Bonaventure asserts, is not so much to be found in the legal document confirmed by the Roman pontiff, as in the book of Francis, the document confirmed by Christ the supreme pontiff. Thus the story of the evolution of the rule of the order is not complete without the one document that informs the others, Francis, who is completed and authenticated by the stigmata, the event that confirms him as the Angel of the sixth seal.

As we have indicated, Bonaventure identifies Francis as the Angel of the sixth seal three times in the course of the *Legenda Maior*. We have discussed the first two instances at length: in the prologue, where the sophisticated theology of the *Legenda* is systematically laid out for the reader; and briefly in chapter 4 as part of the climactic image of the stigmata in the sequence dealing with the growth, development, and ultimately the meaning of the order. The third identification comes after Bonaventure has resumed the chronological orientation of the first four chapters with a chapter (13) describing at length the reception of the stigmata. Since the entire chapter is devoted to the event, it is hardly surprising that the sealing of Francis is presented with due elaboration, and that the chapter itself seals one of the most important sequences in the *Legenda*, the eight thematic chapters detailing the timeless virtues of Francis.

As is characteristic of the *Legenda* as a whole, Bonaventure here juxtaposes his detailed narrative and affective description of the appearance of the wounds with theological interpretation. Thus, describing Francis's descent from the mountain of La Verna after receiving the stigmata, Bonaventure connects him both with the Old Testament lawgiver and the apocalyptic angel:

Postquam igitur verus Christi amor in eamdem imaginem transfor-
mavit amantem, quadraginta dierum numero, iuxta quod decreverat,
in solitudine consummato, superveniente quoque solemnitate Ar-
changeli Michaelis, descendit angelicus vir Franciscus de monte,
secum ferens Crucifixi effigiem, non in tabulis lapideis vel ligneis
manu figuratam artificis, sed in carneis membris descriptam digito
Dei vivi. (p. 109)

[When the true love of Christ
had transformed his lover into his image
and the forty days were over
that he had planned to spend in solitude,
and the feast of St. Michael the Archangel
had also arrived,
the angelic man Francis
came down from the mountain,
bearing with him
the image of the Crucified,
which was depicted not on tablets of stone
or on panels of wood
by the hands of a craftsman,
but engraved in the members of his body
by the finger of the living God.]

(p. 307)

Bonaventure temporarily withholds the identification of Francis as the Angel of the sixth seal. The precise equivalence is made explicit only toward
the end of the chapter. The suggestion of the apocalyptic Francis, however, is already implicit in the juxtaposition of the angelic Francis with St.
Michael, the archangel who defeats the Dragon in Apocalypse 12.

Francis is also portrayed as an *alter Christus*, partly through direct
comparison and partly through his typological connection with Moses,
for Bonaventure implies that Francis's descent from La Verna is to be compared to Moses's descent from Mt. Sinai carrying the tablets of the law.
Just as Christ fulfills the Mosaic law in the Sermon on the Mount, so also
does Francis on La Verna. Just as Christ internalizes the Mosaic law in his
sermon, so also does Francis, whose body now bears the marks of Christ's
crucifixion. God's "authorship" of Francis is analogous to, yet in some
ways even more miraculous than, his authorship of the commandments,

for his text is "non in tabulis lapideis . . . , sed in carneis membris descriptam digito Dei vivi" (p. 109) ["depicted not on tablets of stone . . . , but engraved in the members of his body by the finger of the living God" (p. 307)].

Francis has also been transfigured by the reception of the stigmata. The comparison of Francis with Moses coming down from the mountain is therefore conflated with the moment of Transfiguration in the New Testament (Matt. 17), which is in turn reinforced by the subsequent description of the miracles and signs performed by the now-transfigured/stigmatized Francis.[43] This is a conflation justified by the Gospel accounts, for in the Sermon on the Mount the two Old Testament figures who are most prominently brought to mind as Christ talks of fulfilling the law and the prophets are Moses and Elijah. They are in fact present in the Transfiguration, their silent witness proclaiming that Christ is indeed the fulfillment of the law and the prophets. And as we have already seen in the *Legenda*, Francis is repeatedly associated with Elijah and Moses, with Elijah especially in the prologue and with Moses especially during the reception of the stigmata.[44]

Bonaventure now emphasizes that the stigmata is the culmination of the spiritual development of Francis at the same time that it is the witness to his followers of the efficacy of that development. It is at this point that Bonaventure recapitulates the six visions of the cross that have been key signs of Francis's spiritual development, paralleling in this outline the outline that concludes the prologue:

Ecce, iam septem apparitionibus crucis Christi in te et circa te secundum ordinem temporum mirabiliter exhibitis et monstratis, quasi sex gradibus ad istam septimam, in qua finaliter requiesceres, pervenisti. (p. 114)

[Behold
these seven visions of the cross of Christ,
miraculously shown and manifested
to you or about you
at different stages of your life.
The first six were like steps
leading to the seventh
in which you have found your final rest.]

(p. 314)

In bringing together these six appearances—"non phantastica visione, sed revelatione caelica" ["not imaginary visions but revelations from heaven"]—Bonaventure explicitly emphasizes how the seventh vision, the reception of the stigmata, is a fulfillment of the first six. The emphasis on seven as the final period of rest, so crucial to the apocalyptic imagination, strengthens all the ways in which this chapter deals with Francis as a figure of completion and fulfillment. Most importantly, it is a fitting conclusion to the apocalyptic progression that ends with Francis proclaimed once again as Angel of the sixth seal:

> Iam denique circa finem, quod simul tibi ostenditur et sublimis simi-litudo Seraph et humilis effigies Crucifixi, interius te incendens et ex-terius te consignans tamquam alterum Angelum ascendentem ab ortu solis, qui signum in te habeas Dei vivi, et praedictis dat firmitatem fidei et ab eis accipit testimonium veritatis. (p. 114)

[Now, finally
toward the end of your life
you were shown at the same time
the sublime vision of the Seraph
and the humble figure of the Crucified,
inwardly inflaming you and outwardly marking you
as the second Angel,
ascending from the rising of the sun
and bearing upon you the sign of the living God.
This vision confirms the previous ones
and receives from them
the testimony of truth.]

(pp. 313–14)

In this last sustained description of Francis as the Angel of the sixth seal, Bonaventure establishes the importance of Francis for all time. The concluding two chapters of the *Legenda* now continue the chronology of the life of Francis, describing his death (chapter 14) and his canonization (chapter 15). Apocalyptic resonances are evident in these chapters as well and are linked with Bonaventure's major concerns throughout the *Legenda*. The introduction to the scene of the death of Francis is particularly significant. In describing the effects of the continual illness that led up to his death, Bonaventure states:

Cum itaque per biennium ab impressione sacrorum stigmatum, anno videlicet a sua conversione vigesimo, multis fuisset agustiantium infirmitatum probativis tunsionibus conquadratus, tamquam lapis in supernae Ierusalem aedificio collocandus et tamquam ductile opus sub multiplicis tribulationis malleo ad perfectionem adductus. (pp. 116–17)

[For two years after the imprinting of the sacred stigmata—that is, in the twentieth year of his conversion—under the many blows of agonizing illness he was squared like a stone to be fitted into the construction of the heavenly Jerusalem and like a work of wrought metal he was brought to perfection by the hammer of many tribulations.] (p. 317)

Francis, who was told to repair the Church, has now physically become part of the Church, repairing it with his own body.

Once again, Bonaventure is concerned with completion. The task that Francis was given in the beginning has now been carried out successfully, for the Francis who took stone and mortar and went to repair the churches that had fallen into ruin has become a stone for the repaired Church that is the apocalyptic heavenly Jerusalem. That Francis is ready to be placed in the New Jerusalem not only anticipates his heavenly reward and canonization, but also establishes him as a figure in apocalyptic history. As is appropriate for the Angel of the sixth seal, Francis becomes, literally, part of the triumph that ends the Apocalypse, in which the heavenly Jerusalem is built from the souls of the saved (Apoc. 21). Thus the early repairing of the churches has become part of a process that can only be fully understood by seeing it as part of the apocalyptic process of *renovatio*.

We have already mentioned one other striking apocalyptic reference supporting the idea of *renovatio* that is present in the final chapter and which forms an appropriate conclusion to the *Legenda Maior* by pointing back to the prologue. Describing the transferral of Francis's body to the basilica constructed in his honor, Bonaventure once again connects Francis to two key Old Testament figures:

Erat re vera condignum, ut quem Deus in vita sibi placentem et dilectum effectum in paradisum per contemplationis gratiam transtulerat ut Henoch, et ad caelum in curru igneo per caritatis zelum rapuerat ut Eliam, eius iam vernantis inter flores illos caelicos plantationis ae-

ternae ossa illa felicia de loco suo pullulatione mirifica redolerent.
(p. 124)

[It was truly appropriate
that he who was pleasing to God and beloved by him
in his life;
who, like Enoch,
had been born into paradise
by the grace of contemplation
and carried off to heaven
like Elijah in a fiery chariot;
now that his soul is blossoming
in eternal springtime
among the heavenly flowers
it was, indeed, truly appropriate
that his blessed bones too
should sprout with fragrant miracles
in their own place of rest.]

(p. 326)

It is truly appropriate, to continue Bonaventure's phrase, that the narrative of Francis's life should end with a comparison to Enoch and Elijah. They are not only Old Testament figures whose lives of contemplation figurally relate them to Francis; they are also, as noted above, those figures most frequently identified with the Two Witnesses of Apocalypse 11:3–13 who will oppose Antichrist in the last days. The figure who has come to battle against the forces of evil in these apocalyptic last times is indeed Francis.[45]

3. The *Roman de la Rose:*
Jean de Meun's Apocalyptic Age
of Hypocrisy

Unlike the *Legenda Maior*, the *Roman de la Rose* does not immediately or obviously call attention to an apocalyptic agenda. Yet this immensely influential poem, which has been called "one of the most significant literary contributions of the entire Middle Ages," and which was probably "the most widely read vernacular poem after the *Divine Comedy*,"[1] can also be characterized by its apocalyptic concerns. As we have already suggested in Chapter 1, these concerns are both present and forceful in the explicit comparison of Astenance Contrainte to the pale and death-like horse that arises from Hell at the opening of the fourth seal of Apocalypse 6:8:

> le cheval de l'Apochalipse
> qui senefie la gent male,
> d'ypocrisie tainte et pale;
> car cil chevaus seur soi ne porte
> nule coleur, fors pale et morte.

> (12,038–12,042)

[the horse in the Apocalypse that signified the wicked people, pale and stained with hypocrisy; for that horse bore no color upon himself except a pale, dead one.]

Of equal or perhaps even greater importance in suggesting the poem's development of the apocalyptic imagination is the fact that Astenance Contrainte's companion, the deceitful friar Faus Semblant, is identified as a follower of Antichrist, in fact, as being no less than one of his "boys":

Je sui des vallez Antecrit,
des larrons don il est escrit
qu'il ont habit de saintee
e vivent en tel faintee.

(11,683–11,686)

[I am one of Antichrist's boys, one of the thieves of whom it is written that they have the garment of saintliness and live in pretense.]

Bonaventure's prologue to the *Legenda Maior*, with its explicit and thorough theological statement placing Francis at a crucial point in salvation history, sets up an expectation that is fulfilled in the body of the text, wherein Francis's life, and thus the *Legenda* itself, is given a consistent apocalyptic meaning. Tracing the influence of the apocalyptic imagination upon the *Roman de la Rose* is necessarily more elusive: the references to Astenance Contrainte and Faus Semblant, as well as the other specific apocalyptic references in the text upon which the analysis of this chapter is built, come in the midst of a vast and sprawling poem. Composed by two authors, Guillaume de Lorris (ca. 1225–35) and Jean de Meun (ca. 1269–78), writing some forty years apart, the poem has thus far successfully defied the attempts of its readers to classify it in terms of its formal unity. It is, furthermore, a poem about which there continues to be heated debate concerning fundamental questions of meaning. Thus an understanding of the apocalyptic resonances of these references in the *Roman* needs to be carried out in tandem with an attempt to see what light they shed on the work as a whole. In short, this chapter asks what is the relationship between these apparently circumscribed apocalyptic references and the meaning of the poem as a whole.

The comparison with Bonaventure provides a useful point of departure for this chapter in another way also. What we have seen in Bonaventure's *Legenda* might be described as the fraternal "school" of the apocalyptic imagination, a biblically charged, eschatologically directed vision that sees Francis as a forerunner of the last times, the Angel of the sixth seal, and a figure of *renovatio* within the Church. This tradition, as we have shown, coalesced in Bonaventure, who opposed two extreme uses of apocalyptic eschatology, both involving mendicancy and both condemned by Pope Alexander IV. The first, condemned in 1255, were the heretical claims of Gerard of Borgo San Donnino's *Liber introductorius in evangelium aeternum*, which radicalized the Trinitarian eschatology of

Joachim of Fiore to support the Spiritual Franciscans in their opposition
to the institutional Church.[2] The second, condemned a year later, were the
virulent apocalyptic writings of Guillaume de Saint-Amour attacking the
mendicants at the University of Paris.[3] Some scholars have questioned
the sincerity of the apocalyptic fervor evident in Guillaume's works, dismissing it as "only a rhetorical device."[4] But Penn Szittya is right in arguing that Guillaume's apocalyptic exegesis "is primary, not rhetorical and
secondary. . . ."[5] In any case, it was certainly taken seriously by Jean de
Meun, who placed Guillaume's eschatological polemics within a larger
narrative framework to comment on the moral crisis of his age. Just as
Bonaventure's *Legenda* became the most important example of apocalypticism in the service of the mendicants, Jean de Meun's continuation of the
the *Roman* became the most popular and influential example of apocalypticism in league with the antifraternal tradition.

Jean de Meun's attraction to the polemical writings of Guillaume de
Saint-Amour is particularly evident in Faus Semblant's long confessional
speech, one of the *Roman*'s major narrative achievements. Ironically
through the words of the "foxlike" friar, Jean explicitly condemns the *Liber
introductorius* of Gerard of Borgo San Donnino as "un livre de par le deable" (11,771) ["a book from the devil"], "bien est digne d'estre brulez"
(11,776) ["indeed worthy to be burned"], and rightly condemned by the
University. Faus Semblant also praises Guillaume de Saint-Amour (11,453–
11,478), explaining that the master had the support of the University and
his preaching audience. He further notes that his mother, Hypocrisy, is
responsible for Guillaume's banishment from the kingdom:

> Ma mere enessill le chaça,
> le vaillant home, tant braça,
> por verité qu'il soutenoit.
> Vers ma mere trop mesprenoit,
> por ce qu'il fist un noveau livre
> ou sa vie fist toute escrivre,
> et voloit que je reniasse
> mendicité et laborasse,
> se je n'avoie de quoi vivre.

(11,479–11,487)

[My mother plotted against him so much, on account of the truth
that he supported, that she chased him into exile. He committed a
great fault against my mother in writing a new book in which he

exposed her entire life, and he wanted me to deny mendicancy and go to work, if I had nothing to live on.]

Support for the position of "the man from Saint-Amour" is thus explicit; in fact, these sympathies are so obvious that one early scribe confused the two Guillaumes, the poet and the polemicist, commenting that Jean de Meun completed the *Roman* at the request of Guillaume de Saint-Amour rather than Guillaume de Lorris![6]

Jean's association of Astenance Contrainte with the pale horse of the fourth seal of the Apocalypse may be borrowed from Rutebeuf's poem, the "Complainte de Guillaume," from which Jean also borrowed Faus Semblant's name.[7] But the image is ultimately based on Guillaume de Saint-Amour's *De periculis novissimorum temporum*, which identifies the pale horse with hypocrisy and the friars, concluding that "quia sub specie pietatis decipient, plus poterunt nocere Ecclesiae Dei, quam aliqui alii homines, huiusmodi speciem non praetendentes"[8] ["Because they deceive under the appearance of piety they are able to harm the Church of God more than some other men who do not feign an appearance of this kind"]. The allusion to the fourth horseman, however, is more than yet another example of Jean's sympathy for the position of Guillaume and his followers in his dispute with the mendicants at the University of Paris. It is not simply a way of establishing Faus Semblant's hypocrisy or extending the poem's attack on the hypocritical friars. The apocalyptic allusion goes beyond Guillaume de Saint-Amour and, as we shall see, even beyond the polemical apocalypticism characterizing the Parisian dispute. It places Faus Semblant—and therefore Amant, his dream, his quest for the Rose, and the poem itself—into a particular scheme of history that is based upon contemporary interpretations of the Apocalypse.

Faus Semblant is usually understood as a figure created to embody the position of Guillaume de Saint-Amour in his quarrel with the mendicants. Many scholars have noted, for example, that Faus Semblant proudly confesses to many of the abuses attacked by Guillaume and his supporters.[9] The danger, however, in seeing Faus Semblant only in terms of the Parisian dispute is that it mistakenly restricts the extent to which the apocalyptic imagination informs Jean's concerns, makes lengthy sections of the poem seem irrelevant to Amant's quest, and raises serious questions about Faus Semblant's inclusion among the barons of love. As a result, Faus Semblant's lengthy confession is often treated as a mere footnote to a contemporary and immediate problem: it becomes of interest to historians, but a nuisance to most readers and a real obstacle to literary criticism. Typical of many critical reactions is William W. Ryding's view that Faus Semblant's presence in the poem is "unfortunate," because it poses for the critic "a very serious problem: it would be difficult enough to explain, let alone justify, the inclusion of so much irrelevant material."[10] The way out of this restricting position is certainly not to deny in any way the importance of the quarrel between the seculars and the mendicants at the University of Paris. Nor is it to deny Jean's obvious interest in the quarrel. Rather, we wish to show that Jean's interest in the quarrel was more than simply historical: we wish to show how this dispute was the conduit through which he drew upon the extraordinarily rich apocalyptic imagination to energize his continuation of the *Roman de la Rose*. Modern scholars have tended to see that quarrel as history rather than eschatology. We submit that the distinction is a modern one, and that it is both history and eschatology at the same time.

Though Jean de Meun borrows his specific polemical stance from Guillaume de Saint-Amour, he follows the more generalized historical model suggested by Bede and established by Anselm of Havelberg and other twelfth-century exegetes and historians. This model, which understood the opening of the seven seals of Apocalypse 5:1–8:1 as revealing a sequence of historical periods from the apostolic Church to Doomsday, identified the pale horse of the fourth seal as the hypocrisy of the contemporary Christian Church and the events of the sixth seal with the final assault of Antichrist. It is important to remember that this model represents just one approach to the Apocalypse that is based on the relatively new historicizing exegesis of the high Middle Ages. To underscore this point, it is worth investigating a somewhat earlier poem alluding specifically to the seven seals of the Apocalypse, the so-called *Apocalypse of Golias*, which was composed toward the end of the twelfth century. A satiric parody of the early chapters of the Apocalypse, in which the visionary narrator is taken up "in spiritu" to see "what only John has seen," the *Apocalypse* refers to the seven churches, the seven candlesticks, and the book with the seven seals in order to attack the moral decadence of the Church hierarchy.[11] Charles Dahlberg has recently speculated that there is "the possibility that some of the satiric extravagances of the *Golias*-poet parallel those of Jean de Meun," but, the satiric brush of the *Apocalypse* is too broad to include any historical details.[12] The *Apocalypse of Golias* parodies the Apocalypse to frame a bitter, ahistorical picture of the Church debased and vicious throughout time.

Its treatment of the seven seals exemplifies the ahistorical character of the *Apocalypse*. The visionary first sees the four creatures of Apocalypse 4:6–8—a lion, ox, eagle, and man—but rather than symbolizing the four Gospels, they represent an evil pope, bishop, archdeacon, and dean. Each of the seven seals is then opened as the narrator describes the various offices of the Church, attacking those offices symbolized by the four creatures and continuing with attacks on parish priests, vicars, and abbots. All is depraved. If, as Augustine claimed, the Apocalypse embraces the time "from the first coming of Christ to the end of the world, which will be Christ's second coming," then this new *Apocalypse* is bleak indeed.[13] It lacks any historical movement from the pristine Church of the past to the apocalyptic age of hypocrisy in the present or any grouping of the seals in distinct numerical patterns of four and three or six and one, which might suggest the potential positive role of God's people throughout history and at the end of time. Instead, all are corrupt and cruel, greedy simonists and lecherous gluttons, unrelated except in their evil as categories of a hopelessly depraved Church and differentiated only by their relative places in its perverse hierarchy.

Significantly, there is no apocalyptic expectation of an imminent end to this desperate condition. The sixth seal reveals a corrupt vicar, not a great angel or Antichrist; the seventh seal introduces a drunken abbot, not an ominous silence preceding Doomsday. Unlike the Apocalypse, which always juxtaposes some promise of reward for the righteous and judgment for the depraved, which introduces the peaceful lamb after the persecuting beasts, and which concludes with a vision of the New Jerusalem after the fall of Babylon, the *Apocalypse of Golias* suggests no progress toward either *renovatio* or judgment, but only the generalized immorality of a Church hierarchy. The *Apocalypse of Golias* may be an "apocalypse" in parodic form, but its familiar structure does not develop the rich symbolic imagery of the biblical Apocalypse, the four horsemen, the souls crying out from under the altar, the cataclysmic earthquake, and so forth. Its perspective is not "apocalyptic," furthermore, nor does it reflect the four interpretive keys which, as we saw in Chapter 1, characterize the apocalyptic imagination.

In contrast, as an allegorical dream vision whose introduction alludes to Macrobius (line 7) rather than to John the Revelator, the *Roman de la Rose* in Jean de Meun's continuation draws upon the four keys of the apocalyptic imagination to understand contemporary events. Reflecting the first key, for example, it understands Faus Semblant and Astenance Contrainte not only as allegorical emblems of hypocrisy, but also as specific figures living in the contemporary apocalyptic age of hypocrisy. Their actions and, as we shall see, the actions of other characters in the *Roman* are portrayed as reflecting the second key of the apocalyptic imagination as well. They act as deceitful inversions of the good, so that Faus Semblant's long rambling speech is essentially an inverted false confession, Amant's quest a parody of religious pilgrimage, and the entire landscape of the Garden a world turned upside-down. Understanding the opening of the fourth seal in historical terms, Jean places the false friar and beguine within a scheme of history which reflects the fourth key typifying the apocalyptic imagination, numerical patterns which trace the history of the Church from its first-century foundation to its final victory, concentrating on its historical enemies from Nero and Simon Magus to Antichrist. Finally, developing the third key, Jean links these contemporary representatives of evil by means of allegorical genealogies and apocalyptic imagery to other manifestations of evil prefiguring Antichrist.

This apocalyptic scheme helps explain the lineage of Faus Semblant, his relationship to Astenance Contrainte, and his crucial role among the barons of love in the *Roman*. When we are first introduced to this allegorical couple, Faus Semblant is identified as the son of Fraud and Hypocrisy:

> Baraz engendra Faus Semblant,
> qui va les queurs des genz emblant;
> sa mere ot non Ypocrisie,
> la larronesse, la honie,
> Ceste l'aleta e norri,
> l'ort ypocrite au queur porri,
> qui traist mainte region
> par habit de religion.
>
> (10,437–10,444)

[Fraud engendered False Seeming, who goes around stealing men's hearts. His mother's name is Hypocrisy, the dishonored thief who suckled and nursed the filthy hypocrite with a rotten heart who has betrayed many a region with his religious habit.]

He is the heir, the natural progeny, of those symbolized by the fourth horseman, who, as we noted in Chapter 1, historically represents the hypocrisy of the immediate past and the present. Perhaps alluding to the medieval understanding of vice as growing organically from hypocrisy and becoming ubiquitous in the last days, Jean de Meun identifies Faus Semblant as the contemporary fruit of the vicious coupling of Hypocrisy and Fraud which has characterized the Church in the immediate past. Traditionally, this ecclesiastical hypocrisy is associated with the last days and the imminent appearance of Antichrist and his false prophets. One twelfth-century lyric, for example, complains:

> Amodo siquidem possum asserere
> quia Antichristus creditur vivere,
> cum sic Ecclesiae nunc per circuitum
> vadant ad dedecus et ad interitum.
>
> Puto quod tempora venerunt ultima,
> cum tot ebulliant per mundum scandala,
> et cum jam pseudo-prophetae veniant,
> et jam quae scripta sunt mala incipiant.[14]

> [Now certainly I can assert
> That Antichrist is believed to be alive
> Since the Churches are now going around
> In circles to vice and to destruction.
>
> I think that the last times have come
> Since so many scandals are boiling up
>   throughout the world
> And since the pseudo-prophets are now coming
> And the written about evils are now beginning.]

It is therefore not surprising that, as we have noted, Faus Semblant later claims to be one of Antichrist's boys (11,683). He is the contemporary representative of the great eschatological deceiver, what the apocalyptic imagination identified as a forerunner or prophet of Antichrist. Jerome and later medieval exegetes argued that just as Christ had many forerunners in the past, so Antichrist would be typified by many evil figures.[15]

Like Antiochus Epiphanes, Nero, Simon Magus, and Domitian in the past, Faus Semblant in the present typifies through his deceptive and vicious life the even greater evil of Antichrist expected for the last days. Augustine particularly considered hypocritical Christians in the contemporary Church to be types of Antichrist, because, like the master liar, they claim to support Christ in their words yet deny him by their deeds.[16] As a present forerunner, therefore, the great hypocrite Faus Semblant states that he awaits Antichrist in the future:

> Ainsint Antecrist atendrons,
> tuit ensemble a lui nos tendrona.
>
> (11,815–11,816)

[Thus we are awaiting Antichrist, and we are headed toward him all together.]

Faus Semblant's status as a forerunner of Antichrist is given even greater emphasis later in the poem, after Amant has listened to La Vieille and, following her advice, approaches the gate broken earlier by means of Faus Semblant's deceit. Amant now sees Faus Semblant and a pregnant Astenance Contrainte:

> Ce fu Faus Samblant, li traistres,
> li filz Barat, li faus menistres
> dame Ypocrisie sa mere,
> qui tant est au vertuz amere,
> et dame Attenance Contrainte,
> qui de Faus Samblant est enceinte,
> preste d'anfanter Antecrit,
> si con je truis an livre ecrit.
>
> (14,709–14,716)

[There was the traitor False Seeming, son of Fraud and false minister of Hypocrisy, his mother, who is so bitter toward the virtues; there too was lady Constrained Abstinence, pregnant by False Seeming and ready to give birth to Antichrist, as I find it written in a book.]

Faus Semblant will be the father of Antichrist, a role that is consistent with Amour's repeated references to Faus Semblant as a devil (e.g., 11,085,

11,522). Responding to Faus Semblant's explanation of his parentage, for example, Love praises Fraud and Hypocrisy for their "mout bone engendreure . . . e mout profitable" ["very good engendering . . . and very profitable"] ironically adding, "Qu'il engendrerent le deable" ["since they engendered the devil"] (10,954–10,956).

These references to Faus Semblant as devil must not be reduced to what is in effect simply a good-natured way of taunting a scoundrel. They contribute to the poem's apocalyptic content precisely because in a tradition popular in medieval vernacular literature, the devil is expected to "father" Antichrist near the end of time. The early thirteenth-century *De l'avenement Antecrist*, for example, identifies Antichrist's parents as Beelzebub and a Babylonian whore; similarly, in perhaps the most dramatic version of this tradition, the fourteenth-century *Jour du Jugement* portrays a devil fathering Antichrist on a Jewish whore.[17] Thus, Faus Semblant as devil and Astenance Contrainte as whore are appropriate parents for Antichrist.

As his contemporary representative and progenitor, Faus Semblant also shares many characteristics with Antichrist and in fact is often described by the inverted religious language associated with the medieval Antichrist tradition and typifying the apocalyptic imagination. For example, Adso of Montier-en-Der's *Libellus de Antichristo*, the definitive medieval *vita* of Antichirst, describes Antichrist's life as an inversion of Christ's:

> Ideo scilicet, quia Christo in cunctis contrarius erit et Christo contraria faciet. Chistus uenit humilis, ille uenturus est superbus. Christus uenit humiles erigere, peccatores iustificare, ille e contra humiles eiciet, peccatores magnificabit, impios exaltabit semperque uicia, que sunt contraria uirtutibus, docebit, legem euangelicam dissipabit, demonum culturam in mundo reuocabit, gloriam propriam queret et omnipotentem Deum se nominabit.

> [This is because he will be contrary to Christ in all things, that is, his actions will be contrary to Christ. Christ came as a humble man; he will come as a proud man. Christ came to raise up the lowly, to pass judgment on sinners; he, on the contrary, will cast down the lowly, glorify sinners, exalt the impious and always teach vices which are opposite to virtues. He will destroy the law of the Gospel, bring back

the worship of demons in the world, seek personal glory and call himself the almighty God.] [18]

Like Antichrist, Faus Semblant is proud, an arrogant braggart, and a manipulator of the word, who, by pretending to be holy, is able to gain power and wealth. He is a most vicious trickster, openly confessing that he is a religious in order to trick people (11,187–11,192) and to gain wealth (11,523–11,546).

Furthermore, he is a murderer who uses religious pretense to kill his enemy in the midst of confession. Those critics who are reluctant to consider Amant's quest in moral terms must also gloss over the dispatching of Male Bouche, seeing it as no more than a necessary if slightly sordid step in the achievement of that quest. But this is a part of the poem that simply demands to be read in moral terms: Jean makes Faus Semblant's crime shocking by noting that Male Bouche is truly repentant, by reminding the reader that he is Faus Semblant's host, and by describing the action in the most brutal terms:

> Male Bouche tantost s'abesse,
> si s'agenoille et se confesse,
> car verais repentanz ja ert;
> et cil par la gorge l'ahert,
> a .ii. poinz l'estraint, si l'estrangle,
> si li a tolue la jangle;
> la langue a son rasoer li oste.
> Ainsint chevirent de leur oste,
> ne l'ont autrement enosse,
> puis le tumbent en un fosse.
>
> (12,331–12,340)

[Straightway Foul Mouth got down, knelt, and confessed, for he was already truly repentant; False Seeming seized him by the throat, squeezed with his two hands, strangled him, and then took away his chatter by removing his tongue with his razor. Thus they finished with their host; they did nothing else to kill him, but tumbled him into a moat.]

Noting that in this scene Jean draws "a parallel between hypocrisy and deceit in religious and political life and hypocrisy and deceit in the pursuit of the Lover's kind of love," Dahlberg emphasizes that the pursuit of the Rose through the confession and murder of Male Bouche must be read in moral terms: "The pursuit requires both self-deception and deceit towards others."[19]

In this violent murder the hypocritical Faus Semblant prefigures the master deceiver Antichrist, who in the medieval apocalyptic imagination is expected to mask his murderous intent under the cloak of hypocrisy. In the twelfth-century *Ludus de Antichristo*, for example, Antichrist first appears on stage "dressed in a breastplate which is hidden under his other garments," makes his religious claims, and then, along with Heresy and Hypocrisy, lays aside his robes and attacks the King of Jerusalem with a sword.[20] Faus Semblant similarly disguises his murderous mission by hanging a compassionate look on his face and a Bible around his neck:

> La chiere ot mout simple et piteuse,
> ne regardeure orgueilleuse
> n'ot il pas, mes douce et pesible.
> A son col portoit une bible.
> Empres s'en va sanz esquier,
> et port ses menbres apuier
> ot ausinc con par impotance
> de traison une potance,
> et fist en sa manche glacier
> un bien trainchant rasoer d'acier
> qu'il fist forgier en une forge
> que l'en apele Coupe Gorge.
>
> (12,055–12,066)

[He had a very simple, compassionate face without any appearance of pride, a sweet, peaceful look. At his neck he carried a Bible. Afterward, he went off without a squire, and, to support his limbs, as though he had no power, he used a crutch of treason. Up his sleeve he slipped a very sharp steel razor, that he had made in a forge and that was called Cut-Throat.]

Although Faus Semblant's initial outer sanctity hides his true intent, ultimately he draws his weapon. In so doing, he is a type of Antichrist, for Antichrist and his henchmen are expected to kill those whom he is unable to bribe or convert through his false teaching and miracles.[21] Faus Semblant thus rightly predicts that in the future those who resist Antichrist will lose their lives:

Ainsit Antecrist atendrons,
tuit ensemble a lui nos tendrons.
Cil qui ne s'i vorront aherdre,
la vie leur convendra perdre.
Les genz encontre eus esmovrons
par les baraz que nous covrons,
et les feron deglavier
ou par autre mort devier,
puis qu'il ne nos voudront ensivre

(11,815–11,823)

[Thus we are awaiting Antichrist, and we are headed toward him all together. Those who don't want to join him will have to lose their lives. We will incite people against them by the frauds that we hide, and we will make them perish by the sword or by some other death if they don't want to follow us.]

The poem also draws on specific images typical of the apocalyptic imagination to portray Faus Semblant and his cohorts. For example, after Faus Semblant proudly claims to be one of Antichrist's boys, he states:

si avironnons mer et terre,
a tout le monde avons pris guerre.

(11,689–11,690)

[And we inhabit sea and land. We have taken up war against the whole world.]

This couplet may allude to the origins and power of the three major apocalyptic beasts that are described at the very center of the Apocalypse: the Dragon "qui vocatur Diabolus et Satanas, qui seducit universum orbem" ["who is called the devil and Satan, who seduceth the whole world"] (Apoc. 12:9) and wages war against all the faithful (Apoc. 12:17); the leopard-like seven-headed Beast that receives its power from the Dragon, speaks blasphemously, and rises from the sea (Apoc. 13:1–2); and a third land-based Beast that hypocritically appears benign while ruthlessly combining the worst features of the Dragon and the sea Beast:

Et vidi aliam bestiam ascendentem de terra, et habebat cornua duo similia agni et loquebatur sicut draco. Et potestatem prioris bestiae omnem faciebat in conspectu eius; et fecit terram et habitantes in ea, adorare bestiam primam, cuius curata est plaga mortis. (Apoc. 13:11–12)

[And I saw another beast coming up out of the earth, and he had two horns, like a lamb, and he spoke as a dragon. And he executed all the power of the former beast in his sight; and he caused the earth, and them that dwell therein, to adore the first beast, whose wound to death was healed.]

According to medieval exegesis, these creatures represent Satan, Antichrist, and his False Prophet.[22] They are a parodic trinity of evil that Jean de Meun can appropriately associate with Faus Semblant, "the devil," the father and prophet of Antichrist. Faus Semblant's hypocrisy particularly associates him with the image of the seven-headed sea Beast (Apoc.13:14; cf. Apoc. 20:4), which, according to Augustine, symbolizes "the pretence" of the Beast and of "those people who profess the faith but live the lives of unbelievers. For they put up a show of being what they are not, and they are called Christians, not because of a truthful representation of Christianity, but because of an illusory resemblance to it."[23] Finally, Faus Semblant resembles the lamb-like Beast that rises out of the earth, whose two horns represent, according to Haimo of Auxerre, false innocence and pretended purity.[24]

The preceding verses further underscore Faus Semblant's role as false prophet:

Dehors semblons aigneaus pitables,
dedanz somes lous ravisables.

(11,687–11,688)

[We seem pitiful sheep without, but within we are ravening wolves.]

These lines clearly allude to Matthew 7:15–16, where, in what became a commonplace in medieval condemnations of false ecclesiastics, Christ warned the disciples against false prophets:

Attendite a falsis prophetis, qui veniunt ad vos in vestimentis ovium, intrinsecus autem sunt lupi rapaces; a fructibus eorum cognoscetis eos.

[Beware of false prophets, who come to you in the clothing of sheep, but inwardly they are ravening wolves. By their fruits you shall know them.]

Furthermore, the long disquisition on the many evils of the friars (lines 11,591–11,658) may very well suggest the "fruits" of these false prophets.[25] As we have seen, the apocalyptic imagination understood the appearance of such pseudo-prophets as a sign of the end of the world. These hypocritical deceivers are furthermore associated with Antichrist's deceitful pretensions in the last days to imitate the sanctity of Christ:

Multi enim venient in nomine meo dicentes: Ego sum Christus, et multos seducent. (Matt. 24:5)

[For many will come in my name saying: I am Christ: and they will seduce many.]

Yet, from the earliest development of the Antichrist tradition, exegetes warned that Antichrist would not simply be *ante* Christ—that is, he would not only appear before Christ's second coming—but *anti* Christ— that is, he would also oppose all that is Christ-like and be *Christo contrarius*.[26] As Arnold of Villanova, a younger contemporary of Jean also embroiled in Church polemics, argues, Antichrist is opposite to Christ in every way: "Nam Christus est dominus et alius latro, Christus est pastor et alius lupus, Christus custos et alius fur, Christus est sponsus et amicus, alius vero adulter, et inimicus"[27] ["For Christ is Lord and the other a robber, Christ is shepherd and the other a wolf, Christ is guardian and the other a thief, Christ is bridegroom and friend, the other, in fact, an adulterer and an enemy"]. Note that in addition to contrasting Christ the shepherd to Antichrist the wolf, Arnold contrasts Christ the true bride and friend to Antichrist the adulterer and enemy. Thus the imagery of the Antichrist tradition not only resonates in the self-portrait of Faus Semblant, but also can be applied to the poem's other characters who are hypocritically involved in the quest for the rose: the adulterous Lover and the false Friend.

These apocalyptic associations often lie below the surface of much of what has been perceived simply as Faus Semblant's brazen hypocrisy. For example, Faus Semblant's assertion as he prepares to "confess" and ultimately murder Male Bouche resonates with apocalyptic significance:

Car je sui d'ordre e si sui prestres,
de confessier li plus hauz mestres
qui soit, tant con li mondes dure.
J'ai de tout le monde la cure.

(12,309–12,312)

[For I am from an order and thus am a priest, the highest master of confessing that may be, as long as the world lasts. The whole world is my charge.]

Faus Semblant's proud boast to be the greatest master of confessing "as long as the world lasts" and his claim that the whole world is his charge probably refers both to the often debated question whether the friars should be assigned cure of souls and to the controversial claims of the radical mendicants to be the world's final orders, perhaps even to Gerard's identification of the Spiritual Franciscans with Joachim's new *viri spirituales*.[28] But because the opponents of the mendicants identified them with Antichrist, Faus Semblant's claim may also allude to the common medieval expectation that in the last days Antichrist will gain control of the entire world, his power increasing unabated as long as the world lasts, that is, until he is struck down by Christ at the end of time.[29] In a few short lines, Jean de Meun thus draws on a variety of images from the apocalyptic imagination to associate Faus Semblant with Antichrist, the false prophets who deceive the faithful, and the hypocrisy of the last days.

Jean further places these associations in a larger eschatological context that is developed throughout the *Roman de la Rose* by means of numerous references to other traditional signs of the end, especially to a world turned upside-down by rampant vice in which Christian truth, virtue, and love are hypocritically manipulated. Reason, for example, describes the world as sick, suffering because love is absent and becoming merely a piece of merchandise (5,100–5,124). This concern with the perversion of love is perhaps a contemporary manifestation of the "cooling of charity" that Jesus prophesied would result from the scandals of the last days and the deceit of false prophets:

Et tunc scandalizabuntur multi et invicem tradent et odio habebunt invicem. Et multi pseudoprophetae surgent et seducent multos; et quoniam abundavit iniquitas, refrigescet caritas multorum. (Matt. 24:10–12)

[And then shall many be scandalized: and shall betray one another: and shall hate one another. And many false prophets shall rise, and shall seduce many. And because iniquity hath abounded, the charity of many shall grow cold.]

The "cooling of charity," in fact, is a common complaint about the evils of the last days. In his influential sermons on the Johannine epistles, for example, Augustine explicitly connects hypocrisy and the subversion of charity with Antichrist: "Then whoever violates charity, whatever he says in words, denies by his very life that Christ has come in the flesh: and this is the Antichrist, wherever he is, wherever he goes." [30] Hypocrisy and the absence of *caritas* thus became in the later Middle Ages compelling evidence that the end was imminent. The "cooling of charity" represents, according to Robert Grosseteste, the evening of the sixth age that dawned with the preaching of the evangelists and ends with the persecution of Antichrist: "Huius diei mane fuit predicacio ewangelii; cuius vespera erit persecucio Antichristi, quando refrigescet caritas et habundabit iniquitas" [31] ["The preaching of the Gospel was the morning of this day, whose evening will be the persecution of Antichrist, when charity will cool and iniquity abound"].

In the *Roman* Nature also shares these eschatological concerns. She describes Doomsday and the torments of Hell at great length (19,200–19,338), just before her exclusion of Faus Semblant and Astenance Contrainte from her "salvation" because they are hypocrites, other than what they seem, characters to be feared. Sending Genius to the God of Love, Nature states:

> Dites li que saluz li mant,
> et a dame Venus, m'amie,
> puis a toute la baronie,
> fors seulemant a Faus Semblant,
> por qu'il s'aut ja mes assemblant
> avec les felons orguilleus,
> les ypocrites perilleus,
> des quex l'Escriture recete
> que ce sunt li pseudo prophete.
> Si rai je mout soupeçoneuse
> Attenance d'estre orguilleuse
> et d'estre a Faus Samblant samblable,
> tout samble ele humble et charitable.

(19,312–19,324)

[Tell him that I send greetings to him and to my friend, the lady Venus, and to his entire barony as well, except False Seeming alone, because he always goes congregating with those proud criminals, those dangerous hypocrites of whom Scripture says that they are pseudoprophets. And I consider Abstinence very suspect of being proud and like False Seeming, however humble and charitable she seems.]

Nature thereby condemns Faus Semblant for being in league with the pseudoprophets against whom Scripture warns in some of its most apocalyptically charged passages (cf. Matt. 7:15, Matt. 24:11, Apoc. 13:11).

Thus although the eschatological setting and apocalyptic language of the poem that we have been discussing are clearly important parts of its antifraternal polemic, Jean indeed does more than simply locate Faus Semblant within a specific controversy. Jean develops the figure of the false friar as a representative of Antichrist afflicting the Church in the present and as a link between the present time of hypocrisy and the evils of the last days. He does so not only—we would suggest, not primarily—to join with Guillaume de Saint-Amour in the current polemic, but also to energize the portrait of Faus Semblant and thereby bring the wider concerns of the apocalyptic imagination into the poem. As a forerunner of Antichrist, Faus Semblant has already infiltrated the Church during the apocalyptic age of hypocrisy. According to the medieval tradition, in the last days Antichrist will overturn all aspects of religion, will desecrate all holiness. In fact, his hypocrisy will be so effective that, heeding Christ's warning in Matthew 24:24, Christians believed even the elect will be deceived. Adso's standard *vita Antichristi* makes the point directly:

Nam quando tanta ac talia signa uiderint etiam illi, qui perfecti et electi Dei sunt, dubitabunt, utrum sit ipse Christus, qui in fine mundi secundum Scripturas uenturus est, annon.

[For when they see so many great miracles, even those who are righteous and chosen by God will wonder whether or not he is the Christ who, according to Scriptures, will come at the end of the world.][32]

As we have noted earlier, the second key of the apocalyptic imagination understands evil to be essentially an inversion of good. It thus portrays Antichrist and his minions as false imitations of Christ and his saints, and it develops parodies of religious images, rituals, and language to show how vice deceives virtue. Given how the apocalyptic understanding of history informs the *Roman*'s treatment of the contemporary controversy at the University of Paris, it is not surprising that the apocalyptic imagination also informs the parody of religious language throughout the *Roman de la Rose*. This parody, evident already in Guillaume de Lorris's beginning, is especially emphasized in Jean de Meun's ending. Faus Semblant is not alone in this parody, furthermore. Having accepted Faus Semblant's crucial aid in smashing the gate, Amant imitates Faus Semblant's parodic pilgrimage. Especially at the end of the poem (21,316–21,712), Jean inverts the language of pilgrimage, relics, and saints to suggest that Amant's pilgrimage is also hypocritical:

> Je, qui l'an rant merciz .c. mile,
> tantost, conme bons pelerins,
> hastis, fervenz et enterins
> de queur conme fins amoureus,
> anprés cest otroi savoureus
> ver l'archiere acueill mon veage
> por fournir mon pelerinage,
> et port o moi par grant efort
> escharpe et bourdon roide et fort,
> tel qu'il n'a mestier de ferrer
> por journoier ne por errer.
>
> (21,316–21,326)

[I gave him a hundred thousand thanks for his gift, and straightway after that delicious boon, I set out like a good pilgrim, impatient, fervent, and wholehearted, like a pure lover, on the voyage toward the aperture, the goal of my pilgrimage. And I carried with me, by great effort, the sack and the staff so stiff and strong that it didn't need to be shod with iron for traveling and wandering.]

A. C. Spearing points out that the explicit allegory here "is not only obscene but blasphemous." He rightly comments, however, that the parody "is not necessarily irreligious. It is precisely because the values implied in pilgrimage had a real meaning for the poet and his audience that the profane parody, with its identification of things that ought to be contrasted, was worth elaborating."[33]

In his continuation of the *Roman de la Rose* Jean de Meun suggests that Amant's entire quest is set in the apocalyptic age of hypocrisy. Faus Semblant is unique not because of his hypocritical nature, but because his hypocrisy is so blatant. Our reading of the Faus Semblant episode sees it not as so much extraneous material referring to a contemporary conflict unrelated to the poem's central concerns, but as an explicit gloss on the quest for the Rose: Faus Semblant's pilgrimage culminates in the throttling of Male Bouche, as Amant's pilgrimage culminates in the violent plucking of the Rose.

A similar connection between Amant and Faus Semblant has been made by Penn Szittya in his recent study of antifraternal literature in the Middle Ages. Szittya has called attention to another scriptural linkage, one that is important in medieval apocalypticism and that applies in privileged ways to Faus Semblant because it is central to the tradition of antifraternal satire. It also applies by implication to Amant and to the larger action of the poem:

> The pilgrim Lover then is morally and pictorially another version of the pilgrim Faus Semblant. When he is decked out in metaphorical pilgrim's garb, he reminds us iconographically of the earlier pilgrim who also broke down walls and forced entry into forbidden places. Though Jean de Meun does not quote the verse, William of St. Amour's favorite passage links them together: "ex his enim sunt qui penetrant domos et captivas ducunt mulierculas oneratas peccatis" (II Timothy 3:6).[34]

That one kind of penetration analogously defines the other is surely an example of the kind of wit that is lost by critics who read the quest *in bono* and who fail to see how the poem juxtaposes the cupidinous Lover and the hypocritical friar.

Indeed, such a juxtaposition strongly suggests that even if Amant's hypocritical actions seem to pale in comparison with the hypocrisy of Faus Semblant—a hypocrisy which after all imitates the hypocrisy of Antichrist himself—the fact is that Amant is likewise and in essential ways a hypocrite who uses the cloak of religion to mask his true intentions. One could, of course, argue that the hypocrisy of Amant is not on the same level as that of Faus Semblant because it is essentially private, whereas Faus Semblant's actions have massive implications for all levels of society. But we think that the larger and more significant point is that the Faus Semblant episode highlights something essential to Amant's actions and places it too by association in an apocalyptic context precisely to show that what seems to be purely private does in fact have a public dimension. Bernard of Clairvaux had earlier emphasized the close relationship between private hypocrisy and public corruption and similarly placed such hypocrisy in an apocalyptic context. Condemning the hypocrisy of false ecclesiastics, and the resultant corruption of the Church, he concludes that although "called to be ministers of Christ" such hypocritical ecclesiastics "are servants of Antichrist." It is important to note that, according to Bernard, "this foul corruption" is "all the more dangerous the more it penetrates inwardly."[35]

The same point is made by Jean de Meun when he shows what kind of company Amant must keep in order to accomplish his quest. By having Faus Semblant do Amant's dirty work for him, he not only undercuts Amant's claims to innocence, he shows as well that Amant too can be considered one of Antichrist's boys. It is especially telling that after listening to La Vieille's hypocritical advice and immediately after realizing that Faus Semblant and Astenance Contrainte are about to give birth to Antichrist, Amant prays for these evil characters in gratitude. By recognizing their role in his sexual quest, he associates himself with their hypocrisy:

> Cil la desconfirent sanz faille,
> si pri por eus, vaille que vaille.
> Seigneurs, qui veust traistres estre,
> face de Faus Samblant son mestre,
> et Contrainte Attenance preingne:
> double soit et simple se faigne.
>
> (14,717–14,722).

[Without fail, these were they who overcame the gate. Therefore I pray for them, for whatever that is worth. My lords, he who wants to be a traitor should make False Seeming his master and take Constrained Abstinence. He may then practice duplicity and pretend simplicity.]

We have clearly moved very far from the commonplace that the "real concerns" of the poem are embodied only in the direct movement of the Lover toward the Rose. In fact, the elaborate exemplification of the Faus Semblant episode invites us to see that problems of false and misdirected love characterize the quest as a whole by showing how that quest is informed both by a present social reality and a universal tendency indicative of the last times. It is not surprising, then, that the scriptural texts that define that apocalyptic situation also apply directly to the Lover. One such connection has been made forcefully and articulately (and then largely ignored in subsequent criticism) by John Fleming in his 1969 study of the poem. He sees both Amant and Faus Semblant as *seipsos amantes*:

> Faussemblant exemplifies a major aspect of love, one which he vigorously advances in his preaching and to which his whole being is a living sacrifice. It is, furthermore, the generic manifestation of the same love of which a subspecies, "civilized" sexuality, animates the Lover and his trivial conspiracy. The great scriptural text of antifraternalism from II Timothy, begins as follows: "Hoc autem scito, quod in novissimis diebus instabunt tempora periculosa: erunt homines seipsos amantes, cupidi, elati, superbi, blasphemi. . . ." The phrase *seipsos amantes* to which the antifraternal exegetes returned time and again has obvious relevance to the vile Jacobin who readily confesses, indeed boasts, that his single-minded goal is self-gratification; it should now be no less obvious that its application to Amant, and to his single-minded quest, is equally appropriate. The reader who has followed with some care the course of love's dance as it has been controlled by Guillaume de Lorris and Jean de Meun, and who is prepared to believe that Jean's ideas about sex and love may turn out after all to be predictably medieval rather than surprisingly modern, will see that the ultimate object of Amant's love is not the "lady," not "love itself," not even some fragile and immeasurable mystery of the human heart known only to poets and a few lovers—but himself. Amant's object is *seipsum*.[36]

Short of a book-length study of the *Roman* alone, it is not possible to do justice to all the evidence for Amant's self-love, but surely the mythological accounts of the fountain of Narcissus in Guillaume de Lorris's beginning (1,423–1,623) and the statue of Pygmalion in Jean de Meun's ending (20,787–21,198) both strongly suggest that Amant's self-love is a central issue in the poem. Or perhaps a better way to put the matter, since the interpretation of these episodes is a subject of scholarly dispute, is that our reading of the relationship between Faus Semblant and Amant confirms the moralized reading of these episodes, indeed, suggests that the moralized reading is inevitable. We therefore agree with Marta Powell

Hartley, who, approaching the poem from a different perspective, concludes after a careful analysis of the Fountain of Love that "Guillaume's *Roman* is a statement of some consequence on the destructiveness of the obsessive passion that Narcissus and Amant exemplify, a passion that has its origin in self-love."[37]

We would simply add that by setting Amant's quest during the apocalyptic age of hypocrisy, Jean has made explicit what is only implicit in Guillaume de Lorris. For example, Jean has Pygmalion express astonishment that his own creation—the object of his own worship—has come alive by exclaiming that he is like someone in a very lifelike dream (21,114). Thus the reader is led to see in Pygmalion's idolatry an image of the dreamer's own. Jean also pointedly relates his discussion of Pygmalion to Guillaume's earlier discussion of Narcissus by having Pygmalion himself use the story of Narcissus as a gloss for his own predicament (20,829–20,859). Pygmalion rather pathetically believes that, however hopeless is his own predicament, he is in better shape than Narcissus, because he can at least embrace and kiss his lifeless statue, whereas Narcissus found his reflection somewhat more elusive. The reader, however, has a harder time choosing between two such absolute versions of folly than does Pygmalion, which is perhaps another way that Jean is able to link the two episodes together: the similarities that the reader sees make the differences that console Pygmalion seem relatively inconsequential. Thus in his use of the mythographic tradition in his ending, Jean recalls the mythographic tradition of the poem's beginning, just as his inversion of the language of pilgrimage, relics, and saints recalls Guillaume's earlier description of the religion of love. Both suggest that Amant's actions are hypocritical, self-serving, and idolatrous.[38] At the end of the poem, we are at least in one crucial way pretty much back where we started: Amant may have gained the Rose, but he has not learned anything in the process.[39]

Seeing a connection between the Faus Semblant episode and the quest as a whole may also provide an important clue for the understanding of the poem's other episodes. Hypocrisy often goes unnoticed; by definition it is extremely difficult to identify. The *Roman de la Rose* shows that this is true in art perhaps no less than in life. Unless, of course, one has a good warrant for expecting to find it. And in the *Roman* it can be found ready and waiting once we realize what to expect in an age of hypocrisy, once we realize that the apocalyptic age of hypocrisy is the plane of action of the poem. One place where sharpened expectations might well notice a hypocritical discrepancy between words and deeds is Amant's response to the speeches of Nature and Genius. Central to the current critical debate are questions concerning the authority of Nature and her relationship to Reason. It is not possible here to resolve fully this debate, but it is important to realize that whatever the relationship between Reason and Nature, their spheres are distinctly different and Jean makes it clear that Nature's vision is limited. As Spearing has argued, "by the very fact of being Nature she is precluded from understanding the supernatural, though she knows of its existence. She gives men freedom (as La Vieille previously claimed), but God gives them reason."[40]

Even if a case could be made for the autonomy of Nature in the poem—that is, a Nature not subject to Reason—it is still very important to note that the Lover takes only that part of Nature's teachings that suits his purposes. In the poem's concluding lines, Amant thanks all the barons of love (including Faus Semblant) and explicitly rejects Reason (21,713–21,744), but it would be a mistake to believe that in doing so he is following the dictates of Nature. There is a difference, a pointedly hypocritical difference, between carrying out Nature's command for the good of the species and using the "good of the species" argument as a means to another end.[41] The poem nowhere suggests that Amant's purpose is to father a child; in fact, when he does "scatter a little seed," he seems quite regretful (21,689–21,712). His misappropriation of the command to generate is hypocritical even if we consider Nature to be autonomous; it is *a fortiori* even more hypocritical if we understand Nature as subordinate to Reason. Similarly, Jean makes it clear that Amant only selectively applies the lessons that Genius develops in his sermon. As Winthrop Wetherbee points out, although Nature and Genius play a major role in Amant's quest, "they evoke no perceptible moral awakening, and indeed their positive implications are as nearly as possible repudiated." Wetherbee further argues that "Sexual fulfilment, not as a metaphor for rational self-awareness, but as an end in itself, is the Lover's goal, and it is hard to see his success as affirming anything more positive. There is evidently something amiss in the world of the *Roman* which has no clear precedent in the allegories of the Chartrians."[42] That "something amiss," we maintain, is the poem's setting during the apocalyptic age of hypocrisy.

Even more obvious is the way in which Amant's counselors—both Amis and La Vieille—make hypocrisy the cornerstone of their advice. In the case of Amis, the disjunction between words and deeds is seen in his advising Amant to act hypocritically toward Male Bouche (7,303–7,368), offer bribes and feign tears when necessary (7,401–7,432), lie to the gatekeeper (7,561–7,579), and invent a nonexistent friendship with Bel Acuel (7,689–7,706). Though more disjointed, the speech of La Vieille is no less a counsel to hypocrisy, relying as it does on the absolute primacy of lying in every aspect of the relations between men and women. She is, as Carolynn Van Dyke has recently argued, the "logical successor" of Faus Semblant: "If False Seeming introduces moral and intellectual anarchy, La Vieille manifests moral and intellectual opportunism."[43]

Most important is the hypocrisy involved in the failure to consider Amant's quest in moral terms and instead to see the world of the Lover as a world which somehow exists outside the necessity for moral judgment. However much the surface rhetoric of the poem may lead us in that direction, an awareness of how the apocalyptic imagination informs the poem warns us that we cannot ignore the means by which Amant gains the Rose: the characters with whom he must deal, the deeds he must approve, the lies he has to tell. It is perhaps the poem's most significant exemplification of the age of hypocrisy to suggest that these are somehow accidental or of minor importance and that we can ignore them in our final judgment of what the poem is about. The apocalyptic resonances of the poem are important not chiefly because they take us outside of the poem to comment on the events of Jean's society, but because they are also a guide for understanding what is happening within the poem itself. The Faus Semblant episode is not an atypical episode in the poem where moral criteria cannot be ignored, but rather an episode that helps to provide the criteria that illuminate the moral dimensions of the entire poem.

The quarrel between the mendicants and the seculars is the only part of the *Roman* that is given the specificity of a contemporary setting. It is only at this point, in other words, that the poem appears to go beyond allegory and into history, or to put it in another way, is able to include history within its allegory. In what way is this fact significant? The *Roman* is a poem that includes a great deal that appears merely random, that is curiously digressive, and is difficult to explain; it is a poem that has defied critical attempts to elucidate its unity. Is it any less likely that a genuinely anti-mendicant diatribe—one that takes on the specificity of time and place—should find a place in the poem than should some of its many other subjects? Theologians, moralists, and poets were, after all, much agitated about the friars in the late thirteenth century and often for very good practical reasons. There is no a priori reason to assume that this was not also the case with Jean de Meun. The actions of venal friars might well have been more than enough to cause a shift in the rhetorical strategy of his continuation of the *Roman de la Rose*, since Jean clearly delights in such shifts in any case.

The way to deal with this question is to ask whether the shift to the present necessarily implies the same thing for Jean that it would in our own time. What does it mean for a thirteenth-century poem to be anchored in the "here and now?" If it is true, as this chapter argues, that history cannot meaningfully be divorced from eschatology in the *Roman*, then the poem's allusion to contemporary events must mean something very different than it would to us. That is to say, Jean cannot turn to history without also turning to eschatology. To make a historical statement is to make an eschatological one, because historical events and patterns in the Middle Ages are always understood within the larger philosophy of Christian history that sees history as essentially teleological, to be judged by its ending, from the perspective of eschatology. When Jean moves the action of the poem onto the plane of present-day "reality," it is not the impetuous or even casual move of a part-time reformer who seizes the opportunity to do some literary "friar bashing" because contemporary abuses have him and presumably his audience in an uproar. Rather, it is the studied move of a poet who has thoughtfully considered the significance of those abuses within the larger framework of human and divine action. The fact that this is the only part of the *Roman* that is in the "here and now" thus becomes in itself another clue to the importance of the incident, its very difference suggesting a kind of privileged status for the episode and the possibility that it can serve as an interpretive paradigm for Jean's extensive continuation of the poem.

Those who have argued for the moral inversion inherent in Amant's quest for the Rose have done so by claiming that what is described in the movement of the poem is not merely an excusable fault, at worst the least of the seven deadly sins, but rather an embodiment of the tendency toward sin itself. It should be clear by this time that our own analysis has necessarily taken us in this direction. To make our conclusions even more explicit in this regard, we suggest that yet another level of hypocrisy in the *Rose* is to be discerned in the assumption, already alluded to, that the private world of the Lover has no public implications. If even here, in Amant's private world, there are widespread public consequences, then we must attend to the seriousness of the Lover's actions. By setting the quest during the apocalyptic age of hypocrisy, Jean suggests that what is passed off as trivial can be a deadly serious disorder involving the larger community, all the more serious to the degree that it masks itself as the good.

Dante provides a useful comparison here, for, as the *Inferno* would exemplify a little later on, there is no such thing as a purely private sin: all sins are sins against the commonweal. Francesca, in telling Dante the pilgrim of her sin in canto 5, subtly recreates for her listener a private world of love. But she concludes with a very public statement of hate and revenge which proves that the notion of a private world is in fact a delusion, a studied failure to examine the consequences of one's actions. Though her sin has much in common with Amant's, it might be objected that bringing Dante in as a point of comparison is unfair, because it assumes that Jean de Meun operates within the same moral framework as does Dante, and this is precisely what is disputed in criticism of the *Rose*. Nevertheless, comparing Amant and Francesca is helpful precisely because in the past critics have read their respective affairs with equal approbation. Generations of critics argued that Dante was of Francesca's party despite the moral geography of Hell which he had created, and that we should take Francesca's own estimation of her situation and the pilgrim's swooning response as the final guides to our interpretation of the canto.[44] That Dante critics no longer accept this romantic reading is the result of many interconnected factors. One such factor is that critics now pay much more attention than formerly to the subtexts and to the iconography that informs Francesca's speech. The carefully wrought allusions in *Inferno* 5 to Augustine's conversion, for example, now receive as much attention as does the surface elegance of Francesca's language. Ultimately, critical interpretation depends on the fact that more evidence is now allowed into court.

The "Querelle du *Roman de la Rose*" has heated up considerably in these last days. Witty and playful as it undoubtedly was meant to be, John Fleming's attack on the "Ithacan Heresy" in the opening pages of his recent study of the poem continues a serious polemic that he began well over twenty years ago. And seriously indeed has it been answered in Thomas Hill's review of *Reason and the Lover*.[45] To the extent that we must enter into the "Querelle," we prefer to do so indirectly. Rather than adjudicating directly between the conflicting claims, we wish to suggest that interpretation of the *Roman de la Rose* also depends very much on the kinds of evidence allowed in court. What we hope to have added, of course, is the evidence provided by an understanding of the medieval apocalyptic imagination. If we assert that such evidence has been overlooked in previous studies of the poem, it is not because there is little scholarly attention being paid to the apocalyptic tradition in the Middle Ages—quite the contrary, as is evident in the astonishing number of recent studies cited in Chapter 1 and notes. But when such studies examine works of medieval literature and thought, they usually do so to find examples of change in the tradition, often emphasizing its radical elements. Simply put, the purpose of such studies is to further our knowledge of the tradition of apocalyptic thought, and the texts are a means to that end.

What we have done in this chapter is to reverse the angle of vision, seeing the tradition itself as a means to an end, as part of the intertextuality of the *Roman* that needs to be carefully considered in its interpretation. We are not suggesting that an apocalyptic reading will open up all of its still-hidden mysteries, and certainly not that the poem must now be understood as an apocalyptic poem pure and simple. But it is clear that Jean de Meun draws on the energies of a powerful and resonant tradition to put his characters and their actions in perspective, to set the poem's allegory in the age of hypocrisy, and to give meaning to his poetic structures. Though his sources and ultimately his purposes are different, his method is the same as Bonaventure's in the *Legenda Maior*. Although on opposite sides of the mendicant controversy at the University of Paris, Jean and Bonaventure also share the same goal: to show the relationship between present-day events and an apocalyptically directed vision of history. Thus, to understand fully the *Roman de la Rose* one must also understand the complexity of the medieval apocalyptic imagination and the sophisticated use to which it is put.

4. The *Commedia*: Apocalypse, Church, and Dante's Conversion

The outraged cry of Dante the pilgrim toward the end of *Inferno* 19, in which he assails the corruption and degeneracy of the papacy, contains one of the most striking apocalyptic references in the entire *Commedia*. This grim reminder of how far papal succession had in Dante's time departed from the Petrine ideal is energized by a direct and specific reference to the great harlot of Apocalypse 17:

> Di voi pastor s'accorse il Vangelista,
>   quando colei che siede sopra l'acque
>   puttaneggiar coi regi a lui fu vista;
> quella che con le sette teste nacque,
>   e da le diece corna ebbe argomento,
>   fin che virtute al suo marito piacque.

(19.106–11)

[It was shepherds such as you that the Evangelist had in mind when she that sitteth upon the waters was seen by him committing fornication with the kings: she that was born with the seven heads, and from the ten horns had her strength, so long as virtue pleased her spouse.]

Like the apocalyptic references in the *Roman de la Rose*, this passage, with its allusion to the "meretricis magnae, quae sedet super aquas multas, cum qua fornicati sunt reges terrae" (Apoc. 17:1–2) ["great harlot, who sitteth upon many waters, With whom the kings of the earth have committed fornication"], depends for its interpretation on an understanding of the Apocalypse which finds in contemporary history a fulfillment of biblical prophecy. It is clear that Dante means to include within the condemnation of ecclesiastical corruption figured by this passage not simply simoniacal prelates in general, but the three popes in particular whose nepotism and greed have been woven into the narrative of *Inferno* 19: Nicholas III (1277–80), Boniface VIII (1295–1303), and Clement V (1305–14). Moreover, it is appropriate to point out—again the *Roman de la Rose* provides a parallel—that such a method of interpretaion is not uniquely Dante's. Indeed, by this time the habit of finding the fulfillment of apocalyptic expectation in the events of contemporary history had become an almost unstated assumption of interpretation, indeed an expected and ordinary manner of interpretation. Dante therefore is drawing on a shared tradition that has become part and parcel of the medieval apocalyptic imagination. We will not fully appreciate the richness of the apocalyptic associations in *Inferno* 19 unless we understand that tradition as well as the particular uses to which it is put both in this section of the *Inferno* and the *Commedia* as a whole.

Even though this specific allusion to Apocalypse 17 is far and away the most direct, it is by no means the only such reference in canto 19, which is studded with imagery that has apocalyptic resonances. In particular, Dante evokes the rich tradition associated with the figures of Simon Magus and Antichrist by beginning the canto with a ringing condemnation of Simon Magus himself—invoked by the poet to stress the urgency of the canto's concerns:

> O Simon Mago, o miseri seguaci
> che le cose di Dio, che di bontate
> deon essere spose, e voi rapaci
> per oro e per argento avolterate,
> or convien che per voi suoni la tromba,
> pero che ne la terza bolgia state.

(19.1–6)

> [O Simon Magus! O you his wretched followers that, rapacious, prostitute for gold and silver the things of God which ought to be the brides of righteousness! now must the trumpet sound for you, since you are in the third pouch.]

To show how completely the Simon Magus story is intertwined with the broader apocalyptic concerns of the canto and the *Commedia* is to give further evidence of the pervasiveness of the apocalyptic imagination. These interconnections are, of course, by no means unique to Dante, and it is only by first understanding the richness of the imagination that we will be able to see the richness of Dante's appropriation of it. To do this, however, we will proceed by way of analogy with another work of art, one that draws its energy from the *Commedia* at the same time that it visually portrays the apocalyptic figures of both Simon Magus and Antichrist.

Luca Signorelli's frescoes in the Capella di San Brizio of Orvieto Cathedral, which portray the last days and the end of the world, "constitute the most ambitious treatment of eschatological subjects in Renaissance art."[1] For obvious reasons they are often described as reflecting Dante's *Commedia* or as having a Dantesque quality.[2] Commissioned in 1500 to complete the decoration of the cathedral begun by Fra Angelico and Benozzo Gozzoli half a century before, Signorelli painted—along with such scenes traditionally associated with the Last Judgment as the Resurrection of the Dead, the Damned in Hell, and the Saved in Paradise—two frescoes that portray the deeds of Antichrist and the signs of the end. Together with his illustrations from Dante's *Purgatorio*, also at Orvieto, these frescoes depict the key events of Christian eschatology. The entire cycle reflects, therefore, the artist's awareness of eschatology as encompassing not only the fortunes of the individual soul after death, but also the events that occur in the last days of world history, a view of eschatology that is both personal and universal. It is certainly appropriate to recognize Dante's influence upon the artist, which is acknowledged by Signorelli. He not only included such scenes as the "anti-Inferno" and the suffering of the damned in Hell, but also painted a portrait of Dante in the lower part of the chapel as well as in the frescoes.

Although the subject matter of these paintings was not drawn exclusively from Dante, a knowledge of the *Commedia* clearly helps one better understand the frescoes. Both Dante and Signorelli reflect a concern with the last things which is typical of their times, and along with many other artists and poets, they share a common background in Christian eschatology. Because their individual achievements are in some respects analogous, an understanding of the frescoes can also help us to understand the *Commedia*, even though the painter worked a century and a half after the poet. Moreover, an awareness of some of the interpretive questions connected with the Signorelli frescoes can help shed light on the interpretation of Dante's apocalypticism. Particularly, Signorelli's "Fatti dell'Antichristo" (see Figure 4), a portrayal both of the traditional Christian beliefs concerning the great deceiver of the last days and of late medieval apocalypticism, provides insights into Dante's incorporation of the apocalyptic imagi-

Figure 4. Luca Signorelli, "Fatti dell'Antichristo" [Deeds of Antichrist]. Fresco, Capella di San Brizio, Orvieto Cathedral. (Photograph: Scala Editorial Photocolor.)

nation in his description of the contemporary Church in *Inferno* 19—and throughout the *Commedia*. Both the artist and the poet draw upon long-established Christian iconography and symbolism to infuse their works with an apocalyptic expectancy that places contemporary scenes in a cosmic perspective and thereby underscores their religious significance and ultimate consequence.

It has been consistently noted that in the "Fatti dell'Antichristo" Signorelli has depicted his contemporary world. More specifically, art historians have shown many of those portrayed listening to Antichrist in the foreground of the fresco to be contemporaries of Signorelli or other well-known Florentines—including Dante in the group to the right of Antichrist.[3] Signorelli even includes portraits of himself and Fra Angelico to the far left of the scene. Like the depiction of the visionary John in many illuminated Apocalypses, they stand outside the action but watch the events unfold.[4] Other elements of the fresco adding to its contemporary setting include the central-plan church occupying the background and the Dominican friars preaching behind Antichrist. The church is painted in the High Renaissance style influenced by the revival of classical models, yet it clearly symbolizes the expectation, related to the Antichrist tradition since the early church, that the false Christ will take possession of the Temple in Jerusalem where he will blasphemously claim to be Christ.

Similarly, the friars in the fresco should also be understood to reflect the medieval Antichrist tradition. As we have seen in earlier chapters, the traditional interpretation of the Two Witnesses who oppose the Beast from the abyss (Apoc. 11:3–13) identified them with the Old Testament figures Enoch and Elijah, who in the last days were expected to return from the Earthly Paradise to oppose Antichrist. This interpretation is a commonplace in most exegetical discussions of the Apocalypse through the twelfth century, and it continues to be noted in later medieval exegesis.[5] After the establishment of the mendicants, however, some commentators understood the Two Witnesses to represent Francis and Dominic specifically, or more generally their two orders.[6] This identification simply followed from the apocalyptic understanding of Francis evident in the theology of Bonaventure, for example, and of the apocalyptic meaning of the new orders which we have discussed in previous chapters. Signorelli's inclusion of these friars, then, most probably reflects this new interpretation, for in later medieval illuminated Apocalypses the Two Witnesses of chapter 11 are often portrayed as friars.[7]

For Signorelli, however, the contemporary and the cosmic are fused. Signorelli's portrayal of Antichrist's work among his own contemporaries as he and his mentor Fra Angelico observe the scene suggests that the artist, like many others during his time, believed that he was living in the last days, that corruption in society and the Church reflected the working of Antichrist and his followers, and that the signs of Doomsday could be read clearly in contemporary events. As we have noted in previous chapters, especially from the time of Joachim of Fiore the direct application of apocalyptic exegesis to contemporary events is an important element in European religious and political life, and it remains so for several centuries. For instance, the Antichrist tradition, which had become one of the most important elements of the medieval apocalyptic imagination, continued to be interpreted in historical and contemporary terms. It was applied to specific astrological portents, religious and political leaders, and social and religious conditions. In the early fifteenth century, to take one example, the sermons of the very popular St. Bernardino of Siena drew from that tradition and other apocalyptic expectations to condemn the practice of usury and other vices of the merchant class.[8] Historians, furthermore, interpreted social and economic upheavals, natural disasters, and military defeats as signs of the last days. Local political disputes, earthquakes and plagues, and the growing power of the Turks were all understood within an apocalyptic framework. Writing in 1348, Giovanni Villani, the Florentine merchant chronicler and contemporary of Dante, describes the natural upheavals of his time as "great signs and judgements of God," as the "signs that Jesus Christ, preaching to his disciples, predicted should appear at the end of the world."[9]

Historians in the late fifteenth century continued to infuse contemporary events with apocalyptic significance, both optimistic and pessimistic. On the one hand, Joachimist expectations of the defeat of Antichrist and the establishment of a millennial kingdom circulated widely and had a profound effect, for example, on the Franciscan missionaries sent to the Americas to "convert" the native peoples. Although influenced as well by more conservative sources, Columbus similarly understood his voyages of discovery in apocalyptic terms. An avid collector of prophecies, he considered himself—as he states in a letter to the Spanish court—to be the divinely appointed "messenger of the new heaven and the new earth."[10] On the other hand, ominous astrological predictions and prophecies of imminent cataclysm were also pervasive. One example, the "Toledo Letter," which predicted disaster for Europe and first appeared in 1184, circulated again in the fourteenth and fifteenth centuries, the last version in 1480. It included the very popular Sibylline prophecies of the Last World Emperor and the ubiquitous expectation of the imminent reign of Antichrist, updated to begin in 1516.[11] Another example is the so-called Cedar of Lebanon vision. Although originating in the thirteenth century when Europe awaited the Mongol assault, this "prophecy" gained new meaning and was applied to new villains closer to home as a result of the tumultuous natural, ecclesiastical, and political events of the fourteenth and fifteenth centuries.[12] In Italy, as throughout Europe, in fact, the late fifteenth century was a period of general anxiety, when Renaissance optimism concerning the renovation of the arts and society was coextensive with the resurgence of a pessimism regarding contemporary events and the expectation of Antichrist.[13]

Perhaps the most striking scholarly attempt to understand Signorelli's fresco in contemporary, late-fifteenth-century terms is André Chastel's detailed interpretation, which specifically identifies Antichrist in the painting with the apocalyptic preacher Savonarola, a Dominican. The identification, which is heavily based upon Marsilio Ficino's condemnation of Savonarola as Antichrist, is fascinating if not totally convincing.[14] But even if one accepts Chastel's interpretation, one needs to be wary of the simple equation of Antichrist and Savonarola. Such an identification can be misleading, especially if it is used as a restrictive model of how the traditional iconography of Antichrist is appropriated to understand visually the contemporary world. Chastel's identification will ultimately result in a narrow interpretation of the fresco, one that fails to take into account the extent to which the iconography is traditional and its meaning universal as well as particular. Thus the inclusion of Antichrist in a series of pictures portraying the last days is not, as Chastel would have it, an innovation, but a reflection of the widespread apocalyptic imagination and of popular eschatological fervor during the late Middle Ages and Renaissance.[15] For example, the important role played by Antichrist in last-day events is illustrated widely in illuminated manuscripts and the early printed block-books of the fifteenth century. These often trace the details of his deceit, continue with the signs of the end, and culminate in the Last Judgment, placing him within the same eschatological perspective developed by Signorelli's fresco cycle.[16]

Antichrist in the "Fatti dell'Antichristo" may allude to Savonarola, whose own prophetic denunciations of contemporary Florence were charged with apocalyptic fervor, although there is little evidence to support this identification.[17] It may also refer to contemporary political developments in Orvieto, even to specific local oppositions between political and religious groups, as Jonathan Riess has recently argued.[18] The apocalyptic tradition portrayed in the fresco, however, probably reflects Signorelli's contemporary world in a much broader sense. If the artist was thinking of the recent career of the fanatic Dominican and other disturbing local events, he clearly understood them as instances in a long line of evils afflicting Italy and the Church. As we will show below, the fresco draws widely from the fertile apocalyptic imagination. Rather than limiting our understanding of it to Florence and Orvieto in the late 1490s, we should recognize in it the painter's apocalyptic outlook on his times and his commentary upon not only his own Italy, but also the earlier Italy of Dante and another Dominican, Fra Angelico. Signorelli views this Italy as suffering from the signs of the end, the corruptions and deceits that culminate in Antichrist's appearance before Doomsday. Like the *Commedia*, therefore, the fresco is not a topical work in the narrow sense nor is its meaning limited to one contemporary event. It is a portrayal of the immediate past and of the present within an apocalyptic framework developed by means of the iconography associated with Antichrist's expected appearance in the imminent future.

Because the details of the Antichrist tradition are related to the apocalyptic concerns of *Inferno* 19 (and of the *Commedia* more generally), they are worth investigating. Signorelli has, in fact, included in the "Fatti dell'Antichristo" much of the traditional iconography of Antichrist. To begin with, the portrayal of Antichrist as a human—as resembling in outward appearance the historical Christ—is typical of later medieval representations of the deceiver. Such representations, evident in the popular artistic *vitae* of Antichrist, particularly emphasize his deceitfulness while simultaneously portraying him (as does Signorelli) as devil inspired.[19] The fresco includes the terrors associated with Antichrist, including the soldiers on the church steps and the decapitation of his opponents. Signorelli also carefully portrays the deceiver's several means of winning converts, the four methods by which he gains power: through false doctrine, through false miracles, through threats and persecutions, and especially through gifts and bribes. As regular features of the medieval imagination, these methods were commonly developed in literature and art since Adso's *Libellus de Antichristo*. They are evident, for example, in the Anglo-Norman Apocalypses which include several scenes from Antichrist's life.[20] The influential Apocalypse of the Pierpont Morgan Library (MS M. 524) shows the deceiver working a miracle (pointing to an upside down tree) in one scene (fol. 7^r), whereas in another he blasphemously sits in the Temple in Jerusalem claiming to be God while his followers distribute treasures to his converts and threaten those Christians who remain faithful (fol. 7^v).[21]

Although the arrangement of details is quite different, Signorelli similarly includes these methods by which Antichrist gains power in the last days. In the fresco's central scene, Antichrist stands on a pedestal, inspired by a devil, preaching his false doctrine in which he claims to be Christ, while to the far left, also in the foreground, the righteous faithful are killed for not accepting him. In the central background, in the midst of the piazza, Antichrist—imitating Christ's most popular miracle—heals the sick or perhaps raises the dead. These marvels were attributed to him in the medieval tradition, even though theologians routinely emphasized that these were false, accomplished only through devilish powers.[22] Significantly, the result of this deception, as the fresco clearly shows, is Antichrist's acceptance by Christians, who now worship him. Signorelli particularly emphasizes Antichrist's effective use of bribes. This method of gaining power, in fact, is given precedence in the fresco. Below the pedestal on which Antichrist stands lies a cache of valuables, which represents his chief means of winning converts. In the group listening to Antichrist on the left are shown two of his followers, one offering money to the other, who accepts, apparently in return for his promised loyalty. Thus, while including many scenes which the apocalyptic imagination associated with Antichrist and his career, the fresco concentrates on his ability to gain power and emphasizes especially his ability to purchase the loyalty of Christians who are concerned more with worldly than with spiritual wealth. Signorelli highlights the means by which he believes Antichrist most readily will gain control of the Church and convert Christians to his false doctrines during the last days.

The fresco also portrays, in the left background, Antichrist's death. Because its depiction provides the most telling linkage with Dante, it is important to sketch some of the details of this visual treatment, all the more so in that it is here that Signorelli is most dependent on the traditional iconography of Antichrist rather than on specific contemporary events. The representation of the headlong fall of Antichrist affirms that Signorelli conceives of him as the eschatological deceiver who plays such a prominent role in the apocalyptic imagination, not a contemporary false prophet. Antichrist is portrayed falling through the sky to his death below. He has just been struck down by the Archangel Michael, here representing the agent of Christ, who alone can destroy the deceiver.[23] Having attempted to ascend to heaven in his ultimate blasphemous and parodic imitation of Christ, Antichrist is finally struck down, destroying himself and many of his followers. Signorelli's decision to portray Antichrist at this particular point draws heavily from traditional iconography. Such is how Michael Wolgemut portrays him in the woodcut printed in Hartmann Schedel's *Liber chronicarum* (1493), the so-called *Nuremberg Chronicle*, which art historians sometimes cite as a possible source for Signorelli (see Figure 5).[24] Yet he need not have seen that particular illustration, for Antichrist's death is often so shown, especially after the fourteenth century.[25]

For our purposes it is important to note that Antichrist's death was not so depicted in earlier illustrations, which instead drew upon the key apocalyptic texts dealing with the destruction of the eschatological deceiver, 2 Thessalonians 2:8 and Apocalypse 19:20–21 and 20:9–10. In pictures following the Pauline version, such as the short life cycles inserted in illustrations of chapter 11 of the Anglo-French Apocalypses, Antichrist is consumed by fire or some other destructive force from heaven: "Et tunc revelabitur ille iniquus, quem Dominus Iesus interficiet spiritu oris sui et destruet illustratione adventus sui" (2 Thess. 2:8) ["And then that wicked one shall be revealed whom the Lord Jesus shall kill with the spirit of his

Figure 5. Michael Wolgemut, "The Fall of Antichrist." Woodcut printed in Hartmann Schedel's *Liber chronicarum* [*Nuremberg Chronicle*] (1493). (Photograph: Regenstein Library, University of Chicago.)

mouth; and shall destroy with the brightness of his coming"]. Because exegetes interpreted the "spirit" as signifying Christ's agent, an angel wielding a sword is sometimes shown killing Antichrist, who is usually crowned and enthroned at the height of his glory. Such, for example, is how his death is portrayed in the church of Santa Maria in Puorto Fuori, Ravenna.[26] In illustrations of Apocalypse 19, on the other hand, a victorious Christ, portrayed with a two-edged sword extending from his mouth, defeats the Beast and the false prophet (the seven-headed sea-Beast and two-horned lamb-like Beast of Apoc. 13). Symbolized by these hypocritical beasts, Antichrist is shown cast into the mouth of Hell, where he is punished along with the Dragon and the false prophet.[27]

The portrayals of Antichrist's death in the fifteenth-century block-book *vitae*, the *Nuremburg Chronicle*, and Signorelli's fresco as a headlong fall after an attempted rise into Heaven thus clearly reflect a shift in the traditional iconography of Antichrist. The source for this shift may be discerned in Adso's early medieval *Libellus de Antichristo*, which organizes exegesis of scattered biblical passages to create a brief "biography" of Antichrist modelled on the life of Christ.[28] This highly influential *vita Antichristi* provided an outline that later theologians, poets, and artists could stuff with details as they enlarged and enriched their imaginative understanding of the final deceiver. Thus, if the life of Antichrist is essentially understood to be—following the second key of the apocalyptic imagination—an inversion of Christ's life, it is logical that his death should result from his parodic attempt to reenact the Ascension. His spiritual heritage as "son of the Devil," furthermore, allowed artists to borrow events and details from the iconography of Satan as well. Thus the portrayal of Antichrist's self-serving attempted rise into Heaven and immediate fall into damnation not only inverts Christ's true and selfless Ascension and ultimate return as judge, but also reenacts the fall of Lucifer into Hell following his hubristic challenge of the divine. This event, which opens the late medieval cycles of English mystery plays, is represented in such typologically structured works as the popular *Biblia Pauperum* and *Speculum Humanae Salvationis* manuscripts and block books.[29]

Another important impetus for the development of the Antichrist tradition in the later Middle Ages was the gleaning of images and details from the popular biblical and apocryphal narratives dealing with earlier figures of evil. These, according the the third key to the apocalyptic imagination, were identified as types of Antichrist. As we have seen earlier, the most influential type was Simon Magus, the great opponent of Peter and

Paul, whose legend remains both popular and important throughout the Middle Ages and into the Renaissance.[30] His death is described as part of the legend of St. Peter in the immensely popular *Legenda aurea* of Jacobus da Voragine (c. 1260–70):

> But later on Simon returned to Rome, and regained Nero's favour. One day he called the people together, and declared that because he was much offended by the Galileans, he was about to abandon the city, which hitherto he had shielded by his presence, and that moreover he would ascend into Heaven, since the earth was no longer worthy to hold him. On the appointed day, therefore, he climbed to the top of a high tower, or, according to Linus, to the summit of the Capitoline hill; and thence he rose in flight, with a laurel crown upon his head. And Nero said to the two apostles: "Simon says sooth! You are both impostors!" And Peter said to Paul: "Lift up thy head and look!" Paul lifted his head, saw Simon flying about, and said to Peter: "Peter, linger not to finish thy work, for already the Lord calls us!" Then Peter cried out: "Angels of Satan, who hold this man up in the air, in the name of my Master Jesus Christ, I command you to hold him up no longer!" And straightway Simon was dashed to earth, his skull was split, and he died.[31]

The dramatic death of Simon Magus was repeatedly illustrated in the visual arts as well. Though the legend is rich and varied, the earliest known and most prevalent illustration of Simon Magus represents his plunge from the heavens after being cursed by Peter.[32] Throughout medieval art, he is shown falling headlong through the sky from the arms of the devils by whose power he has attempted to rise to Heaven in imitation of Christ. The scene is popular enough to have been illustrated in historiated capitals, altarpieces, stained glass, mosaics, and illuminated manuscripts. And in some of these, such as the thirteenth-century Sienese panel painting now in the Pinacoteca of Siena (see Figure 6, top), Simon's fall is placed within a cycle depicting the life of St. Peter.[33]

It is to this well-known scene of Simon's upside-down fall that Dante alludes when he portrays the simoniac popes in *Inferno* 19. Charles Singleton was the first to urge that the iconography of Simon Magus be considered in interpreting the invocation to Simon.[34] For a full understanding of the apocalyptic resonances of this canto, however, the relationship between Simon Magus and Antichrist implied by this scene must also be

Figure 6. *Top:* "Life of Saint Peter." Panel painting, Pinacoteca, Siena. (Photograph courtesy of William R. Cook.) *Bottom:* Fall of Simon Magus. Lower left panel of "Life of Saint Peter," Pinacoteca, Siena. (Photograph courtesy of Wes Kennison.)

taken into account. Since, according to the Simon Magus legend, the deceiver of the early Church claimed to be Christ and attempted to prove himself divine in opposition to Peter by working miracles and rising to Heaven, he was quite early identified by exegetes as a type of Antichrist, the deceiver of the last days. As we have previously indicated, exegetes and theologians recognized numerous types of Antichrist in the Old and New Testaments and throughout Church history, characters who precede his appearance in the last days and who foreshadow Antichrist's great evil by means of their tyranny and hypocrisy. In the very earliest Christian literature Antichrist and Simon are compared, and in later literature, often homiletic, the two deceivers are likewise associated by their ability to work false but effective miracles. Thus in medieval exegesis the thought of one often suggested the deeds of the other.[35]

An important example of the close identity of the two in the later Middle Ages is developed in a work whose importance we have already noted in our introductory discussion of the way in which Simon Magus becomes a part of the apocalyptic tradition. As we have shown, Bonaventure's seminal *Collations on the Hexaemeron* identifies the two in his discussion contrasting Christ and Antichrist and showing how each is reflected in the twelve principal Christian mysteries. Discussing the eleventh mystery, which deals with the gifts of the Holy Spirit, Bonaventure states that the Antichrist is symbolized by Simon the Magician:

> In mysterio undecimo, scilicet diffusionis charismatum, signatur per Simonum magnum, qui voluit emere Spiritum sanctum et in altum ascendit et postea cecedit, qui daemonia invocavit. Erat enim mendacissimus, et veniat in signis et prodigiis mendacibus.

> [In the eleventh mystery, the diffusion of charismatic gifts, he is symbolized by Simon the Magician, who wanted to buy the Holy Spirit, who rose up to great heights and then fell, who called upon evil spirits. For he will be the worst liar: he will come with deceitful signs and prodigies.][36]

In this short passage Bonaventure refers to several of the features that link Simon Magus and Antichrist and that are illustrated by Signorelli. Both opponents of Christianity abuse the charismatic gifts, for instance. According to Acts 8:18–19 Simon attempted to purchase the Holy Spirit, and according to the standard interpretation of Apocalypse 13:13, Antichrist will simulate Pentecost by bringing down fire upon the heads of his converts.[37] Both are deceivers, claiming "Ego sum Christus" (Matt. 24:5); both prove their supposed divinity by false miracles, by depending upon evil spirits, and by rising into the heavens.

The shared iconography of the two deceivers was elaborated in great detail by the medieval apocalyptic imagination. We have already shown, for example, that in the later Middle Ages, when artists began illustrating the complete *vita* of Antichrist in picture cycles separate from the biblical texts, portrayals of Simon's headlong fall served as models for illustrations of Antichrist's death. But in addition to this scene, manuscript illustrations point to other similarities between the two deceivers. The Gulbenkian Apocalypse interprets the miracles performed by the two-horned Beast of Apocalypse 13:14–15 by picturing both a winged Simon Magus and a regal Antichrist raising the dead (see Figure 3). Both hold scrolls proclaiming their miraculous powers over death. The manuscript also illustrates the silence that accompanies the opening of the seventh seal (Apoc. 8:1) with a picture of the fall of Simon Magus (see Figure 7).[38]

Figure 7. Fall of Simon Magus. *Gulbenkian Apocalypse* illustration of Apoc. 8:1. Lisbon, Museu Calouste Gulbenkian MS L.A. 139, fol. 16ʳ. (Reproduced by permission, Calouste Gulbenkian Foundation Museum.)

Usually the Anglo-French Apocalypses note that this silence represents a short period of peace to follow the death of Antichrist, perhaps a period of forty or forty-five days during which Christians may repent for worshiping the deceiver.[39] However, here the Gulbenkian Apocalypse gloss identifies the period of silence as representing a past brief time of peace experienced by the Church between the rule of Augustus and Nero. The illustration portrays the end of this earlier time of peace by showing a crowned Nero holding a sword and watching Simon Magus fall from the hands of devils. Peter and Paul watch the scene and then are killed at the hands of the tyrant. But in much medieval exegesis and in many of the illuminated Apocalypses this scriptural passage is interpreted not only as an account of the past persecutions of the Church by Nero, but also as a foreshadowing of the future persecution under Antichrist. Nero in this illustration, therefore, should be understood as typifying Antichrist, who is closely associated with Simon Magus. In fact, Christian exegesis often identified Nero, as well as Simon Magus, as a type of Antichrist.[40] Peter and Paul, the two apostles of the early Church who challenge the pseudo-Christ Simon Magus and are killed by the tyrant Nero, therefore, appropriately typify Enoch and Elijah, the two prophets of the last days who will challenge the pseudo-Christ and be killed by the tyrant Antichrist.

The Gulbenkian Apocalypse, as is typical of the third key of the apocalyptic imagination, thus links Antichrist and Simon Magus by drawing parallels between their careers. Each seeks to imitate events from the life of Christ in order to mislead the unwary, and each opposes the representatives of Christ during a time of crisis in Church history. Simon battled against the first leader of the apostolic Church, Peter; Antichrist will attack the Church's last defenders, Enoch and Elijah (or, as the later tradition has it, the embodiment of the Two Witnesses in the fraternal orders). Although standing at opposite ends of Church history, Simon Magus and Antichrist are thus closely related in the apocalyptic imagination. In fact, in his depiction of the simoniac popes in *Inferno* 19, Dante argues that their common methodology of pretended holiness masking devil-inspired works and bribes represents the major evil plaguing the contemporary Church. Within the apocalyptic framework of the later Middle Ages, that Church, led by followers of Simon Magus, anticipated and indeed reflected in its decadence the workings of Antichrist in the last days. Like Simon Magus in the New Testament, in other words, these hypocritical religious can be identified as types of Antichrist. In portraying the lamentable condition of his Church, Dante was thus able to draw on a rich and complex iconography to infuse his work with apocalyptic expectancy. By means of this tradition, the poet's apostrophe to Simon Magus at the outset of the canto is connected with the pilgrim's apocalyptic outburst towards the end (19.106–11). As we will show, the entire canto links an especially significant episode in the personal journey of the pilgrim to a universal scheme of history.

In *Inferno* 19 this journey begins when the pilgrim descends from his vantage point on top of a bridge arching a bolgia and discovers that the livid stones full of holes which he saw from a distance actually contain burning and twitching legs. These are visible remains of what he soon finds out are the simoniacs, punished by being embedded upside down in rock. Encountering the most prominent of these, he learns that he is standing next to Pope Nicholas III. Mistaken at first by Nicholas for Boniface VIII—who is to be Nicholas's successor in punishment in Hell even as he was his successor in simony on earth—Dante listens to Nicholas's sordid and self-damning confession of nepotism and greed and then responds with his impassioned and apocalyptically charged harangue against simony and the abuse of papal power. The condemnation of the simoniac popes in this canto, both explicit and implicit, draws together a very wide range of sources to highlight the inversion between matter and spirit which defines their nepotism and greed.

The sources are biblical, apocryphal, and sacramental.[41] The descent of the Holy Spirit in tongues of fire at Pentecost, the occasion when the Church first began exercising its priestly duties, is parodied in the flame of punishment on the feet of these modern-day upside-down apostles. It is also parodied in the encounter between Dante and Pope Nicholas, which recalls through inversion the life of the Spirit as outlined in the description of Pentecost in Acts 2. The scriptural texts establishing the primacy of Peter (especially Matt. 16:18), first pope and therefore the standard for papal ideals, are also appropriated in the language of the canto. Just as the Sienese altarpiece (Figure 6, top) parallels the manners by which the two first-century figures—the archetypal simonist and the archetypal pope—died, Dante recalls Peter's martyrdom by inverted crucifixion in the punishment of the simoniac popes embedded upside down in rock. The effect shows how in their thirst for wealth these popes have overturned the role of shepherd entrusted by Christ to Peter and his successors and how in their pursuit of material rather than spiritual gain they have become the successors of Simon Magus rather than Simon Peter. These foraging shepherds have also failed in their duties as priestly ministers empowered to preserve the proper relationship between material and spiritual reality through the proper administration of the sacraments. The canto thus also recalls details of sacramental theology and ritual to reinforce Dante's criticism of these upside-down successors of the apostles, the first high priests of Christendom. With typical thoroughness Dante alludes to the seven sacraments, providing within the fabric of this especially rich and dense canto clear references to the ideal which simony inverts.

The density of this traditional iconography is heightened by an awareness that these sources all have strong apocalyptic associations. Since our discussions of the tradition in Chapter 1 and of Signorelli's fresco in this chapter have already shown how the medieval apocalyptic imagination connected Simon Magus and Antichrist, we can now elaborate on how Dante develops these apocalyptic associations by further demonstrating the pervasiveness of the figure of Simon Magus within the canto. The ringing invocation which calls on Simon Magus at the same time as it tells the reader that the canto will be concerned with his successors, his *miseri seguaci*, is of course the first and most obvious example of his importance within the structure of the canto:

> O Simon mago, o miseri seguaci
> > che le cose di Dio, che di bontate
> > deon essere spuose, e voi rapaci
> per oro e per argento avolterate,
> > or convien che per voi suoni la tromba
> > pero che ne la terza bolgia state.

$$(19.1-6)$$

[O Simon Magus! O you wretched followers that, rapacious, prostitute for gold and silver the things of God which ought to be the brides of righteousness! now must the trumpet sound for you, since you are in the third pouch.]

The importance of the magician continues well beyond this initial invocation, however. The scriptural account from Acts depicts Simon attempting to buy the gifts of the Holy Spirit from Peter and John in a blatant inversion of the nature of spiritual power. Peter's reply, "Pecunia tua tecum sit in perditionem" (Acts 8:20), is appropriated by Dante in the structure of the canto: this reply carries with it something of the flavor of "take your money to hell with you."[42] This, of course, is precisely the fate of the simoniac popes in *Inferno* 19, who are literally "pursed" down in the bolgia even as they put money in their purses above:

> e veramente fui figliuol de l'orsa,
>   cupido si per avanzar li orsatti,
>   che su l'avere, e qui me misi in borsa.

(19.71–72)

[and I was truly a son of the she-bear, so eager to advance the cubs that up there I pursed my gains, and here I purse myself.]

The account of the fall of Simon the Magician, definitively rendered in the apocryphal *Acts of Peter* and popularized in the *Legenda aurea*, was more widely known in the Middle Ages than was the biblical story, for in these versions the slim scriptural account was fleshed out and Simon was given a more complete narrative history. As we noted above, his fall is the climax of that history. After escalating the spiritual warfare which he has been waging against Simon Peter, Simon Magus—no longer satisfied with simply trying to buy the gifts of the Spirit—now tries to defraud the people with his false spirituality, his magic. In his climactic demonstration of his power, Simon Magus flies above the city of Rome to the astonishment of the crowd, until Peter, calling on Jesus Christ, challenges these demonic pretensions by causing Simon to fall from the sky.[43] It is this scene that is so frequently recreated in medieval art, definitively rendering the fate of pride and the triumph of the spiritual over the material. And it is this scene that is exactly recreated in the placement of Dante and the upside-down Nicholas, which suggests through their analogous positions how Nicholas is indeed a follower of Simon Magus and how Dante the pilgrim has become the true follower of Simon Peter.

Of the many examples from the visual arts which recreate the fall of Simon the Magician, the thirteenth-century Sienese panel painting (Figure 6, top) is especially interesting because it both relates and opposes Simon Magus and Simon Peter. It provides a striking parallel for the scene in *Inferno* 19, emphasizing the very way in which the opposition between Simon Magus and Simon Peter is brought out in the canto. In the painting the central figure of Peter is flanked by six scenes representing crucial events in his life. In the bottom two panels, the fall of Simon Magus on the left (Figure 6, bottom) is balanced by the apostle's upside-down crucifixion on the right, so that these two upside-down events—one signifying foolhardy pride, the other spiritual humility—are clearly contrasted. Similarly, both events come together in the positioning and suffering of the upside-down Nicholas in Hell, a barren parody of Peter's martyrdom. As the Sienese panel painting reminds us, according to tradition Peter was martyred by being crucified upside-down in order to acknowledge his unworthiness to be crucified in the same manner as his master.[44] The tormented simoniac popes embedded upside-down in the rock surely parody Peter's martyrdom, showing at once their failure to follow both Peter and Christ. This is fitting, for just as Peter's crucifixion was a sign of his humility, the simoniac popes, as Nicholas's speech makes clear, are defined by their pride.[45] It is this pride that likewise makes Simon Magus such an appropriate contrast to Peter, for it is this pride that is crushed in his fall. In the Siena panel, the fall of Simon Magus (Figure 6, bottom) is clearly to be interpreted as both a physical and spiritual inversion of the scene to which it is juxtaposed, the crucifixion of Peter. And just as the painting defines the meaning of the magician's damnation by juxtaposing it with Peter's saving act, so Dante is able to evoke both resonances through the positioning of the figures in canto 19. The suffering Nicholas parodies Peter's crucifixion and at the same time recreates the fall of Simon the Magician.

Because Christian tradition closely associates Simon Magus and Antichrist—following the third key of the apocalyptic imagination, which links the historical and eschatological figures of evil—Dante's pervasive allusions in the canto to the magician also suggest Antichrist's potential role within the text as well. Thus, as we will show, these popes are not only followers of Simon Magus; they are also types of Antichrist. Like Signorelli's fresco, the canto draws on contemporary apocalyptic expectations to portray the present conditions of the Church. In other words, it deals not only with specific simoniac popes, but also with the more disturbing and ominous problems typical of the last days. Not surprisingly, once this apocalyptic dimension is recognized in the canto, a number of details that might otherwise go unnoticed take on greater meaning. Not simply Simon Magus, but many other details which make the *contrapasso* of this canto so rich can be understood in the light of the apocalyptic imagination.

The same iconographic configuration that suggests a parody of Peter's crucifixion and the fall of Simon Magus contains further apocalyptic suggestions in addition to those linking Simon and Antichrist. In this configuration Dante, a layman, has taken over the position of priest and is about to hear the "confession" of a corrupt high priest. As the poet puts it, the pilgrim is in the position of a friar about to hear the confession of an assassin, for, as glosses to these lines commonly point out, it was Florentine custom to execute such assassins by burying them alive upside down:

> Io stava come 'l frate che confessa
>   lo perfido assessin, che, poi ch'e fitto,
>   richiama lui per che la morta cessa.
>
> (19.49–51)

[I was standing there like the friar who confesses the perfidious assassin who, after he is fixed, recalls him in order to delay his death.]

Thus Dante himself must leap into the breach caused by the Church's failure, through the greed and corruption of her high priests, to observe and fulfill her sacramental function.[46] But as we have already seen, the connection between the simoniac popes and Simon Magus likewise links these popes to Antichrist and to other figures associated with his expected appearance in the last days, such as the prophets Enoch and Elijah. Later medieval illuminated Apocalypses portray these prophets in the garb of contemporary friars, suggesting that to at least some artists and exegetes in the thirteenth and fourteenth century, the coming of the friars signified the coming of Enoch and Elijah in the last days. The simile ("Io stava come 'l frate" [19.49]) linking Dante to the friars, then, may also link him to these latter-day prophets. Such a reading would support John Block Friedman's analysis of Geryon, the beast of *Inferno* 16 and 17. Friedman has argued that a figural relationship exists between Enoch and Elijah and Vergil and Dante throughout the *Inferno*. In demonstrating a figural connection between Geryon and Antichrist—which is the major thrust of his study—Friedman likewise shows how Vergil and Dante, "the two persons who do something with Geryon," stand in a figural relationship to the Two Witnesses of the Apocalypse, Enoch and Elijah: Enoch, like Vergil, was a virtuous man who lived before the law; Dante, like Elijah, is taken to the spiritual realm while still in the body.[47]

In *Inferno* 19 that relationship too is recalled by the position of Vergil and Dante, who have descended the pit together to do battle with the precursor of Antichrist, Nicholas III. The subsequent direction of the canto reinforces this set of associations. Dante does in fact hear a confession from Nicholas III, the confession of his nepotism and greed. But it is a parodic false confession, a sacramentally invalid confession without either contrition or satisfaction. It highlights for both pilgrim and reader the fact that these simoniac popes, in their thirst for wealth, have neglected their duties as chief ministers of the saving rites of the New Law. So instead of bringing the absolution of Dante as a friar hearing an assassin's confession, it brings instead the stinging rebuke of Dante as a friar prefiguring Elijah. Thus it is appropriate that the pilgrim does indeed do battle against the forces of Antichrist toward the end of the canto, using the same weapon to be used by Elijah in the last days, the weapon Dante knows best: the word. His denunciation of papal corruption in lines 90 to 117 is one of the fiercest and most highly charged of the entire *Commedia*. It contains, for reasons we will show shortly in more detail, exactly that same combination of zeal and prophetic fervor that he is urged to use as his crusader's weapon by his crusading great-great-grandfather Cacciaguida in the central cantos of *Paradiso* (i.e., 17.118–143) when the pilgrim is given the most sustained and explicit statement of his mission as prophet and poet.

Dante's denunciation of papal corruption in *Inferno* 19 also clearly invokes the doctrine of papal succession from Simon Peter, the first pope, as yet another way to show what has been inverted by these successors of Simon Magus. Nicholas III, the current infernal occupant of the upside-down *cathedra petri*—the pun on Peter's name works especially well here in the rocky bolgia—will soon give way to his successor in simony, Boniface VIII. This the reader discovers when Nicholas mistakes Dante's arrival with that of Boniface, and thus adds false prophecy to the list of ways in which he has perverted the gifts of the Holy Spirit:

> Ed ei grido: Se'tu gia costi ritto,
>   se'tu gia costi ritto, Bonifazio?
> Di parecchi anni mi menti lo scritto.
>
> (19.52–54)

[and he cried, "Are you already standing there, are you already standing there, Bonifazio? By several years the writ has lied to me."]

Nicholas further explains that Boniface will give way in turn to Clement V:

> Ma piu e 'l tempo gia che i pie mi cossi
>   e ch'i'son stato cosi sottosopra,
>   ch'el non stara piantato coi pie rossi:
> che dopo lui verra di piu laida opra
>   di ver' ponente, un pastor sanza legge,
>   tal che convien che lui e me ricuopra.

(19.79–84)

[But longer already is the time that I have cooked my feet and stood inverted thus than he shall stay planted with glowing feet, for after him shall come a lawless shepherd from the west, of uglier deeds, one fit to cover both him and me.]

To this sequence of unapostolic succession we can add the very mechanism of that succession, which also in a literal and parodic way suggests the same inversion. Each new occupant of this inverted *cathedra petri* will literally push his predecessor through the rock, thus assuring that in Hell just as on earth the chair of St. Peter is occupied by only one pope at a time.[48] The ideal of papal succession is contrasted with Hell's grim reality, where popes succeed each other only as practitioners of simony.

Yet this grim reminder of how far papal succession has departed from the Petrine ideal in Dante's time must also be seen in terms of apocalyptic associations that transcend Dante's own time. As we noted in Chapter 1, the first key of the apocalyptic imagination understands the personal in universal terms, on the one hand, just as it expects the cosmic to be manifested in the individual historical instance. At this point in the *Commedia*, then, where Dante is at his most specific, he implies that individual judgment must be rendered in terms of the universal framework provided by apocalyptic associations present both in the language of the canto and in contemporary apocalyptic writing that denounces these popes. Thus Dante's use of the apocalyptic imagination is crucial to the canto. Charles T. Davis underscores the importance of the apocalyptic frame of *Inferno* 19 by noting the link between these popes and the image of the Whore of Babylon (Apoc. 17) present in the lines quoted at the beginning of this chapter. He also points out that polemical works roughly contemporary with Dante link these popes to apocalyptic concerns:

It is worth observing that there Dante denounces the simoniac popes primarily because they have disrupted the Church, although he does not forget that they have harmed the empire as well. His words are violent, and recall those of the more energetic of the contemporary Joachite and Franciscan theorists and reformers. Affinities with their views have been perceived in *Inferno XIX*, where the crimes of the evil pastors Nicholas III, Boniface VIII, and Clement V are associated with the great whore of the Apocalypse.[49]

Apocalyptic language is present elsewhere in the canto as well. As Robert E. Kaske has pointed out in his detailed study of the apocalyptic and eschatological elements connected with the two cruces, "DXV" and "Veltro," such language is present in the denunciation of papal simony earlier in the canto. Even in his mistaken identification of Dante for Boniface, Nicholas uses language with strong apocalyptic resonances:

> "Se' tu si tosto di quell'aver sazio
>   per lo qual non temesti torre a 'nganno
>   la bella donna, e poi di farne strazio?"

> (19.55–57)

["Are you so quickly sated with those gains for which you did not fear to take by guile the beautiful Lady, and then to do her outrage?"]

In this passage, Nicholas, no mean simoniac himself, accuses Boniface of having done outrage to *la bella donna*. As Kaske's exegesis of the passage has it:

> The "bella donna" corrupted by Boniface I take to be a meaningful fusion of the *sponsa* of the *Canticum* and the *mulier amicta sole* of Apoc. 12, both traditionally interpreted as the Church. As a result of her corruption, she reappears as the "puttana sciolta" of *Purg.* 32. 144ff., obviously corresponding to the *meretrix magna* of Apoc. 17. This connection between "bella donna" and "puttana sciolta" seems supported by the reference to physical violence in the passage just quoted; by the further allusion in *Inf.* 19 to the *meretrix* herself (106–8) along with a loss of virtue (106–11); by the popular figurative theme of the seduced and corrupted *sponsa* and its frequent eschato-

logical ties; and by an explicit statement in the *Arbor Vite* of Ubertino da Casale.[50]

Thus in the denunciation of papal corruption apocalyptic language is present throughout, with Dante's direct condemnation of Nicholas and his successors at the end of the canto completing Nicholas's indirect address to Dante in the beginning. The change from the use of such language *in bono* to its use *in malo* implicit in the first passage is made explicit in the second, where, as Kaske tells us, the bride of Christ becomes the Whore of Babylon.

Kaske and Davis, in the passages quoted, alike suggest a connection between Dante's appropriation of apocalyptic language in *Inferno* 19 and the writings of the so-called Spiritual Franciscans, an unofficial group of Franciscans who continued to insist on the literal observance of the *Rule* and the *Testament* of Francis. In earlier chapters discussing Bonaventure's *Legenda Maior* and Jean de Meun's continuation of the *Roman de la Rose*, we noted the apocalyptic expectations and even heretical claims of earlier radical and rigorist Franciscans. Similarly, the polemical writings of later Spirituals, especially those of the most radical group, the Fraticelli, provide a fruitful source for investigating the apocalyptic associations connected with the three popes of *Inferno* 19. These documents were generally well-known and, of more importance, were well-known to Dante, as scholars have attested.[51]

Despite the efforts of Bonaventure to unify the Franciscan order during his tenure as minister general, the problems he addressed continued after his death. In Chapter 2 we argued that Bonaventure succeeded in giving the world a definitive portrait of Francis in the *Legenda*, but his version of Francis and the order was not accepted universally. After Bonaventure, for example, the Spirituals saw only corruption in whatever concessions were made to the increasing size of the movement. Like their predecessors in the 1250s, they nurtured a marked strain of radical apocalypticism in their writings. Denouncing what they took to be the present-day evils in the order and in the Church, they once again appropriated the teachings of Joachim of Fiore (and some heretical teachings mistakenly attributed to him) to the contemporary Church. However complicated the history of the Spirituals, their literary legacy is relatively easy to trace: in terms of literary eminence the three most prominent were Peter John Olivi (c. 1248–98), Angelo Clareno (d. c. 1323), and Ubertino da Casale (1259-c. 1338).[52] Each of these three may well have provided Dante with a wealth of material for the *Commedia*. It is in no way necessary to believe that Dante agreed with the more extravagant claims of the Spirituals—claims that may or may not be present in the writings of these three—on such matters as the poverty question or the stages of history to see in these writers a rich source for his apocalypticism.[53]

It was, of course, the poverty question that put the Spirituals in direct conflict with the papacy. Out of this conflict came a number of prophecies written by the Spirituals which looked forward to a so-called Angelic Pope, a pope whose future reign would redress the grievances endured by the friars from the actions of the popes in the present.[54] One series of prophecies, which emphasized the intolerable actions of contemporary popes, was the *Vaticinia de summis pontificibus*. Following Herbert Grundmann, scholars have generally held that the Latin pope prophecies were transmuted versions of the Leo Oracles, which detailed a succession of Greek emperors, and that this Byzantine tradition was appropriated in the early fourteenth century by Fra Liberato, the leader of the Fraticelli, or by his best-known follower, Angelo Clareno. Recently, Robert Lerner has argued that the transformation was accomplished by an unknown Englishman named Rabanus, and that originally the Latin prophecies were not the work of a Spiritual Franciscan. Lerner comments that "resentment of papal grandeur and hopes for eschatological change were not Franciscan or heretical monopolies in the late thirteenth and early fourteenth centuries."[55] Lerner here underscores an argument that we have made throughout this study: apocalypticism, even when appropriated for polemical purposes, is not necessarily radical or heretical.

Nevertheless, once the papal prophecies were popularized, they were seized by the Spirituals for their own purposes. These included the condemnation of popes hostile to their cause as well as praise of the elderly Celestine V (pope, 1294), an "angelic" hermit who abdicated the papacy after five months and was succeeded by the hated Boniface VIII. According to Marjorie Reeves, the first series of *Vaticinia* "consists of fifteen prophecies, each representing a pope by means of a picture, a key phrase, an enigmatic description. The series begins with Nicholas III, and the 'unholy' portraits are identifiable as far as Boniface VIII."[56] In these prophecies, then, both Nicholas and Boniface are linked to apocalyptic expectations, as two examples of the bearers of the tribulation that must be endured before the final peace brought by the Angelic Pope. Moreover, the connection between these prophecies and *Inferno* 19 may be both precise and direct. When Nicholas identifies himself in the canto it is not by name but, significantly, by his membership in the Orsini family: "'e veramente fui figliuol della' orsa,'" (19.70) ["'and I was truly a son of the she-bear'"]. This identification is precisely the key phrase that describes Nicholas in these prophecies: "ursa catulos pascens"[57] ["a she-bear feeding her whelps"].

The implication of this series of prophecies is that Nicholas and Boniface are to be seen as forerunners or types of Antichrist. Boniface is actually equated with Antichrist in the most important work of another of the Spiritual Franciscans known to Dante, the *Arbor vite crucifixe Jesu* of Ubertino da Casale.[58] Because Ubertino is cited in *Paradiso* 12 as one who was too strict in his application of the Franciscan rule, it is clear that Dante did not endorse all of Ubertino's vision. Yet of the influence of the *Arbor Vite* on the *Commedia* there can be little doubt. As Charles Davis has put it, "although Dante certainly seems to have borrowed from the *Arbor Vite* some of the important positive elements in the *Commedia*, and to have been indebted to Ubertino for his conception of Francis and Dominic and the historical mission of the orders they instituted, he does not seem to have regarded the Franciscan as a safe guide in other things, notably in his criticism of the *ecclesia carnalis*."[59] One borrowing, as Davis points out, is in Dante's conception of Francis and Dominic. For example, the life of St. Francis in *Paradiso* 11, particularly the marriage of Francis to Lady Poverty, was influenced by the *Arbor vite*.[60] This mystic marriage, symbolizing the true poverty of the Church as embodied in Francis, should be seen as a figural counterpart to the greed of the simoniacs in *Inferno* 19, a greed expressed in the corruption of a true marriage—the marriage between Christ and his Church—at least three times in the canto (lines 1–4, 55–57, 106–111).[61] With this contrast in mind, Ubertino's direct equation of Boniface with Antichrist provides more evidence of the various ways in which the medieval apocalyptic imagination resonates in Dante's portrayal of the simoniac popes in *Inferno* 19.[62]

The papal prophecies indicting Nicholas III and Boniface VIII make no reference to Clement V, the third simoniac pope of *Inferno* 19, for they were written before his election to the papacy.[63] Contemporary writings, however, are packed with apocalyptic references connected with his reign as well. He was perhaps most noted for moving the seat of the papacy from Rome to Avignon in 1309, and, as we noted in Chapter 1, the apocalyptic associations of this move were not lost on his contemporaries. The Avignon papacy was often called the "Babylonian Captivity," with all the attendant apocalyptic associations connected with the reign of Babylon.[64]

Petrarch was not the only contemporary who made these associations explicit, although his identification of the Avignon papacy as the Whore of Babylon is one of the most striking condemnations drawing on apocalyptic symbolism:

> De l'empia Babilonia ond' e fuggita
>> ogni vergogna, ond' ogni bene e fori,
>> albergo di dolor, madre d' errori,
>> son fuggito io per allungar la vita.

> From impious Babylon, where all shame is dead,
> All goodness banished to extremest bounds,
> Nurse of black errors, lair of brutish hounds,
> I, too, in hope of longer life have fled.[65]

Equally striking, the imagery of the canto itself reinforces the apocalyptic associations of Clement's reign by referring to his very election to the papacy as a kind of simony. He is compared to Jason of 2 Maccabees, who bought the office of high priest which rightly belonged to his brother:

> "Nuovo Iason sara, di cui si legge
>> ne' Maccabei; e come a quei fu molle
>> suo re, cosi fia lui cui Francia regge."

(19.85–87)

> ["A new Jason he will be, like him we read of in Maccabees, but even as to that one his king was pliant, so to this one shall be he who governs France."]

Jason did in the Old Testament what Simon Magus attempts in the New—he buys a spiritual office with money:

> Sed post Seleuci vitae excessum, cum suscepisset regnum Antiochus, qui nobilis appellabatur, ambiebat Iason frater Oniae summum sacerdotium. Adito rege, promittens ei argenti talenta trecenta sexaginta et ex redditibus aliis talenta octoginta. (2 Macc. 4:7–8)

[But after the death of Seleucus, when Antiochus, who was called the Illustrious, had taken possession of the kingdom, Jason the brother of Onias ambitiously sought the high priesthood: And went to the king, promising him three hundred and sixty talents of silver, and out of other revenues fourscore talents.]

Moreover, once he gained control of the priesthood, Jason tried to disrupt the practices of the Jewish religion and to introduce Hellenistic customs and the worship of Greek divinities in their place (2 Macc. 4:13–16). Thus the comparison of Jason to the foreign pope Clement V in particular—the *cui Francia regge* of line 87, who owed his papal election to the good favor of Philip the Fair—and to the simoniac popes in general is both powerful and apt.

This comparison of the damned popes with Jason not only provides yet another example of priestly simony but also reveals another dimension of the apocalyptic imagination at work in the canto. According to medieval exegesis, Jason and his kingly supporter, Antiochus, are apocalyptically charged figures. Here Dante develops a complex analogy in which Clement's figural relationship to Jason the high priest is paralleled by the implied relationship of Philip the Fair to Antiochus, the king mentioned in Maccabees. As Benvenuto da Imola's commentary on *Inferno* 19 concisely states: "Nam sicut Jason obtinuit summum pontificatum simoniace a rege Antiocho qui opprimebat terram sanctam tirannice; ita iste Clemens obtinuit summum pontificium simoniace a rege Franciae Philippo, qui tirannice et impie conculcabat ecclesiam sanctam, occiso Bonifacio"[66] ["For as Jason obtained the high priesthood through simony from king Antiochus, who oppressed the holy land through tyranny; so did this Clement obtain the papacy through simony from King Philip of France, who tyranically and impiously trampled on holy Church after the death of Boniface"]. Once Jason and Antiochus are both understood typologically, moreover, the analogy is further enriched. Just as Clement is compared to Jason, who is a type of Simon Magus, Philip is compared to Antiochus, who is identified throughout medieval exegesis as one of the most important types of Antichrist. Jerome's extremely influential *Commentary on Daniel* is undoubtedly the most important source for this identification:

Sicut igitur Saluator habet et Salomonem et ceteros sanctos in typum aduentus sui, sic et Antichristus pessimum regum Antiochum, qui sanctos persecutus est templumque violauit, recte typum sui habuisee credendus est.

[And so, just as the Savior had Solomon and the other saints as types of His advent, so also we should believe that the Antichrist very properly had as a type of himself the utterly wicked king, Antiochus, who persecuted the saints and defiled the Temple.][67]

In addition to its other resonances, therefore, Dante's charged analogy compares the simonist Clement with the simonist Jason as priests in the service of a foreign and persecuting tyrant. The apocalyptic resonances, moreover, link the Old Testament and the contemporary manifestations of these evil religious-secular allies, implying that Philip is also a type of Antichrist. As is outlined in the chart below, Dante draws on the third key of apocalyptic interpretation to show how the contemporary representatives of Antichrist are inextricably linked both historically and apocalyptically.

Contemporary History		*Old Testament History*	*Apocalyptic Figures*
Priest:	Clement	Jason	Simon Magus
Tyrant:	Philip	Antiochus	Antichrist

In his rebuke to Nicholas, Dante the pilgrim comes to realize that the Church's involvement with simony must be traced all the way back to the Donation of Constantine. This gift of land that the Emperor Constantine was thought to have given to Pope Silvester in the fourth century is usually considered to be the beginning of the Church's appropriation of secular power and privilege and therefore, for medieval reformers and critics, to be the source of ecclesiastical corruption. For example, Anima in *Piers Plowman*, condemning the sad condition of the fourteenth-century Church, relates a popular anecdote concerning the Donation:

> "Whan Costantyn of curteisie Holy Kirke dowed
> With londes and ledes, lordshipes and rentes,
> An aungel men herden an heigh at Rome crye,
> '*Dos ecclesie* this day hath ydronke venym,
> And tho that han Petres power arn apoisoned alle!' "[68]

Given the popularity of such views in the later Middle Ages, it is not surprising that Dante the pilgrim concludes his condemnation of papal corruption with an apostrophe to Constantine. It also appropriately and carefully balances the poet's opening apostrophe to Simon Magus:[69]

> "Ahi, Costantin, di quanto mal fu matre,
>   non la tua conversion, ma quella dote
>   che de te prese il primo ricco patre!"
>
> (19.115–117)

> ["Ah, Constantine, of how much ill was mother, not your conversion, but that dowry which the first rich Father took from you!"]

Significantly, it is Constantine's material gift, not his spiritual conversion, that Dante bemoans, for throughout much of the later Middle Ages the contemporary papacy was unfortunately more attracted to the former than the latter. Drawing on this familiar imagery, for example, Bernard of Clairvaux had earlier made a similar charge in his immensely influential *De Consideratione*. Opposing Peter to Constantine, Bernard accuses the contemporary papacy with worldly excesses appropriate not for the Church but for the empire: "In this finery you are the successor not of Peter, but of Constantine."[70]

In the high Middle Ages the Donation of Constantine came to play a major role in the apocalyptic imagination. Guido da Pisa's commentary on *Inferno*, for example, places the Donation of Constantine and Dante's reference to it within an apocalyptic context. Commenting on the lines just quoted (19.115–17), he says:

> Pia exclamatione autor invehit in Constantinum, dicens: Non tua conversio fuit mater tanti mali, sed illa dos quam a te recepit primus dives pater, idest beatus Silvester, cui primo bona temporalia ab ipso imperio sunt concessa; propter quam dotem Romana Ecclesia, quia male utitur ipsa, in Apocalypsi, ut dictum est, meretrix nominatur.[71]

> [By this conscientious exclamation the author inveighs against Constantine, saying: the mother of such great evil was not your conversion, but that gift which the first rich father received from you, namely blessed Silvester, to whom temporal goods were granted by this very

command. On account of this gift the Roman Church, because she used it wickedly, is called a whore, as it is said in the Apocalypse.]

Moreover, some writers in the Middle Ages, often heretical ones, went even further than did Guido da Pisa, whose perception is that the Donation of Constantine fixes that moment when *ecclesia* turned from *sponsa* to *meretrix*. They saw the Donation as the actual beginning of the reign of Antichrist and accused Sylvester I of being Antichrist for accepting the Donation.[72] Thus not only the abuses of Dante's contemporary papacy, but also the historical "fact" that Dante saw as the forerunner of these contemporary abuses were understood within an apocalyptic framework. Taken together, the evidence which suggests that these three popes are to be associated with Antichrist and his types is remarkably consistent. It is an association, furthermore, that reinforces the logic of the entire canto. The strong relationship between the figures of Simon Magus and Antichrist appropriately establishes the same relationship between Antichrist and these followers of Simon Magus. Dante shows the apocalyptic associations of simony to be a current that runs deep.

We have shown how elements of the medieval apocalyptic imagination permeate the canto: in the use of language drawn from the Apocalypse, in the pervasive presence of the figure of Simon Magus, in Dante's embodiment of simony through three popes who were associated with prophecies and treatises on Antichrist, in the figurative association of the pilgrim as friar to suggest the apocalyptic figure of Elijah, in the typological connections of contemporary pope and king to Jason and Antiochus, and in the reference to the Donation of Constantine. Still another way in which apocalyptic associations are present is evident in the canto's inversion of the iconography of Pentecost. Drawing on the second key of apocalyptic interpretation to depict the agents of evil as inversions of good, Dante parodies the suffering of the simoniac popes, suggesting that the flames on the feet of these upside-down apostles mimic the flames on the heads of the first apostles at Pentecost.[73] The canto extends this parody by inverting the scriptural account of Pentecost, which describes the first effects of the descent of the the Holy Spirit (Acts 2:4−47). Among these effects are the gift of tongues (vv. 4−13), Peter's first sermon (vv. 14−36), mass conversions (vv. 37−43), and the establishment of the newly formed Church holding all goods in common ownership (vv. 44−47). In stark contrast to this description of the Pentecostal Church, the Church depicted in *Inferno* 19 has denied, in its works, the gifts of the Holy Spirit. In their study of the sacramental inversion at work in the canto, Herzman and Stephany emphasize this denial:

> The gift of tongues suggests that the good news is to be preached to all people, but the simoniac popes have turned their attention narrowly to their own interests, confining their zeal to an eagerness to fill their own and their relatives' coffers. Peter's first sermon begins by proclaiming the arrival of that day foretold by Joel when the son of God will prophesy. That Nicholas III, no son of God, is unable to prophesy is clear in his misunderstandings about the coming of his successor Boniface VIII (XIX, 51 ff). Finally, the failure of the simoniacs to perceive the church's property as communal is self-evident in the entire Canto's depiction of their greed and nepotism. Since Pentecost was the occasion on which the Apostles first began exercising their priestly duties, and since the simoniac popes as high priests are successors of the Apostles, the popes' failure to serve as an instrument of the Holy Spirit is significant.[74]

Thus not only the flames falling on the feet of the simoniac popes, but also many of the details of the canto reflect an inversion of Pentecost. These false leaders have rejected the gifts of the Holy Spirit in order to gain the worldly and material rewards of ecclesiastical office. By so preferring the example of Simon Magus to that of Simon Peter, they associate themselves with Antichrist rather than Christ. They once again become identified as predecessors or types of Antichrist, who, as we noted in Chapter 1, is expected to execute a false Pentecost in order to deceive his disciples and to resemble Christ.

This pseudo-Pentecost is depicted by the fire summoned from heaven by the two-horned false-prophet Beast, as is evident in the illustration of Apocalypse 13:13 in the Moralized Bibles (see Figure 2). According to medieval exegetes, this fire symbolizes a *spiritus malignus* that outwardly resembles the *spiritus sanctus* of Pentecost, so that Antichrist's disciples may even speak in tongues.[75] This pseudo-Pentecost, another example of Antichrist's ability to work wonders and of his parodic imitation of events connected with Christ, became an important part of later medieval treatments of Antichrist. The Velislav Bible, for example, pictures small winged devils hovering over the heads of Antichrist's followers as fire and stones descend from the sky. The explanatory rubric states: "Faciet et ignem de celo descendere in terram et lapides de celo cadere et malignum spiritum super suos descendere ut loquuntur variis linguis"[76] ["He will make fire descend from heaven onto earth and stones fall from heaven and an evil spirit descend upon his people so that they speak in various tongues"]. The block-book *vitae* of Antichrist consistently include an illustration of the devil-inspired fire from Heaven, usually after portraying Antichrist's pretended death and resurrection; and the fifteenth-century *Coming of Antichrist*, the play preceding *Doomsday* in the Chester Corpus Christi cycle, stages the pseudo-Pentecost in a similar sequence.[77] The parodic misuse of Pentecost, which typifies the terrible effectiveness of the deceiver, is another means by which he is expected to gain control of the Church in the last days. It is also a particularly powerful reminder of the vividness of the medieval apocalyptic imagination and the intensity of its understanding of last-day events in parodic terms.

Taken together, the associations developed in *Inferno* 19 between the simoniac leaders of the contemporary Church, Simon Magus, and the apocalyptic pseudo-Christ suggest something of the richness of the apocalyptic imagination in the Middle Ages as well as Dante's incomparable ability to mine it. Yet it still remains for us to say something about the question "Why?" What energies are released by Dante's incorporation of these rich apocalyptic traditions in *Inferno* 19? To attempt to answer this question is to move from meaning within the canto to meaning beyond it, to make some connections with the larger concerns of the *Commedia*. It is to talk, at least in a tentative way, about the importance of the apocalyptic imagination to the *Commedia* as a whole. In his own analysis of the tradition of Antichrist and apocalypticism in Dante, Kaske dealt with the problem of identifying possible political allegory in the *Commedia*:

> such allegory in literature, if it is to become more than a series of arbitrary and imaginatively jejeune equations, must by its very nature draw on other more fundamental and universally significant meanings, already somehow implicit in the figures it is made to inhabit. If this observation is sound, it does not seem impossible that in passages like that mentioned above [in particular, the "DXV" crux of *Purgatorio* 33], in the most profound poem of the Middle Ages, the Apocalyptic imagery may be primary and consistent, the political allegory secondary and sporadic.[78]

This observation provides a good beginning for assessing the importance of the apocalyptic imagination in the *Commedia*. By placing the events of the canto within an apocalyptic frame, Dante is able to draw on traditions of significant and universal meanings to energize the canto. Recovering these energies, therefore, connects this canto with the apocalyptic resonances pointed out by such scholars as Davis, Kaske, and Friedman; it adds to their work by suggesting that indeed apocalyptic resonances are more pervasive than was previously thought.

There is, however, a significant difference between the insights of Kaske and Friedman and those of this chapter. In both cases, these scholars were led to an analysis of apocalyptic sources and traditions in an attempt to deal with what are among the most enigmatic puzzles in the *Commedia*: "DXV" and "Veltro" for Kaske, and the beast Geryon in *Inferno* 16–17 for Friedman. Puzzles such as these, however, do not pose a challenge for understanding *Inferno* 19, for here the characters are unambiguously clear. The identity of the simoniac popes who are its subject has never posed a problem for readers of the poem; it is the way in which the apocalyptic imagination gives them significance which requires attention. In this respect *Inferno* 19 once again can be profitably compared to Signorelli's "Fatti dell'Antichristo" analyzed at the beginning of this chapter. Even if one grants that the events surrounding Savonarola were the immediate impetus for the fresco—a position that we and others have questioned—these local events are energized by the artist's placement of them within a universal context. This context, which informs the fresco by drawing upon the apocalyptic concerns of the time, gives the local event wider significance. The immediate event is understood as characteristic of Italy and the Church in the last days. Similarly, the local is energized by the universal in *Inferno* 19. As is typical of the apocalyptic imagination, Dante emphasizes both the contemporary and the eschatological, the simoniac popes and Antichrist. To put the matter specifically into the critical vocabulary often applied to the *Commedia*—the language of fourfold interpretation—in this canto Dante emphasizes the anagogical level in order to heighten the impact of the allegorical.

One clue to this dual focus of bringing together present and future in a typological relationship is the way in which, like Signorelli's fresco, the canto is framed by references to judgment. At Orvieto, the Antichrist fresco is accompanied by paintings of angels blowing judgment trumpets, of the signs of Doomsday, and of the Last Judgment. Similarly, the canto begins with an obvious allusion to judgment and ends with a subtle one. It has frequently been noted that the trumpet that begins the canto is a trumpet announcing judgment:

or convien che per voi suoni la tromba,
pero che ne la terza bolgia state.

(19.5–6)

[now must the trumpet sound for you, since you are in the third
pouch.]

What has been noted only recently, however, is that the canto also ends
with an allusion to an equally powerful apocalyptic sign of judgment, the
separation of the sheep from the goats: "et congregabuntur ante eum
omnes gentes, et separabit eos ab invicem, sicut pastor segregat oves ab
haedis" (Matt. 25:32) ["And all nations shall be gathered together before
him, and he shall separate them one from another, as the shepherd sepa-
rateth the sheep from the goats"]. As Vergil takes Dante on his breast to
remount the path they have so recently descended, they pass easily over a
rugged and steep crag:

Quivi soavemente spuose il carco,
    soave per lo scoglio sconcio ed erto
    che sarebbe a le capre duro varco.

(19.130–32)

[Here he gently set down his burden, gently because of the rugged
and steep crag, which would be a hard passage for goats.]

The literal sense of this passage is that Vergil and Dante were fortunate to
be able to climb a path which would have been difficult even for such good
climbers as goats. But it is possible to read this image in a quite different,
though complementary, way: this would have been a hard climb for goats,
not because the path is steep and rugged, but simply because they are
goats. Dante and Vergil are able to negotiate the path, and easily at that,
"because they were not goats at all; the goats are those who have been left
in the valley, embedded in rock, separated for eternity from the sheep by
God's judgment, and shown to us by Dante's."[79]

Thus the canto presents us with the immediacy of Dante's judgment
on these sinners, a judgment echoing God's own. He has been called upon
to give this judgment by no less an authority than St. Peter, who, in
Paradiso, commissions Dante to carry back to earth his condemnation
of those who have used the bride of Christ "'ad acquisto d'oro'" (27.42)

["'for gain of gold'"]. But these two signs—the trumpet and the separation of the sheep from the goats—signify judgment because they are part of the iconography of the apocalyptic Last Judgment, the final coming of Christ in majesty to which the appearance of Antichrist is prelude. These clear echoes of the Last Judgment give strength to Dante's present and "local" denunciation of the perversion of the Spirit in his own time by giving it the definitiveness and finality of the consummation of Christian history. Here too, as in the iconography of Antichrist and throughout the medieval apocalyptic imagination, the universal gives power to the local, events in the present foreshadow the future.

It is easy to overlook the fact that it is not only the simoniac popes who are judged in this canto, but also Dante himself. If the goats are left behind, Dante is a sheep who continues on his journey. This is a crucial consideration for both the canto and the poem, for the idea of judgment as it relates to the pilgrim is also—like the judgment on the simoniac popes—one which can be seen from both allegorical and anagogical perspectives, from the perspective of the present and the perspective of the future. From the perspective of the present, Dante in this canto comes to a greater awareness of the nature of sin which allows him to distance himself from the sinners, literally and figuratively. At the same time the canto points forward toward those future moments in the *Commedia* when judgment becomes a more explicit theme for the pilgrim. What is given an apocalyptic and hence universal framework within this canto is not simply the condemnation of an especially heinous and destructive group of sinners, but the journey of the pilgrim from ignorance to knowledge, from self to God.

As soon as one turns attention from the sin of simony to the pilgrim's growth within this canto, further reasons for its apocalyptic structure come into focus. Though the *Commedia* as a whole is about the growth of a pilgrim who begins in a dark wood of error and who finishes the journey with a direct apprehension of God, at certain points the stages of that growth are made more explicit than at others. For the *Inferno*, canto 19 is such an explicit moment, perhaps *the* explicit moment. Until this point, the pilgrim's reaction to the sins he has seen has been mostly acquiescence of one sort or another: he swoons for Francesca; he engages in heated partisan debate with Farinata; he agrees with Brunetto's craving for a barren earthly fame. In *Inferno* 19 acquiescence turns to anger, debate turns to denunciation. More than any other canto in the *Inferno*, then, this is a microcosm of the poem as a whole. Not only does it embody the pilgrim's growth, but its prophetic proclamation at the end may be seen as a figure for another prophetic proclamation, the *Commedia* as a whole.

In *Inferno* 19 the pilgrim moves from literal incomprehension, not knowing whom or what he is looking at as he first descends the bolgia, to spiritual vision as he comes to understand the correct relation between the material and the spiritual, the relation that has been precisely inverted by the simoniac popes. The structural symmetry of the canto, in which the initial apostrophe to Simon Magus is balanced by the final apostrophe to Constantine, also strongly reinforces this movement to spiritual awareness. The opening apostrophe, announcing the concerns of the canto, is made by the poet, a fact that becomes evident once the reader sees that at this point the pilgrim is merely groping about, not yet able to understand the literal let alone the moral geography of the bolgia. Thus the second apostrophe, that to Constantine (19.115), shows that the pilgrim's moral awareness has caught up with the poet's. It becomes a precise measurement of his growth within the canto, which corresponds to the pilgrim's growth throughout the poem as a whole, wherein the pilgrim in the dark wood of error catches up with the poet who is retelling the experience. The canto which most clearly spells out the nature of the experience of the pilgrim takes pains to link his individual destiny with a pattern of universal and cosmic meaning.[80]

The poem's thorough linking of the pilgrim's individual destiny to eschatological concerns is nowhere more evident than in the cantos connected with the appearance of Beatrice at the end of the *Purgatorio*. There Beatrice's judgment of the pilgrim becomes part of a universal drama and forms a climactic statement about the nature of his growth. No work of literature, let alone medieval literature, so consistently and energetically evokes the Christian apocalyptic imagination as do the concluding cantos of the *Purgatorio*. As Robert Kaske has shown, these cantos present nothing less than a pageant of all Christian history, developing their imagery and symbolism directly from the Apocalypse. Canto 29 includes a series of symbolic scenes recapitulating the various *aetates* of salvation history that are drawn from and reminiscent of exegesis of the Apocalypse and its numerical patterns. Canto 32 presents a seven-part history of the tribulations of the Church suffered during its various *tempora*. This history shifts in canto 33 to a veiled prophecy of the Second Coming, once again consistently using the language of the Apocalypse.[81]

Throughout these three cantos we are reminded of the vision of the New Jerusalem which is in effect the subject of what follows in the *Para-*

diso. It is important to remember, furthermore, that the appearance of Beatrice, which is so central to these cantos and to the entire *Commedia* and which becomes for the pilgrim a second coming carefully fashioned by the poet to parallel the apocalyptic Second Coming of Christ in judgment, does not initiate the process of judgment in the poem, but rather continues and expands a process begun in *Inferno* 19. It is indeed as Dante's judge that Beatrice comes, and the reader is made conscious of the difference between this appearance and her first incarnation to the poet while she was in the flesh, which is the subject of the *Vita Nuova*. And yet without in any way diminishing the universal and public character of these eschatological concerns, these cantos also contain what are among the most personal revelations of the *Commedia*, certainly the most personal up to this point. For they are the most explicit moments of the personal conversion of the pilgrim, and include a history of that conversion which is uniquely his, from his earliest life to the fictional present. His sins, his repentance, and his purification are as much the center of these cantos as is the eschatological pageant. Moreover, Beatrice, who is his personal judge and savior, is conspicuously unlike the universal symbols drawn from the Apocalypse. Both as character and as symbol she is the invention of the poet, someone whose very existence for us depends on the fact that Dante has written her into his poem and given her such a significant place within a universal drama.[82]

With less fanfare but with no less exactness, Dante aligns the particular and the universal by drawing upon the apocalyptic imagination in *Inferno* 19. Perhaps the one question that remains, however, is "why there?" What makes the condemnation of these particular sins the proper occasion for the pilgrim's growth to be brought into such high relief? The *Commedia* is both the experience of Dante's journey as it is unfolding in time, and the record of that journey in his memory after it has taken place, after the golden fleece has been captured and brought back to his readers. Because of this dual structure, our reading of the poem constantly works retrospectively. Only after we have been with Dante at the moment of final vision can the whole poem be illuminated. Thus present and future are continually brought together: we see Dante putting into the book of memory what he has learned from the book of experience even at a later point in his journey. In *Inferno* 19 he denounces the corrupt popes already in hell with especial prophetic urgency. In *Paradiso* 27 the pilgrim learns in the book of experience from Peter how to recognize specifically those "le piu alte cime" (*Par.* 17.134) ["upon the loftiest summits"] against whom the poet must direct his zeal: Peter's own corrupt successors. In *Inferno* 19 he carries out his charge in the book of memory.

More importantly, in the central cantos of *Paradiso* (14 to 18) he learns from his great-great-grandfather, Cacciaguida, that he must become a prophet. He comes to understand not only that he must match his verses to his vision in fullest truth, but also that only through an acceptance of this prophetic calling can his conversion be complete and his identity established. Here Dante learns what it means to transform exile into pilgrimage, to be a warrior whose weapon is the pen rather than the sword, to be a prophetic voice whose chief credential is his own conversion. Accordingly, these cantos too fuse the personal and the cosmic, explicitly placing Dante's journey within an apocalyptic vision of history. It is not necessary to trace in detail the eschatological resonances of these cantos because that task has already been accomplished with erudition and insight by Jeffrey Schnapp, who argues in his study that "in the Cacciaguida cantos the term 'history' encompasses everything from the poet-pilgrim's personal history to the particular history of a city (Florence) to the universal drama of human history in its progress towards apocalypse."[83] But it is worth mentioning that once again it is during those very moments that are the most personal in the entire *Commedia*—those most explicit in shaping the identity of the pilgrim—that a fusion with the eschatological takes place. Schnapp has shown, by an extended analysis of the eschatological implications of the central image of the circle of Mars, the cross, that eschatology is a key to understanding the process of conversion throughout the entire poem. As is typical of the apocalyptic imagination throughout the Middle Ages and particularly in Dante, the universal and the individual are here linked as the concerns of cosmic eschatology are merged with those of personal conversion.

Prophets have been given the burden of seeing the world from God's point of view. What authenticates the prophetic zeal of Dante is that he has completed his journey, has corrected his vision, and has seen the world and its inhabitants *sub specie aeternitatis*. That this vision remains in the book of memory is proven for us by his incorporation of various apocalyptic elements in *Inferno* 19. The canto is not only proof that Dante has put into practice in the book of memory what he has learned in the book of experience; it is also proof that he has understood, in the manner of a true prophet, the relation of his contemporary world to the working of God's purposes in history. As we have argued above, Dante achieves true prophetic stature in his denunciation of papal corruption in *Inferno* 19. This prophetic denunciation typifies, furthermore, that prophecy which is the poem itself, just as the pilgrim's growth within the canto typifies the record of that growth which is also the poem itself.

In the polemical apocalypticism of the Spiritual Franciscans, the imminence of Antichrist signifies both the timeliness and rightness of their position and their willingness and obligation to battle all opponents. Dante's apocalypticism, although it may sometimes draw from these radical sources, is less polemical and more orthodox, more reflective of the central concerns of the medieval apocalyptic imagination. It is the apocalypticism of Bonaventure, who is probably the most important direct source for Dante's apocalyptic understanding of history. It is not an accident that Dante gives Bonaventure equal time with Thomas Aquinas as a spokesman in the circle of the Sun in *Paradiso* 11, nor that when Thomas relates the life of Francis he follows with care Bonaventure's *Legenda*.[84] Like Cacciaguida, Francis becomes a model for Dante, an *exemplum* who helps shape his identity. The poet must not only learn from Cacciaguida to become a prophet and pilgrim, he must also learn from the life of Francis analogous ways of becoming a mendicant and peacemaker as the necessary conditions for turning his exile into pilgrimage.[85] The shaping of the pilgrim's identity thus is informed not only by the personal eschatological journey through the landscapes of the afterlife which is the very matter of the *Commedia*, but also by the universal eschatological significance of Bonaventure's Francis that we discussed in Chapter 2. The personal and the universal are balanced in Dante. Although he burns with a prophetic zeal few have matched, he also has the calm perspective of someone who remembers the final vision of *Paradiso*. Although he wishes the reader to understand the apocalyptic elements of his prophecy as a sign that he sees things according to God's plan, he never uses them as an opportunity to rearrange God's plan to suit the exigencies of the present. Rather he uses them to show how the personal and the cosmic, twin focuses of the poem, come together; he uses them to show that the story of the pilgrim and the book of the universe are one.

5. *The Canterbury Tales:* Apocalypticism and Chaucer's Pilgrimage

Ever since the publication of Morton Bloomfield's *Piers Plowman as a Fourteenth-century Apocalypse*, there has been no scarcity of analyses of the apocalyptic elements of *Piers Plowman*.[1] Generally the poem is approached as a dream vision rather than as an "apocalypse," and it apparently does not even allude to the Apocalypse of John.[2] Nevertheless, there is no question that it thoroughly reflects a fully developed apocalyptic imagination, as is evident especially in its numerous cryptic prophecies, in its hopeful if problematic early millenarian visions of a reformed society, in its polemical portrayal of the friars as false prophets, and in the admittedly ambiguous arguments of specific characters such as Need.[3] The most obvious apocalyptic elements are evident in the attack of Antichrist that concludes the poem's final vision.[4] It is important to realize, however, that from its very beginning *Piers Plowman* is set in an apocalyptic context.

In the Prologue Will falls asleep in springtime on a bank of a river, but unlike Amant in the *Roman de la Rose*, he does not dream of a lush garden of love. Instead, he finds himself in a wilderness:

> Thanne gan I meten a merveillous swevene—
> That I was in a wildernesse, wiste I nevere where.
> A[c] as I biheeld into the eest an heigh to the sonne,
> I seigh a tour on a toft trieliche ymaked,
> A deep dale bynethe, a dongeon therinne,
> With depe diches and derke and dredfulle of sighte.[5]

The radical vertical separation of the world between the tower and the pit is, as we have seen in previous chapters, typical of the dualism so characteristic of the apocalyptic imagination. As is the case in the Apocalypse, furthermore, the eternal spatial division between Heaven and Hell leaves room—as long as history lasts—for a middle, the world in which the forces of good and evil struggle. Represented in the poem by the wilderness of wandering, it is populated by the fair field full of folk:

A fair feeld ful of folk fond I ther bitwene—
Of alle manere of men, the meene and the riche,
Werchynge and wandrynge as the world asketh.

(Prol. 17–19)

This folk, moreover, comprises two moral categories, so that even those in the middle are affiliated in time—if not yet placed eternally—with the competing forces of Heaven and Hell:

And somme putten hem to pride, apparailed hem therafter,
In contenaunce of clopynge comen disgised.
In preieres and penaunce putten hem manye,
Al for the love of Oure Lord lyveden ful streyte
In hope to have heveneriche blisse—

(Prol. 23–27)

They are engaged in all the vivid and boisterous activity of contemporary society, but their state reflects the apocalyptic age of hypocrisy that characterizes the last days.

Much of the poem is devoted to the ways in which the religious systematically replace the striving for moral values with the pursuit of material possessions. The avaritious corruption of the religious is thus particularly condemned. In the wilderness of middle earth witnessed in vision by Will, friars preach for profit and "Glosed the gospel as hem good liked" (Prol. 60), a pardoner presents his false bull to deceive the unlearned, and priests leave their plague-ridden parishes for London to "syngen ther for symonie, for silver is swete" (Prol. 86). That Langland interprets these ecclesiastical abuses in apocalyptic terms is particularly evident in the poem's final vision, when Will witnesses the attack of the eschatological Antichrist.

The attack is accompanied by the usual physical ravages of nature—including the ubiquitous pestilence—that throughout the tradition signify the end of time, and it reveals the thorough corruption of civil government. As is increasingly typical of the apocalyptic imagination, especially in the late Middle Ages, furthermore, Antichrist is supported by friars and other religious, who are instrumental in his overturning "al the crop of truthe" (20.53). Thus Coveteousness, who along with Pride is Antichrist's most stalwart warrior, engineers an attack that depends for its success on several factors characteristic of the religious disarray of the apocalyptic age of hypocrisy:

> Thanne cam Coveitise and caste how he myghte
> Overcome Conscience and Cardinale Vertues,
> And armed hym in avarice and hungriliche lyvede.
> His wepne was al wiles, to wynnen and to hiden;
> With glosynges and with gabbynges he giled the peple.
> Symonye hym s[ue]de to assaille Conscience,
> And [pressed on] the [pope], and prelates thei hem maden
> To holden with Antecrist, hir temporaltees to save.[6]

As is usually the case with Antichrist's minions—whether they be the false prophets who were his predecessors in the New Testament or the vile Jacobin, Faus Semblant—Coveteousness depends upon false interpretation of Scripture, deceitful preaching, and, most significantly, upon simony to gain power. His purpose is to ally the pope and his court to Antichrist and thus preserve the temporal power and material wealth of the Church, which Langland, like Dante, repeatedly condemns as the primary source of ecclesiastical abuses.

The portrayal of simony in the two poems varies significantly, however. As is typical of this complex dream vision that mixes its moral allegory with historical, contemporary, and eschatological elements, *Piers Plowman* portrays Simony as an all-powerful ahistorical personification whose vicious influences are evident throughout the Church and who is in the forefront of the avaricious attack on Conscience. In *Inferno* 19, Dante, on the other hand, identifies the historical Simon Magus who in the early Church challenged Peter, the first pope, with specific contemporary simoniac popes, whom the poet contrasts to Peter. Although the apocalyptic imagination manifests itself variously in these two allegorical and historical works, nevertheless Dante and Langland agree that the pervasiveness of simony is clear evidence that they are living *in novissimis diebus*. Like Jean de Meun—and, as we will argue below, like Chaucer—these poets identify the ecclesiastical corruption that replaces the spiritual with the material as clear evidence that the contemporary Church is suffering the persecutions of the apocalyptic age of hypocrisy.

In thinking about the apocalyptic elements of *Piers Plowman*, therefore, one cannot help but see how they stand in high relief, inescapable to anyone looking intently at the poem. They are brought to the attention of readers of the poem in somewhat the same way that they are brought to the attention of "readers" of medieval thought, who cannot avoid seeing how eschatology and millenarian thought stand out in high relief in the study of radical and heretical movements. But it is especially important to be reminded at this point that the apocalypticism of *Piers Plowman* is thoroughly orthodox. Derek Pearsall, who calls Langland "a prophet and a visionary" and cites his "mood of apocalypse," states that the poem attempts "nothing less than an immense revolution in the moral and spiritual life of the individual, including his own, and of society." Mary J. Carruthers, moreover, notes that "Eschatological Christianity places a believer like Langland in the radical, though non-revolutionary, position of being in the world but not of it, a pilgrim whose true home lies elsewhere."[7] This call for a moral "revolution" and a "radical" stance in relation to secular society, however, is thoroughly orthodox for all those Christians who understand the true meaning of *conversio* and who— measured by the standards of the world and of Antichrist's followers— are "fooles" (*Piers Plowman* 20.61–63). In fact, theologically the poem's apocalypticism is conservative. This point is stressed by Robert Adams, who has recently analyzed in detail the evidence for the possible influence of Joachist and other heterodox apocalypticism in *Piers Plowman*. He concludes that Langland's intense criticism of ecclesiastical corruption does not lead him toward revolutionary solutions or heretical millenarianism but that instead his "social and theological conservatism are such that when he grasps for comprehensive solutions to these problems, he invariably turns to apocalypse. Only supernatural or preternatural intervention can totally reverse the hellbent course of human society."[8]

This orthodoxy, furthermore, should not be surprising, since we have been arguing from the beginning of this study that the apocalyptic imagination at work in the great literary works of medieval culture is orthodox.[9] Studies that have concentrated on radical apocalyptic movements have been misleading to the extent that they have routinely failed to note that in and of itself apocalypticism is neither revolutionary nor unorthodox, that eschatology is a key aspect of ordinary Christian thought, and that it influenced many works that were not overtly eschatological and many authors who were thoroughly orthodox in their understanding and expectation of the last days. Without this reminder it would be impossible to associate Chaucer with apocalyptic concerns without similarly implying that he was somehow a poet on the fringes—a thought that critics who have rightly admired his essential and deep-rooted sanity have conspicuously wanted to avoid.

In fact *The Canterbury Tales* reflects several ways in which apocalyptic and other eschatological thought informs medieval poems that are not explicitly or obviously apocalyptic and provides a signal example of how readings that bear such thought in mind can provide suggestive insights and interpretations. Some scholars already have noted apocalyptic incidents and suggested eschatological allusions at work in specific tales, although generally critics have been reluctant to consider any kind of pervasive eschatological perspective in the poem as a whole.[10] Once again, the reasons are not hard to find. Even though recent criticism has brought a whole range of newer theoretical perspectives to bear on Chaucer's great masterpiece, for the most part it continues to be studied and admired primarily as a triumph of realism, the particular, and the contemporary. Any attempt to fit the great variety and complexity of the *The Canterbury Tales* into a restrictive, all-encompassing structure, or any attempt to impose an artificial construct from without is regarded with great suspicion by those who wish to preserve the sense of "Chaucer the realist." The structure provided by an awareness of the medieval apocalyptic imagination, however, is neither all-encompassing nor restrictive. Rather, it directs attention to the important eschatological implications of the poem's dominant pilgrimage motif and to apocalyptic allusions, inversions, figures, and patterns that broaden our understanding of this immensely rich poem and increase our appreciation of the poem's wealth of detail, vividness of description, and contemporaneity of setting.

In recognizing the apocalyptic imagination at work in *The Canterbury Tales* by approaching the poem from the perspective of medieval eschatology, we begin with a reminder and an example. The reminder, stressed in various ways in the previous chapters, is that in Christian theology eschatology always has both a personal and an universal dimension, and that in fact eschatology unites the personal and the universal. The example is from a contemporary of Chaucer, Thomas Wimbledon. His well-known sermon preached about 1388 in Paul's Cross, London, stresses this as well as other aspects of medieval eschatology that are likewise present in Chaucer, although Wimbledon does so in ways that are much more obvious and straightforward than is Chaucer, who is no less subtle in his use of eschatology than in the other facets of his literary art. Wimbledon begins with the obvious, namely that the last things apply to each individual Christian as well as to all mankind as part of salvation history. He emphasizes that there are two judgments—the first after an individual's death and the second for every person after the general resurrection: "To the first eueriche man shal be cleped aftir oþer, as þe world passiþ; to þe secunde alle schulle come togidere in þe strook of an eiȝe."[11] What is striking about Wimbledon's lengthy comparison of these two judgments is their essential parallelism, the similarities the preacher draws between personal and universal eschatology, between individual death and the death of the world. For example, in a long passage (pp. 99–109) he describes the "þre somoners" that call all to the first judgment: sickness, old age, death. Similarly, three general summoners also issue the call to the universal judgment:

> And riȝt as þe oþere þre messageþ a mannes ende, so þese telleþ þe ende of þe world. Þe firste is þe worldlis sykenesse; þe secunde is feblenesse; and þe þridde is his ende. And þe sekenesse of þe world þou schalt knowe by charites acoldyng; his elde and his feblenesse þou schalt knowe by tokenes fulfillynge; and his ende þou schalt knowe by Antecristis pursuynge. (p. 109)

An investigation of these three summoners will show that for Wimbledon and his contemporaries the apocalyptic imagination infuses the contemporary scene with eschatological expectations. For example, the first summoner, the world's sickness, is evident in the "cooling of charity," a reference to Matthew 24:12 often identified as a sign of the end of the world and specifically of Antichrist's work.[12] Wimbledon recognizes such a condition in the contemporary perversion of human love. Arguing that since mankind is one body whose love ought naturally to be directed toward God and fellow Christians, Wimbledon concludes that when this love "is litle and feynt and þe loue to worldly þyngis and to lustes of þe flesch is gret and feruent" (p. 110), there is a "cooling of charity." Avarice and lust are repeatedly condemned by contemporary writers and are considered signs of the end, especially after the great devastation of the plagues that so wracked fourteenth-century Europe.[13] Thus the prominence of these vices and the subsequent cooling of charity "warneþ al þe world þat þe day of rekenynge drawþ toward" (p. 111).

The second summoner, the world's old age and feebleness, is similarly evident in numerous contemporary signs. Wimbledon, as a careful and orthodox preacher, argues that only the Father knows the hour of doom.

Nevertheless, he states, "we moweþ by auctorite of holy writ, wiþ resounes and exposiciones of seyntis, wel and openly schewe þat þis day of wreche is nyȝe" (p. 112). One of the surest signs of the end, now fulfilled, is a corrupt priesthood. Quoting John Chrysostom, Wimbledon states: "But whan þou seest prestes, þat beþ put on þe hiȝe coppe of spiritual dignites, þat schulde be as hilles aboue þe comune peple in parfit lyuynge, þat dirkenesse of synnes haþ take hem, who douteþ þat þe world nis at þe ende?" (p. 113).

The third summoner of the world—its end—is Antichrist, whose appearance is imminent. Drawing on what we have identified as the keys of the apocalyptic imagination, Wimbledon explicates symbols and focuses on the agents of evil as inversions of good. He comments, for example, on the opening of the seven seals of the Apocalypse to explain "þe staat of þe chirche fro tyme of Crist into þe tyme of Anticrist" (p. 117). Once again, the most visible sign of Antichrist is the condition of the contemporary church, which is clearly suffering from the afflictions of the apocalyptic age of hypocrisy. Like Jean de Meun and others in the exegetical tradition represented by Anselm of Havelberg, Wimbledon interprets the opening of the fourth seal in Apocalypse 6:7–8 to argue that the time just before Antichrist is the time of hypocrisy in the Church (pp. 119–20). Earlier, as a sign of hypocrisy Wimbledon points to avaricious prelates who ignore their duties in order to gain wealth. Although they occupy the place of Peter, Paul, Thomas, and Martin, they act like Judas among the apostles and Simon Magus among the disciples (p. 79). Avaricious prelates are aptly compared to the two great deceivers of the early Church who were damned for confusing the spiritual with the material: Judas, who treacherously bartered God the Son for thirty pieces of silver (Matt. 26:16), and Simon Magus, who blasphemously attempted to purchase God the Holy Spirit (Acts 8:9–24). Since selling and purchasing the spiritual are forms of simony, both Judas and Simon Magus prefigure the false religious simoniacs of the apocalyptic age of hypocrisy. They also prefigure Antichrist, who was expected to gather avariciously for himself the treasures of the world and to bribe many false Christians—especially the religious— to support his deceitful claims to be Christ and his attempts to manipulate the Holy Spirit.

The association of simony and the false religious with Antichrist is, as we have shown previously, hardly uncommon in the fourteenth century. In Chapter 4 we considered at length Dante's treatment of this theme in *Inferno* 19, where the poet vociferously condemns the simoniac popes by developing the rich traditional imagery associated with Simon Magus and Antichrist, and in the introduction of this chapter we noted that Simony is central to Antichrist's attack on Unity in the final passus of *Piers Plowman*. Similarly for Wimbledon the contemporary simoniac priesthood not only recalls the false religious of the past, but also foreshadows the great false prophet of the future, Antichrist, who will appear, according to an unnamed doctor cited by Wimbledon, in 1400, only twelve years hence (pp. 116–17). Because of their disobedient and hypocritical lives, the false religious leaders will be damned at Doomsday (p. 80).

The relationship that Wimbledon draws between contemporary conditions and apocalyptic signs reflects the conjunction of the personal and the universal in eschatological thought and a tendency typical of the medieval apocalyptic imagination to criticize the present while awaiting the imminent end. These aspects are related and developed in a variety of literary works as well as in sermons. *Piers Plowman* 20.165–98, for example, parallels the attack of "elde" on Will (that is, of old age on the individual) with the attack of Antichrist on Unity (Langland's Holy Church). This comparison comes at the end of Will's long personal quest and also at the end of the two passus outlining Church history, so that the personal "signs" of Will's approaching death are juxtaposed with the most important apocalyptic sign indicating the end of salvation history. In its conclusion the poem links the individual and the universal, the contemporary and the apocalyptic. A similar, although perhaps more sophisticated, example of this relationship is evident in Dante's *Commedia*. As we have shown, those cantos that contain what are among the most personal revelations of the poem—including the poet's meeting with Beatrice at the end of *Purgatorio* and his meeting with Cacciaguida in the central sections of the *Paradiso*—are usually presented in tandem with an exposition of the universal and public character of Dante's eschatological concerns.

In dealing with Chaucer's eschatological concerns, it is a good idea to begin with the conclusion of *The Canterbury Tales*, which is informed by a similar conjunction of the universal and the individual, the apocalypic and the contemporary. These concerns are somewhat less personal than in the *Commedia*, for although Chaucer is, like Dante, a character in his own work, throughout his poem he remains a self-effacing one. They are somewhat more subtle than in *Piers Plowman*, which, as we have seen, is set unambiguously within an apocalyptic framework. Nevertheless, *The Canterbury Tales* reflects a conscious awareness of apocalyptic concerns. What Wimbledon preaches, Chaucer, with his seemingly effortless grace, weaves into the fabric of his story.

In the prologue of the Parson's Tale, the sense of an ending, of antici-
pation, and of change is intense. The setting and imagery is highly suggestive. The pilgrim's shadow, as one critic has commented, is "stretched
on the ground as in a grave."[14] The sun is setting and Libra—typically a
symbol of judgment—is ascending.[15] The Host notes that only one tale
remains to be told, that each social rank has had its due, and that "Almoost
fulfild is al myn ordinaunce" (X.19). He next asks the Parson to "knytte up
wel a greet mateere" (X.28). Refusing to relate a fable, the Parson, following the advice of Paul, promises a prose tale of "Moralitee and vertuous
mateere" (X.38) in order "To knytte up al this feeste and make an ende
(X.47). He then requests the help of Jesus to show the pilgrims the true
meaning of pilgrimage:

> And Jhesu, for his grace, wit me sende
> To shewe yow the wey, in this viage,
> Of thilke parfit glorious pilgrymage
> That highte Jerusalem celestial.
>
> (X.48–51)

The Host, to this point the leader of the Canterbury pilgrims, tells him to
hurry, adding to the sense of urgency:

> But hasteth yow; the sonne wole adoun;
> Beth fructuous, and that in litel space,
> And to do wel God sende yow his grace!
> Sey what yow list, and we wol gladly heere.
>
> (X.70–73)

These are the final words of the loquacious Host. Like Vergil in *Purgatorio*, he gives up his position as guide and interpreter. He hands over his
admittedly flawed and comic leadership of the pilgrimage to the Parson,
who relates a long treatise on penitence. The poet's fictional creation, the
Parson—like Beatrice for Dante—becomes a judge of the poet narrator as
well as for the other pilgrims. His exhortations to penitence are followed
by Chaucer's so-called "Retraction," which concludes with a request for
grace "that I may been oon of hem at the day of doom that shulle be saved"
(X.1092).

The "Retraction" seems to flow inevitably not only from the Parson's
Tale but from all that precedes it—the insistence within the fictional frame
on understanding the Canterbury pilgrimage from an eschatological per-

spective. Yet critics have done nearly everything in their power to avoid dealing with the implications of this perspective, sometimes simply dismissing the "Retraction." For David Aers, for example, the "Retraction" of Chaucer "shows that at the point of his life and in the mood in which he composed it, the productions of the creative imagination seemed of little importance to him."[16] That the "Retraction" for many critics is the most enigmatic passage in *The Canterbury Tales* is at least partly due to our modern difficulty in accepting what would be a commonplace in the Middle Ages: a great pilgrimage poem should conclude with an explicitly eschatological perspective since pilgrimage itself is a form of penance. Thus the connection the Parson makes between pilgrimage and eschatology is not unusual. His understanding of the ideal Christian pilgrimage as one leading to a vision of the heavenly Jerusalem is based on the eschatological doctrine that this world is not the home of Christians but a temporary residence. The particular imagery summoned by the Parson clearly alludes to Apocalypse 21, where the angel guide directs John's attention to the New Jerusalem.

The Parson's statement not only reminds the pilgrims of the ideals of pilgrimage, but also points to the significant symbolism and basic structure of pilgrimage. Yet only recently (and it would seem reluctantly) has scholarship investigated the serious implications of this symbolism and structure for *The Canterbury Tales*.[17] Once again, the verisimilitude of Chaucer's characters and the abundance of descriptive and narrative details are so appealing to modern readers that this fictional "journey" often continues to be treated as a stunning example of the rise of literary realism. The understanding of the poem as a "roadside drama," which for so long motivated interpretation of the tales, has tended to treat the pilgrims as if they were "real people" interacting with one another on a "real" pilgrimage to Canterbury; as a result criticism has emphasized the "realism" of the pilgrimage and the ways in which the tales psychologically reflect the characters of their tellers.[18] Similarly, the tendency of historians to treat the poem as a document recording the intriguing sidelights and particular abuses of late medieval pilgrimages has failed to recognize the workings of the apocalyptic imagination in the poem. For many historians the vivid portraits in the General Prologue continue to represent the "unruly pilgrims" that characterized pilgrimage in its decline, with individual characters such as the Wife of Bath becoming "the epitome of the worldly, pleasure-seeking pilgrim."[19] It is as though the resonances of the "idea" of pilgrimage could not transcend the rich realistic and historical details without also denying them.

But Chaucer's practice confirms what we have come to recognize as typical of the apocalyptic imagination, namely that it is not necessary to choose between naturalistic detail and a powerful sense of immediacy, on the one hand, and rich symbolism evoked through traditional contexts on the other. As Donald Howard has noted,

> the nineteenth-century obsession with novelistic realism (and the twentieth century's acceptance of this obsession as providing the norm for all fiction) has made the "documentary" aspects of Chaucer's pilgrimage poem particularly attractive to literary historians who have tended to see the *Canterbury Tales* either as social fact or novelistic fiction. More recently, students of Chaucer have had to "discover," slowly, tentatively, that the pilgrimage frame of *The Canterbury Tales* is not after all local color but an allegory or metaphor of human life, at base religious. To some, this seems to make *The Canterbury Tales* abstract and dogmatic. But the antinomy belongs to us, not to the Middle Ages. The work, like medieval art in general, is at once realistic and abstract. We can have it both ways. A real live pilgrimage to any medieval man *was* a metaphoric one-way journey to the Heavenly Jerusalem, and none the less real for that.[20]

Like the fifteenth-century masters who vivify their traditional subjects by placing them in contemporary Flemish settings and by portraying the received iconography in sharply focused detail, Chaucer gives new life to the idea of pilgrimage, making this particular fictional pilgrimage of interest in its own right. It is, however, no less necessary to consider the traditional implications of pilgrimage in studying *The Canterbury Tales*.

D. W. Robertson, who argues that pilgrimage is the "most important" scriptural concept in *The Canterbury Tales*, comments on its serious implications: "Any pilgrimage during the Middle Ages, whether it was made on the knees in a labyrinth set in a cathedral floor, or, more strenuously, to the Holy Land, was ideally a figure for the pilgrimage of the Christian soul through the world's wilderness toward the celestial Jerusalem."[21] In reminding ourselves of these implications, therefore, we should begin with the goal of pilgrimage, reaching the New Jerusalem. Because the religious goals of pilgrims were not achieved fully until they reached their destination, until the pilgrimage reached conclusion, the teleological implications of pilgrimage were particularly strong. Pilgrimage became associated with the Christian sense of an ending, with both personal and universal eschatology. Thus in innumerable Christian writings, pilgrimage is the standard metaphor for the course not only of the life of the individual Christian journeying through the world's wilderness toward the celestial Jerusalem but also of Christian history from creation to the Last Judgment. Both metaphorical applications are scriptural:

> Iuxta fidem defuncti sunt omnes isti, non acceptis repromissionibus, sed a longe eas adspicientes et salutantes et confidentes quia peregrini et hospites sunt super terram. Qui enim haec dicunt significant se patriam inquirere. Et, si quidem ipsius meminissent de qua exierunt, habebant utique tempus revertendi. Nunc autem meliorem appetunt, id est caelestem. Ideo non confunditur Deus vocari Deus eorum; paravit enim illis civitatem. (Hebrews 11:13–16)

> [All these died according to faith, not having received the promises, but beholding them afar off, and saluting them, and confessing that they are pilgrims and strangers on the earth. For they that say these things, do signify that they seek a country. And truly if they had been mindful of that from whence they came out, they had doubtless time to return. But now they desire a better, that is to say, a heavenly country. Therefore God is not ashamed to be called their God; for he hath prepared for them a city.]

The notion that Christians are "peregrini . . . super terram" is the dominant metaphor in Augustine's *De Civitate Dei*. Individuals who are righteous are citizens of the City of God and thus pilgrims in this world who can depend only on God. The first was Abel, "a pilgrim and stranger in the world."[22] This ideal, significantly, informs Chaucer's short lyric subtitled, "Truth," his "Balade de Bon Conseil":

> Her is non hoom, her nis but wildernesse:
> Forth, pilgrim, forth! Forth, beste, out of thy stal!
> Know thy contree, look up, thank God of al;
> Hold the heye wey and lat thy gost thee lede,
> And trouthe thee shal delivere, it is no drede.[23]

Chaucer's reference to this world as a wilderness, which recalls the field full of folk at the beginning of *Piers Plowman*, explicitly reminds us that the second important spiritual understanding of pilgrimage—as a symbol for salvation history—is also biblically based. It takes as its model the Old Testament Exodus, during which the people of God wandered through the wilderness in quest of the promised land. Throughout history the elect are seen as a *populus peregrinus*, in the world but not of it.[24] For example, Augustine calls the City of God "the pilgrim City of Christ the King," which from its very beginning to its ultimate end in this world suffers temptation and persecution but also the protection of God:

> In this manner the Church proceeds on its pilgrim way in this world, in these evil days. Its troubled course began not merely in the time of the bodily presence of Christ and the time of his apostles; it started with Abel himself, the first righteous man slain by an ungodly brother; and the pilgrimage goes on from that time right up to the end of history, with the persecutions of the world on one side, and on the other the consolations of God.[25]

Abel thus represents the first stranger in an evil world on the individual's pilgrimage of life and the founding father of the *populus peregrinus* on the historical pilgrimage from Creation to Doomsday.

Having argued that the pilgrimage cannot be understood fully if divorced from its eschatological implications, we believe that it necessarily follows that *The Canterbury Tales* must also be examined in terms of those implications as well. For the individual pilgrims, the pilgrimage suggests the journey of life, a full cycle from morning, "whan that day bigan to sprynge" (I.822), to evening. It is a movement from birth, suggested by the imagery of procreation in the opening lines of the General Prologue, to the approach of death, implied by the setting of the Parson's Tale, its penitential theme, and Chaucer's "Retraction." Moving from a tavern in the rather disreputable suburb of Southwark to a saint's shrine in the cathedral city of Canterbury, the pilgrimage is a journey from the worldly to the otherworldly. Considering the pilgrims from the perspective of personal eschatology adds a seriousness to their portraits and tales and invites a search for deeper implications, irrespective of the conventional distinction between serious and comic in the form of the tales. Harry Bailey's enterprising plans, calling for a return to the Tabard Inn, tell us only about the inadequacy of the Host as spokesman for the pilgrimage.[26] This pilgrimage poem encompasses, like the pilgrimage of life, a one-way journey. As Howard has convincingly argued, "the journey takes place unrealistically in one day: the gathering darkness of the Parson's Prologue signals the end of the life of man. What we have in the ending of *The Canterbury Tales* is the unworldly aspect of pilgrimage, the metaphor and the idea."[27]

Its eschatological framework encourages us to view *The Canterbury Tales* as a microcosm of salvation history, the journey of Augustine's "pilgrim city of Christ the King." The poem moves from the natural to the supernatural, from Creation, suggested by the springtime imagery of the poem's opening lines, to Doomsday, implied by the setting of the Parson's Tale. It is true that *The Canterbury Tales* does not conclude, as do *The Pearl* and the *Commedia*, with a vision of the New Jerusalem or a journey into Paradise. It is also true that, unlike Langland, Chaucer does not present his world set against the apocalyptically charged backdrop of tower and pit. He concludes his great *summa* of human nature and imagination within this world but with compelling signs that this world is to be judged from the perspective of the next. There is a sense that the journey of human history is on hold, that it is near its conclusion, but not quite there, that what *The Canterbury Tales* provides is "only a typological Pisgah sight from which the promised land can be seen but not reached before death."[28]

As the most common of Chaucerian commonplaces has it, on this pilgrimage of history we meet a full panoply of individuals, so that at the end the Host can say, "we han herd of ech degree" (X.18). Yet, as in real life, it is not always clear which of the Canterbury pilgrims are following "the wey, in this viage, / Of thilke parfit glorious pilgrymage / That highte Jerusalem celestial" (X.49–51), to quote the Parson, and which are "wandrynge by the weye" (I.467), to use Chaucer's scripturally charged description of the Wife of Bath. That the devout and the debauched are together led by the Host from Southwark to Canterbury reminds us of Augustine's statement that before the end of time the City of God and the city of the world are inextricably joined, the members of each interwoven until their "separation at the last judgment."[29] An arresting but nonetheless accurate way of putting this is to say that, no less than is the idea of pilgrimage, each pilgrim is charged with eschatological possibilities. Each pilgrim is in this sense, therefore, both an individual and a type. Divine judgment does not take place in the poem, which on its literal level sticks to the realistic details provided by Chaucer as pilgrim narrator. The carefully drawn characters of the General Prologue thus remain ambiguous.

But the apocalyptic imagination makes possible a judgment of their characters and the characters inhabiting their tales, especially when the Parson replaces the Host and underscores the poem's eschatological perspective, warning all who care to listen to "drede of the day of doom and of the horrible peynes of helle" (X.157). It is not coincidental that the Parson's Tale is a compendium of the sins implied by Chaucer's detailed portraits of his pilgrims and acted out by the various characters in their tales. As John Wall has noted, the tale provides "the means for judging consistently the examples of the pilgrims and their tales told in a world where, although (as in Langland's work) Redemption has definitively taken place already in Christ's death and resurrection, salvation has yet to be worked out in successive ages and individuals."[30] It thus serves as a fitting conclusion to the entire poem. To understand it as such is not "to read the whole of *The Canterbury Tales* in the light of the Parson's Tale, as though all the other narratives were merely partial expressions of its truth."[31] It is, instead, to recognize that the Parson's introductory comments and sermon make explicit the eschatological perspective that infuses *The Canterbury Tales* by virtue of the fact that it is a pilgrimage poem.

Considering the pilgrims and their tales from the perspective of universal eschatology, furthermore, reinforces a general pattern of movement in *The Canterbury Tales*. Although scholars continue to debate "Chaucer's own final arrangement" of the tales, the two poles are firmly established.[32] The first storyteller is the Knight, who, according to the fiction, is selected by chance, "by aventure, or sort, or cas" (I.844); the last pilgrim to speak is the Parson, who is, significantly, chosen to "knytte up wel a greet mateere" (X.28). The Knight's Tale, the great epic poem of pagan wisdom, asserts in tragic form the necessity of human acceptance of divine judgment apparently beyond, and perhaps unrelated to, individual worth and specific action. It suggests that life is a pilgrimage, but strips that notion of its specifically Christian connotations. As Egeus, the father of Theseus, states:

> "This world nys but a thurghfare ful of wo,
> And we been pilgrymes, passynge to and fro.
> Deeth is an ende of every worldly soore."
>
> (I.2847–49)

The Knight's Tale is the poem of the Earthly City, at once embodying the accomplishments of reason and rule—making the strongest case for these pagan virtues—yet suggesting their limitations as well.[33] The Boethian structure of the Knight's Tale reveals the limits of pagan wisdom and asserts its ultimate insufficiency, but it also steers the pilgrims in the right direction by pointing beyond itself. In the crucial "prime mover" speech of Theseus, the Knight's medieval audience is allowed a vantage point not available to the ancient pagans, because the prime mover in true Boethian fashion represents more than the celestial hierarchy of pagan antiquity. What this speech tells Chaucer's pilgrims is that they must embark on the pilgrimage that ends with the spires of Canterbury.[34] They must move from the Earthly City—symbolized in the tale by Thebes, which destroys itself through fratricide—through the limited perspective of human reason, represented in the tale by Athens and Theseus, finally to the Heavenly City.

Dante's Vergil operates in much the same way within the *Commedia*. Even as the insufficiency of his vision becomes more and more apparent in the climb up the purgatorial mountain, we learn that it was his light that brought his fellow poet Statius to Christianity (*Purgatorio* 22)—his teaching, like Theseus's, meant more to others than it did to himself. The comparison with Vergil is also useful in that it shows how Chaucer, no less than Dante, gives reason its due at the beginning of his "epic." For both poets, grace builds on nature.

The Parson's Tale is the treatise of the Heavenly City. Unlike the Knight's Tale it insists that divine judgment is intimately connected with individual worth and that penitence makes all the difference. As we have seen, it too understands life as a pilgrimage, but a pilgrimage that leads to "the righte wey of Jerusalem celestial" (X.80). Between the overtly pagan position of the Knight's Tale and the unambiguously Christian position of the Parson's Tale, a wide variety of tales (and their tellers) exemplify individual judgment in the light of ultimate universal judgment. The middle, though, is muddled, so that the astonishing variety of tellers and tales and the very complex relationships between them do not move the reader clearly or directly to the heavenly Jerusalem in the manner of Dante. Chaucer's form instead may be compared to the variety and complexity of another pilgrimage "poem"—the Bible. In medieval commentary, the Bible is characteristically conceptualized as the story of salvation history ranging from creation to final judgment. Just as with *The Canterbury Tales*, its two poles are clearly established. Its middle, furthermore, is characterized by a wide variety of literary types, a wealth of characters, and complex interrelationships between individual books. Combining these two scriptural perspectives is perhaps the best way to think about *The Canterbury Tales*. Like the biblical stories embodying God's relationship to particular historical figures, Chaucer's tales deal with a full spectrum of individuals, from saints to scoundrels. For example, the tales concerned with the diffi-cult relationships of the sexes include not only the stories of Constance and Griselda—who, representing Christian virtues, seem more allegorical than real—but also the more naturalistic tales told by the Nun's Priest, the Wife of Bath, and the Merchant. In these the characters are less simplistic, the situations more complex. Their implications are no less serious, how-ever, and beneath the surface of the narrative one perceives allusions to the key events of salvation history, to Adam's fall as well as to the second Adam, to redemption and judgment.

The Nun's Priest concludes his tale with the exhortation:

> But ye that holden this tale a folye,
> As of a fox, or of a cok and hen,
> Taketh the moralite, goode men.
> For Seint Paul seith that al that writen is,
> To oure doctrine it is ywrite, ywis;
> Taketh the fruyt, and lat the chaf be stille.

(VII.3438—43)

No matter how many levels of irony are to be found in this exhortation that comes at the end of one of Chaucer's most elusive tales, we would be wrong to assume that this advice is not meant to be heeded or that Chau-cer is merely being ironic. The exhortation is based, after all, on the Pau-line injunction once again pronounced in the "Retractions": "For oure book seith, 'Al that is writen is writen for oure doctrine,' and that is myn entente" (X.1083). That the exhortation concludes a tale that asserts the limitations of rhetoric by exemplifying the false uses of rhetoric is yet an-other example of Chaucer's subtlety, suggesting that being able to separate fruit from chaf is no small achievement. But it does not mean that they cannot or should not be separated. As we shall argue below, an eschato-logical reading suggests that serious fruit can be detected in the patterns of inversions of salvation history that are abundantly evident in the comic tales, and, furthermore, that detecting these patterns in no way minimizes their outrageous good fun.

In fact, from an eschatological point of view, the comic tales may fit more easily into the framework of the Canterbury pilgrimage than do the allegorical tales. It is not simply that readers are able to have it both ways within this form, reading the comic tales seriously while keeping all the jokes. The use of inversion and even sacred parody that is a dominant feature of these tales and a major source of their humor is—as we have seen in previous chapters—one of the key features of the apocalyptic imagination, and this relationship is not fortuitous.[35] Moreover, of equal importance in understanding *The Canterbury Tales* is the recognition that the comic tales are conspicuously set not in the mythological or historical past but, like the polemical apocalypticism of Guillaume de Saint-Amour and Bonaventure's apocalyptic Francis, *in novissimis diebus*. Their characters—as is typical of the apocalyptic imagination—are clearly linked to earlier figures from salvation history, moreover. The contemporaneity of detail featured in such tales as those told by the Miller and Reeve, Friar and Summoner, and Shipman and Pardoner functions in much the same way as the quarrel between the Mendicants and the Seculars in the *Roman de la Rose*. It is a forceful reminder of the urgency of the present viewed from the perspective of both the past and the future.

The comic tales are in some ways Chaucer's most appropriate vehicles for embodying apocalyptic concerns, and this (among many other reasons) helps confirm that they are his most remarkable artistic achievement.[36] Given this perspective, we can see how the specific details of individual tales reinforce the larger pattern. Just as the general judgment depends on the particular, so the eschatological pattern depends on specific details, allusions, and images, what Gail Gibson has felicitously called "the dramatic icons, compressed symbolic and allusive playing, which lie beneath the literal surface of the narrative."[37] Without in any way claiming to be complete, the following examples are suggestive of how Chaucer presents an inverted version of salvation history, the real as an inversion of the ideal, the present as a parody of the past.

In the Miller's Tale Nicholas, among other roles, becomes a comic false prophet who interprets "Goddes pryvetee" for John the Carpenter. To attain the "pryvetee" of John's wife (cf. I.3164), he predicts a catastrophic one-day flood that "shal mankynde drenche" (I.3521). V. A. Kolve, speaking here for a long line of critics who emphasize the self-contained nature of game and play within the tale, asserts that for his comic purposes Chaucer deliberately distances this one-day flood from the traditional associations of the Flood with Doomsday: "Chaucer prevents Nicholas's Flood game from bringing into the tale anything resembling the moral weight and doctrinal richness of its original—the Flood as recounted in the Book of Genesis, as understood in patristic commentary upon that text, or as represented (sometimes even in comedy, though ultimately toward a serious end) on the medieval pageant stage."[38] Kolve is surely right to emphasize the fabliau justice and the comedy of the tale, but it does not follow that Chaucer sought to avoid invoking "to any serious religious end" the meaning of the Flood, especially its prefiguration of Doomsday.[39] Here, as throughout the tales, the comic and the serious are subtly related.

To laugh at the outrageous lecherous "prophet" and modern-day Noah is rather to affirm than deny that their actions are to be judged ultimately from an eschatological perspective. Their vices, however foolish, exemplify *in novissimis diebus* those of the sinners who lived in the days of Noah and prefigure the last days:

Sicut autem in diebus Noë, ita erit et adventus Filii hominis. Sicut enim erant in deibus ante diluvium comedentes et bibentes, nubentes et nuptui tradentes, usque ad eum diem quo intravit Noë in arcam, et non cognoverunt, donec venit diluvium et tulit omnes; ita erit et adventus Filii hominis. (Matt. 24:37–39)

[And as in the days of Noe, so shall also the coming of the Son of man be. For as in the days before the flood they were eating and drinking, marrying and giving in marriage, even till that day in which Noe entered into the ark, And they knew not till the flood came, and took them all away; so also shall the coming of the Son of man be.]

The Miller's Tale recreates the days of Noah not simply by parodying elements of the Flood as part of its ingeniously elaborate comic mechanism, but by embodying in contemporary England—in Oxford, no less—the very conditions that led God to unleash the flood in the first place and that will be present again as a sign of the last times.[40] Míčeál Vaughan has further underscored this eschatological reading by recognizing that the imaginative one-day "flood" prophesied by Nicholas probably alludes to the flood predicted in the very popular tradition of the Fifteen Signs before Doomsday.[41] Both traditions—Noah's flood as Old Testament type and the flood of the last days as contemporary sign—point to the ultimate eschatological judgment.

The Miller's Tale is answered by the Reeve's Tale, an equally comic, although rather intensely bitter, tale also set in contemporary England and also developing inversions of the pattern of salvation. For example, the mill that provides both the locus of the action and a metaphor for the sexual play of the tale may be understood as an inversion of the so-called "mystic mill," an important image of salvation history that can be traced back to the fathers of the Church and that can be found in both verbal and artistic sources. As this icon is presented in sculpture (for example, at St.-Lazare,

Autun), Moses places the grain of the Old Law into the hopper, and St. Paul, through the transforming power of the mystic mill, receives the flour of the New Law.[42] The Reeve's Tale begins with a relatively lengthy discussion of oldness (I, 3867–98). It catalogues the characteristic sins of *elde*, that individual and collective harbinger of the end that Wimbledon and Langland show to be central to eschatological concerns and that, along with his literal age, characterize the Reeve. Furthermore, the sins that are exemplified throughout the tale in Symkin's viciousness and the madcap revenge of the scholars all exemplify "Pauline oldness." It is the result of refusing to accept the transformation of the individual from the old man to the new. On the personal level it is analogous to rejecting the universal pattern of salvation history from the Old to the New Law and is thus an exact inversion of the idea embodied by the "Mystic Mill." Moreover, in another resonant allusion, Symkin the Miller is both in name and in deed a simonist. John H. Fisher, in pointing out that the name "Symkin" is a diminutive of Simon, has suggested that the name alludes to Simon Magus. This connection is totally appropriate because the carpenter's wealth comes through a form of simony: his wife, the illegitimate daughter of a parish priest, has received Church goods and property unlawfully.[43] It may well be, expanding Fisher's observation, that in the very structure of the tale itself, the rising and falling fortunes of Symkin subtly and wittily echo the well-known story of the fall of Simon Magus. As we have noted in earlier chapters, Simon Magus is a major type of Antichrist whose apocalyptic resonances Dante effectively develops in *Inferno* 19.[44] As in the Miller's Oxford, so too in the Reeve's Cambridge, a contemporary setting is energized by the richness and depth of an apocalyptic tradition.

Other comic tales are informed by parodic allusions to salvation history as well. The Shipman's Tale shows Chaucer's concern with a world in which every single human relationship has been reduced to the level of a financial transaction. Clearly Chaucer is meditating on the implications of a new money economy in this tale, and his references to banking and trade are studded with contemporary allusions, highlighting, among other things, the relevance and the urgency of the problem. Yet this same tale, which deals with adulterous affairs and payments, also alludes by means of inversion to a central New Testament event that exemplifies Christian love freely given. On "the thridde day" (VII.75) the monk daun John rises early to walk in the garden, where he meets the merchant's "goode wyf." The meeting is reminiscent of the so-called *Noli me tangere* scene very popular in late medieval and Renaissance art. Christ's appearance to Mary

Magdalen in the garden is a key moment of recognition following the Resurrection: "Dicit ei Iesus: Noli me tangere, nondum enim ascendi ad patrem meum. Vade autem ad fratres meos et dic eis: Ascendo ad Patrem meum et Patrem vestrum, Deum meum et Deum vestrum" (John 20:17) ["Jesus saith to her: Do not touch me, for I am not yet ascended to my Father. But go to my brethren, and say to them: I ascend to my Father and to your Father, to my God and your God"]. But as Gail Gibson has pointed out, in the Shipman's Tale Chaucer turns the woman in the garden into an inverted Mary Magdalen, wherein "the prostitute-made-saint is replaced by a contemporary Magdalen who will contract to prostitute herself both within and without marriage."[45] Unlike Mary Magdalen, who is commanded, "Noli me tangere," the wife is caught "by the flankes," embraced "harde" and kissed "ofte" (VII.203–204). Unlike Christ, who sends his follower to proclaim her garden experience openly to all, daun John sends his "owene lady deere" (VII.196) to leave the garden "al stille and softe" (VII.204).

Of course, daun John takes both Christ's place in the parodic inversion of the garden scene on the first Easter and the husband's place in this brilliant fabliau. Unlike the Miller, the Reeve, or the Merchant, the Shipman does not relate a tale about the familiar opposition between youth and age; instead, in a rich variation on the love triangle that is at the heart of all Chaucer's fabliaux, the Shipman's Tale reverses the roles of husband and monk. The monk not only takes the place of the husband in bed, but becomes a successful merchant as well, whereas, in an equally ironic reversal, the merchant proves himself to be a "monk" in the new "monasticism" of the new economic order. The merchant's countinghouse, for example, becomes his cell, where he spends long hours in contemplation "Of thilke yeer how that it with hym stood, / And how that he despended hadde his good" (VII.79–80). He remains in his cell undisturbed, his silence punctuated only by the traditional monastic call to prayer:

And eek he nolde that no man sholde hym lette
Of his acountes, for the meene tyme;
And thus he sit til it was passed pryme.

(VII.86–88)

His contemplation is connected as well with another traditional monastic virtue, fasting: "'What, sire,'" his wife exclaims, "'how longe wol ye faste?'" (VII.215). And, as the wife also makes clear, the merchant is "guilty" of the virtue of chastity, above and beyond what is required by the marriage debt. After the monk has hinted that perhaps the wife is tired from laboring with her husband all night, she enticingly describes her husband's "chastity" and her own desperate frustration:

> "Nay, cosyn myn, it stant nat so with me;
> For, by that God that yaf me soule and lyfe,
> In al the reawme of France is ther no wyf
> That lasse lust hath to that sory pley.
> For I may synge 'allas and weylawey
> That I was born,' but to no wight," quod she,
> "Dar I nat telle how that it stant with me."
>
> (VII.114–20)

The eager monk, whose thoughts make him "wax al reed" (VII.111), is of course ready to provide for her more generously than has her husband.

The merchant does not systematically exemplify the entire Rule of Saint Benedict in parodic form, but his new "order" does highlight some of its key features such as reclusion and contemplation, fasting and abstinence, and chastity. His "monastic" behavior, furthermore, recalls the three most obvious deviations from the Benedictine rule that characterize the Monk of the General Prologue, who is never in his cell, who abstains only from fasting (his preference for a fat swan serves as an icon of all that the Rule proscribes in both letter and spirit), and who has mastered the art of "prikyng" in its many forms. Meanwhile, in a systematic exchange of roles, daun John, who should uphold the ideal of the old monasticism, has embraced the ideals of the new as eagerly as he has embraced the merchant's wife. Indeed, one of the most obvious and delightful ironies is that the monk is clearly the best businessman in the tale. He manages to cheat the husband of both his wife and his money, even as he manages to get the wife to pay twice for the same "hundred frankes" (VII.181). His shrewd business sense is evident not only in the tale's climactic stratagem, but also early in the tale in his subtle negotiations with the wife in the garden. In proving to be the better businessman, the monk rejects both poverty and chastity and, like the Monk in the General Prologue, the "old and somdel streit" monastic rule:

> The reule of Seint Maure or of Seint Beneit—
> By cause that it was old and somdel streit
> This ilke Monk leet olde thynges pace,
> And heeld after the newe world the space.
>
> (I.173–76)

Delight in the richness of the irony of the Shipman's Tale, however, ought not to keep us from recognizing the seriousness of Chaucer's indictment of the new order. In this tale, with its parodic inversion of the *Noli me tangere* Easter-morning scene, of conversion, and of the monastic vows of poverty and chastity, the love of money has replaced the love of God and the "privetee" of adultery has replaced the joyous proclamation of charity. The "cooling of charity" (Matt. 24 : 12) characterizes the world of the Shipman just as it characterizes the apocalyptic age of hypocrisy portrayed in Jean de Meun's continuation of the *Roman de la Rose*. The forms by which the love of God are channeled in the monastic ideal are appropriated to serve a new master. The merchandising of erotic love is just one feature of this inversion of values during an age in which, as Langland complains, "charite hath ben chapmen":

> Sith charite hath ben chapmen and chief to shryve lordes
> Manye ferlies han fallen in a fewe yeres.
> But Holy Chirche and hii [the friars] holde bettre togidres
> The mooste meschief on molde is mountynge up faste.
> (Prol.64–67)

Although Chaucer's tale is more localized and less explicitly apocalyptic than are the antimendicant attacks in Langland's prophecy and Jean de Meun's polemic, its portrayal of the new order is typical of the apocalyptic imagination, reflecting the inversion of values that characterizes the apocalyptic age of hypocrisy and the last days. The Shipman's innocuous and commonplace conclusion thus takes on eschatological force:

> Thus endeth my tale, and God us sende
> Taillynge ynough unto oure lyves ende. Amen.
> (VII.433–34)

The Shipman's Tale also suggests that the ideal of pilgrimage has been undermined. The monk's journeys to "Seint-Denys" from Paris are not to honor France's patron saint but "to doon plesaunce, and also greet costage" (VII.45). The merchant's new "monasticism" requires him to take not one but two "pilgrymages," to Bruges and to Paris, but it is clear that in his "order" pilgrimage for profit has replaced pilgrimage for salvation. As the Parson reminds us, the idea of pilgrimage is closely connected to individual conversion; the two cannot really be understood apart from each other, because the two are the universal and individual poles of the same reality. But in the garden the wife takes advantage of her husband's preparation for his "pilgrymage" (VII.234) to Bruges to begin her conversion to prostitution. Her inverted "conversion" in the garden scene recalling Mary Magdalen's encounter with the resurrected Christ is particularly significant. It inverts Mary Magdalen's rebirth from prostitute to saint, one of the most important biblical exemplars of conversion.[46]

Another scriptural allusion to conversion that follows the Shipman's Tale in this parodic version of salvation history is evident in the Friar's Tale, whose very plot is a demonic version of the scriptural "Road to Emmaus." In the Middle Ages Christ's appearance to two of his disciples while walking along the road to Emmaus, their ultimate if belated recognition of him, and their acceptance of his Resurrection became a model of Christian conversion. The most important of the post-Resurrection appearances after the *Noli me tangere* scene, it has been called "the paradigm for the patterned existence of a pilgrim people."[47] According to Luke 24:13–32, the two disciples fail to recognize Christ even as they walk along with him. Similarly, in the Friar's Tale, the Summoner, a disciple of the devil, does not recognize his master even as they walk together until it is too late and "Body and soule he with the devel wente" (III.1640).

The correspondence between the two versions of these mini-pilgrimage stories is, moreover, brilliantly exact. In the biblical account one of Christ's most significant actions is to explain the meaning of Scripture to his disciples, beginning with Moses and the prophets. Yet even here at what should be for them a moment of recognition, the disciples ironically fail to recognize their master. In the Friar's Tale, much of the action is taken up with the devil's witty exposition of demonic lore. This is an even more pointedly ironic scene because the devil consciously describes the very tactics that he is at that moment using on his uncomprehending victim, who fails to recognize in his companion an identity and motive obvious to even the most mildly perceptive reader (III.1424–1522). In the biblical account recognition finally comes at the end of the story, during the significant moment when Christ breaks bread with his disciples, using language that recalls the language establishing the Eucharist at the Last Supper.[48] In the Friar's Tale the recognition comes somewhat earlier in the story, though too late obviously for the Summoner, who remains conspicuously unrepentant even after the devil has made his identity known. But in Chaucer's version the Eucharistic resonances of the biblical recognition scene may also be discerned. The presence of a real devil may be a subtle and witty allusion to the doctrine of the real presence, the affirmation that the body and blood of Christ are truly present under the appearance of bread and wine. As is true with the accidents of the Eucharist, the substance is hidden: the reality of the devil is similarly masked by the utter realism of his disguise. In every way the devil is indistinguishable from the Summoner, his human counterpart and companion.[49]

Since this allusion is less a matter of direct correspondence with the biblical account and more a matter of inference, one might view it as speculative. Whether or not one is inclined to accept this oblique allusion to the Eucharist and the real presence, however, the larger point to be seen through the devil's disguise is of fundamental importance both to the meaning of the tale and to the wider argument of this study. The effectiveness of the disguise—its surface realism, the devil's correspondence both with the garb and the practices of an actual fourteenth-century summoner—guarantees that the eschatologial and the contemporary are radically, if unperceptively, intertwined. The mechanics of the story become an image for the reading of *The Canterbury Tales* as infused by the apocalyptic imagination, the reading we propose in which the contemporary is informed by the eschatological. For in this tale not only does the eschatological emerge from the contemporary as the Summoner is brought to judgment, but the entire action of the tale depends on the fact that they are indistinguishable to the Summoner until then. If the Road to Emmaus story is fundamentally about conversion, then surely the point of its demonic parody is to highlight the Summoner's stubborn refusal to convert or repent:

> And whan the devel herde hire cursen so
> Upon hir knees, he seyde in this manere,
> "Now, Mabely, myn owene mooder deere,
> Is this youre wyl in ernest that ye seye?"
> "The devel," quod she, "so fecche hym er he deye,
> And panne and al, but he wol hym repente!"
> "Nay, olde stot, that is nat myn entente,"
> Quod this somonour, "for to repente me
> For any thyng that I have had of thee."
>
> (III.1624–32)

After these parodies of Christ's appearances to Mary Magdalen and to the disciples, the next event in this comic yet deadly inversion of salvation history is developed in the Summoner's Tale, which depicts a sacrilegious "Pentecost" and a unique scatological judgment. The descent of the Holy Spirit to the twelve apostles at Pentecost is, as several scholars have shown, parodied in the elaborately scholastic explanation of the division of Thomas's fart among twelve friars. It is a climactic joke that is anticipated by many allusions to Pentecost throughout the tale and that "hinges on the scatologically subtle relationship" between the winds of the fart and the inspiring winds of the Spirit at Pentecost.[50] The false Pentecost, which, as we have seen in earlier chapters, the apocalyptic imagination expected as one of the signs of the end, becomes comically present in the *novissimus diebus* of late fourteenth-century England.[51]

The Friar's Tale is about a corrupt summoner, whereas the Summoner's Tale is about a venal friar. Taken together, the two are about the corruption of penitential practice in Chaucer's time. In this scathing depiction of the abuse of the penitential system—unique among the tales with the significant exception of the Pardoner's Tale, to be discussed below—an eschatological perspective also emerges. As John Fleming has put it, the two tales form a "grotesque literary diptych" in which we have "an agonizing tableau of the profound crisis of late medieval Christendom, an episode in the sickness unto death of the old world."[52] Fleming's phrase captures something of the apocalyptic urgency of the tales, as well as their eschatological dimension. Penance, by definition, occupies a central place in Chaucer's pilgrimage. The medieval understanding of pilgrimage as an exterior enactment of an interior conversion links the tales to penance in that the normal way in which such a conversion is effected is through the sacrament of penance. From the point of view of the eschatological perspective of *The Canterbury Tales*, these penitential tales are of central importance.

Near the end of the tales, the Canon and his Yeoman join the pilgrim band as they approach Canterbury, shortly before the Parson brings into focus the poem's many eschatological perspectives. A figure of great curiosity to Chaucer and the other pilgrims, the Canon nevertheless forsakes the pilgrimage once his Yeoman begins to reveal the deceitful character of this "too wise" man, whose false claims, effective temptations, supernatural skills, and direct dealings with the "feend" (VIII.916–19) associate him with Antichrist.[53] Between the Summoner's Tale and the Canon's Yeoman's Tale—between the parodic allusion to Pentecost and the brief appearance of the Antichrist-like deceiver—the pilgrims hear from a more subtle deceiver, the Pardoner. Within the biblical pattern of salvation history that we have been outlining, the Pardoner's position is analogous to the position of Simon Magus, who after the miracles following Pentecost attempted to purchase the Holy Spirit, and who became in medieval exegesis one of the most significant types of Antichrist. The Pardoner's character and tale most clearly illustrate the insights to be gained by recognizing the Chaucerian apocalyptic imagination and by approaching *The Canterbury Tales* in eschatological perspective.

The Pardoner and his tale reflect the subtle mixture in *The Canterbury Tales* of the universal and the personal elements of eschatology and the interconnection between its concerns with both apocalyptic and contemporary time. The tale develops a common theme found in many sermons concerned with personal eschatology and in many of the other tales as well: the moral blindness that is the result of sin leads inevitably to death and hellish damnation. It too, like the Friar's Tale, encompasses a pilgrimage poem within a pilgrimage poem. The three debauched rioters set off on a quest to kill death, a foolhardy and literal-minded reenactment of the perverted spiritual journey represented by their sinful lives.[54] Blinded by their "false felicity," they are unable to recognize what Wimbledon identified as the three "summoners of doom": sickness, old age, and death. They depart from a village suffering from the "pestilence" (VI.679) and soon meet the archetypal Old Man, who directs them to the pot of gold. As a result, as the Pardoner states in one of Chaucer's most ironic lines, "No lenger thanne after Deeth they soughte" (VI.772), because they have found death, or at least it has found them. Thus the Pardoner's Tale highlights the personal warnings inherent in orthodox Christian eschatology. Nor should we overlook the apocalyptic warnings suggested by the Pardoner and his tale. Set during the plague, it emphasizes the debauchery of characters who live as did the doomed in the days of Noah before the first destruction of the world.[55] They embody the moral decline that many contemporary chroniclers believed resulted from the devastation of the pestilence and indicated the imminence of the end.

The portrayal of the Pardoner also powerfully underscores these apocalyptic suggestions. One of Chaucer's richest characters, the Pardoner exerts his fascination by an intricate combination of hypocrisy, gamesmanship, boasting, and arrogance, through which we are able to see in its most developed form a catalogue of contemporary ecclesiastical abuse. As spokesman for and embodiment of a Church turned upside-down, the Pardoner is the heir to a rich tradition. Chaucer criticism long ago recognized that the literary ancestor of the Pardoner is to be found, like so many of Chaucer's characters, in the *Roman de la Rose*, and that in fact he is no less a figure than Faus Semblant. Both in terms of his aggressive confessional technique and his blatant hypocrisy, the Pardoner is clearly a direct literary descendent of Jean de Meun's apocalyptically charged hypocrite. Once these similarities have been noted, however, critics usually emphasize the difference between Faus Semblant and the Pardoner, noting in particular how Chaucer has moved from an allegorical mode to a realistic one.[56] Yet moving too quickly from the similarities to the differences overlooks precisely the similarity that we wish to underscore: the Pardoner clearly inherits the apocalyptic pedigree of his ancestor. He too, no less than Faus Semblant, is a major player in the apocalyptic imagination, embodying the apocalyptic age of hypocrisy. He brings both to his confession and to his tale the apocalyptic resonances of hypocrisy that we detailed in our study of the *Roman de la Rose* in Chapter 3.

Thus in addition to being the vehicle through whom Chaucer embodies many contemporary criticisms of ecclesiastic abuses, the Pardoner fits into a long tradition of spiritual hypocrites, a tradition most often identified with Simon Magus and Antichrist. H. Marshall Leicester, Jr., although his approach to the *The Canterbury Tales* differs from our own significantly, has recently made a similar point about the Pardoner: "His self-presentation throughout the tale constantly stresses his culpability, and as the tale proceeds he seems to take this culpability with increasing seriousness, to regard himself as truly exemplary and symbolic of the evil, corruption, and sinfulness of the world—finally, perhaps, as a type of the Antichrist."[57] That he is a type of Antichrist is clear, for he is modelled on Simon Magus, one of the most powerful actors inhabiting the apocalyptic imagination.

As we will see, the Pardoner, through his sacrilegious mixing of money and grace, is portrayed as a contemporary version of Simon Magus. We have already sketched the main outlines of the Simon Magus tradition in connection with its use by Dante—all the ways in which he is the first great spiritual challenger of the early Church and all the ways in which he typifies the final challenger, Antichrist. This sketch can be fleshed out at this point by adding the words of an especially appropriate source, Chaucer's Parson. He refers explicitly to Simon Magus in his discussion of the sin of avarice:

> Certes symonye is cleped of Symon Magus, that wolde han boght for temporeel catel the yifte that God hadde yeven by the Hooly Goost to Seint Peter and to the apostles. And therefore understoond that

bothe he that selleth and he that beyeth thynges espirituels been cleped symonials. (X.783–84)

That Chaucer meant this definition to reflect the conduct of his own Pardoner can hardly be doubted. The discussion of avarice in this section of the Parson's Tale not only describes the very sins of which the Pardoner is guilty, it describes as well those subheadings of avarice that make up the action of his tale:

> Now comth hasardrie with his apurtenaunces, as tables and rafles, of which comth deceite, false othes, chidynges, and alle ravynes, blasphemynge and reneiynge of God, and hate of his neighebores, wast of goodes, mysspendynge of tyme, and somtyme manslaughtre. Certes, hasardours ne mowe nat been withouten greet synne whiles they haunte that craft. Of Avarice comen eek lesynges, thefte, fals witnesse, and false othes. (X.793–95)

Although at first it is easier to see how these sins as practiced by the rioters lead directly to the tale's denouement than it is to see that they are directly related to avarice, the Parson's sermon makes the connection explicit.

Yet there should be nothing especially surprising about this equation, since critics of the late medieval Church often argued that pardoners practiced simony. Not only did these critics condemn the selling of false pardons for personal profit, but some of Chaucer's contemporaries condemned the very act of taking money for a pardon. While not denying the validity of an indulgence, they argued that such commerce made the pardon false and cursed both the seller and the purchaser, perhaps one reason why the Host reacts so violently to the Pardoner's final blasphemous offer: "'Nay, nay!' quod he, 'thanne have I Cristes curs!'" (VI. 946).[58] For example, the lengthy treatise "Of Prelates," sometimes ascribed to Wyclif, explicitly connects the selling of pardons with simony, condemning it with apocalyptic fervor and identifying simony and pardons with Antichrist.[59] Nor are such contemporary associations limited to Lollard polemics. Throughout late medieval sermons and literature, the hypocrisy of the priesthood, particularly evidenced by its practice of simony, is a sign, as we have seen in Wimbledon's sermon and in *Piers Plowman*, of the appearance of Antichrist. The Parson similarly condemns simony, which he labels "the gretteste synne that may be, after the synne of Lucifer and Antecrist" (X. 788). With subtle virtuosity, Chaucer makes the tradition of Simon Magus and his association with Antichrist present to his concerns in the portrait of the Pardoner and in his tale.

The contrast between Parson and Pardoner—the ideal and its inversion—is enhanced by allusion to the traditional way in which Simon Peter is inverted by Simon Magus. This inversion is noted by the Parson in his definition of simony quoted above and is supported by the traditional imagery of the good versus bad spiritual rule that he develops in this same section of his sermon:

> And, as seith Seint Augustyn, "They been the develes wolves that stranglen the sheep of Jhesu Crist," and doon worse than wolves./ For soothly, whan the wolf hath ful his wombe, he stynteth to strangle sheepe. But soothly, the pilours and destroyours of godes of hooly chirche ne do nat so, for they ne stynte nevere to pile. (X, 768–69)

The point here is not simply that the Parson brings to our attention the gospel ideal of pastoral rule, as stated in such important texts as Christ's admonition to Peter (John 21:15–18) or the parable of the Good Shepherd (John 10:15–18). More significant is the fact that the Parson is himself described as a good shepherd in his portrait in the General Prologue, and thus is spiritually a successor of Saint Peter. Through such direct references to the Pardoner in the Parson's Tale and through his portrayal of the contemporary opposition between Pardoner and Parson, Chaucer effectively echoes and updates the contrast between Simon Magus and Simon Peter.[60]

It is not surprising, therefore, that a systematic look at the apocalyptic traditions associated with Simon Magus and Antichrist will reveal much about many aspects of the Pardoner and his tale. Like Simon the Magician who is portrayed in the *Acts of Peter* and like Antichrist in such late-medieval works as the Chester cycle *Coming of Antichrist*, the Pardoner is clearly a showman of no small accomplishment, an aspect of his character that has been given extensive treatment in recent criticism.[61] Like Simon—whom Chaucer includes among the crowd of magicians, tricksters, and witches in the *House of Fame* (1259–81)—and like Antichrist, the Pardoner dazzles the crowds with his false magic and preaches blasphemy cloaked in doctrine. Like Antichrist and his late-medieval representatives portrayed in the *Roman de la Rose* and *Piers Plowman*, he glosses Scripture not only for personal gain but for the sheer pleasure of deceit.[62] This aspect of his character is all-pervasive in that his tale is a virtuoso performance, even as his

prologue is a kind of behind-the-scenes peek at the nature of his performance, as he essentially reveals to the pilgrims the secrets of his dismal
trade. The Pardoner is nothing if not theatrical.

The Pardoner also resembles Simon Magus and Antichrist in encouraging their followers to idolatry. According to early accounts, Simon established a statue of himself on the banks of the Tiber inscribed *Simoni deo
sancto* and set "himself up for the Messiah."[63] Similarly, the apocalyptic
imagination expected Antichrist to establish an image of himself in the
temple of Jerusalem and claim, "Ego sum Christus."[64] The idolatry of the
Pardoner, although less blatant, is no less serious. At the end of his tale,
the Pardoner moves immediately into his sales pitch, encouraging his audience to pay up while they are still reeling from the force of his powerful
exempla. The Pardoner's routine includes as well a witty and subtle reference to one of the most powerful scriptural examples of idolatry, the worship of the golden bull-calf by the pilgrim people of Israel (Exodus 32:4):

> Myn hooly pardoun may yow alle warice,
> So that ye offre nobles or sterlynges,
> Or elles silver broches, spoones, rynges.
> Boweth your heed under this hooly bulle! (VI.906–909)[65]

The Pardoner, of course, wants the pilgrims to "worship" the bull as the
papal document that has the force of compulsion, a bull that compels his
audience to pay him what he wants. In this he deliberately makes it something other than what it is. Rather than simply being a document that
gives him the authority to preach, in the Pardoner's rhetoric this bull is a
command to give him money. But the witty pun that equates one kind of
bull with another—a papal bull with a golden calf—implies that his own
avarice is indeed nothing other than a species of idolatry. It leads him to
worship the money that he wins from his preaching. As a corrupt priest
he stands in the place of Aaron, his scriptural counterpart, responding to
the urge to idolatry of the people by presumably giving them what they
want. As such, he tempts them to the same idolatry. The Pardoner's request that the pilgrims hand over to him their jewelry recreates Aaron's
request that the Israelites bring him their gold rings and earrings to be
fashioned into the Golden Calf (Ex. 32:3), whereas the furious reaction of
the Host, the fallible leader of this fourteenth-century exodus, parallels
Moses's violent reaction upon to the worship of the bull-calf (Ex. 32:19).

As is typical of the apocalyptic imagination, which intimately associates all who share the pedigree of evil, in the Pardoner's Prologue and Tale Chaucer develops these parallels to associate the Pardoner with a series of false spiritual leaders from the Old and New Testaments. These parallels are particularly appropriate, furthermore, because avarice and idolatry are definitively connected in the Pauline epistles (Eph. 5:5; Col. 3:5). Finally, they become yet another example of the extraordinarily dense relationship between the Pardoner and the Parson, who according to the General Prologue refused to accept money for his spiritual ministry and who in his sermon forcefully equates avarice and idolatry:

> What difference is bitwixe an ydolastre and an avaricious man, but that an ydolastre, per aventure, ne hath but o mawmet or two, and the avaricious man hath manye? For certes, every floryn in his cofre is his mawmet. And certes, the synne of mawmettrie is the firste thyng that God deffended in the ten comaundementz, as bereth witnesse in *Exodi capitulo vicesimo*: "Thou shalt have no false goddes bifore me, ne thou shalt make to thee no grave thyng." Thus is an avaricious man, that loveth his tresor biforn God, an ydolastre, thurgh this cursed synne of avarice. (X. 749–52)

The Pardoner also resembles Simon Magus and Antichrist in his inversion of sacrament and ritual. Simon Magus was guilty of this blasphemous sin in trying to buy the things of the spirit from Simon Peter, the first high priest, a fact that, as we saw in Chapter 4, Dante uses to stunning success in his depiction of the simoniac popes in *Inferno* 19. When Simon offers Peter money to receive the gift of the spirit, Peter's answer is both direct and succinct: "Pecunia tua tecum sit in perditionem, quoniam donum Dei existimasti pecunia possideri" (Acts 8:20) ["Keep thy money to thyself, to perish with thee, because thou hast thought that the gift of God may be purchased with money"]. As we have seen, the apocalyptic imagination also expects Antichrist in the last days to invert sacrament and ritual. He will use money and gifts to purchase spiritual support, parody liturgical language and the Mass, pretend to die and be resurrected, stage his own parodic Pentecost, and finally attempt to rise to heaven in imitation of Christ's Ascension (see Figure 5). Ultimately he too will be cursed to Hell for his blasphemy. Similarly, the Pardoner—like his apocalyptic associates, Simon Magus and Antichrist, and like his literary forerunner, Faus Semblant—repeatedly inverts the sacraments not only in his "confession" but in his tale.

The mysteries of the Eucharist and penance are, not surprisingly, central to this parodic structure. Most obvious is the abuse of penance, since that is in effect the Pardoner's whole life, using as he does the penitential system for his own systematic profit. Only slightly less obvious is the parody of sacramental confession that implicitly underwrites his "confession" to the pilgrims. Recognizing that he is guilty of sin—"But though myself be gilty in that synnne" (VI.429)—the Pardoner confesses his sin in scrupulous detail to the pilgrims. Thus the first inversion is evident in the fact that as a Church official he makes his confession to a group primarily comprised of laity. For any confession to be valid, of course, it must stem from contrition and result in satisfaction. Here is the second and more intense inversion, for quite obviously the Pardoner is anything but contrite. In fact, his boasting about his sins (in effect he says, "see how good I am at being evil") is central to the critical discussion of the tale. In trying to account for the psychology of the Pardoner's boasting, critics have seen him attempting to cover up his own inadequacies, or make the most of his inadequacies, or set up the pilgrims through a deft attempt to make them feel superior. From the perspective of sacramental inversion, however, boasting is simply the most appropriate way of embodying the opposite of contrition; it turns contrition upside-down and calls attention to it.[66] As contrition is inverted, so also is satisfaction. Why the Pardoner should turn on the pilgrims and attempt to defraud them after he has told them in such vivid detail of his fraud and hypocrisy is a much debated question in the criticism of this tale. Once again, from the perspective of sacramental inversion, it is only the logical move, since it takes the sacrament's next stage, satisfaction, and stands it on its head. Rather than give back what he has taken, the Pardoner attempts to take some more.

If penance is the key sacrament in the Pardoner's Prologue and Epilogue, the Eucharist is equally central to the tale itself. According to Thomas Aquinas, the Eucharist is the foretaste of the eschatological banquet present in time and signified in the present in the ecclesiastical unity of all Christians in the mystical body of Christ.[67] Within the tale this unity is broken, disintegrating under the relentless assault of avarice as the three rioters are transformed from being blood brothers to being bloody assassins. The key action of the tale reinforces this disintegration by suggesting a parody of the Eucharist as the three rioters enact a Mass of death, sacrificing their victim at a meal of bread and poisoned wine. Clarence H. Miller and Roberta B. Bosse have systematically detailed the inversion of the Mass present in the tale. They point out, for example, that the vices of gluttony, dicing, and swearing are in the tale all related to the sacrifice of the Mass and of Calvary, a Mass that "culminates when the two who remain alive receive their unholy communion in the poisoned wine."[68]

What is true on the level of plot is also true on the level of language, where blasphemous references to the sacrament are commonplace. Of the many examples that could be adduced, the one that most succinctly captures the nature of the inversion comes in the Pardoner's description of gluttony:

> Thise cookes, how they stampe, and streyne, and grynde,
> And turnen substaunce into accident
> To fulfille al thy likerous talent!
>
> (VI.538–40)

To turn substance into accident is, of course, to transpose the mystery of transubstantiation. This inversion, moreover, rightly parallels the reduction of spirit to matter that characterizes not only the lives of the three rioters in the tale but also the lives of all the representatives of the apocalyptic age of hypocrisy.

The Pardoner's spiritual hypocrisy, showmanship, idolatry, and sacramental inversion all connect him to Simon Magus and therefore to Antichrist. The most visible connection, however, is evident in the way the Pardoner's performance parallels the fatal falls of Simon Magus (see Figures 6 and 7) and of Antichrist (see Figures 4 and 5). The relationship between teller and tale in *The Canterbury Tales* has been much debated by critics, but it is clearly of the first importance in the Pardoner's Tale. What makes it especially acute is the ironic force of a tale whose clear and evident message applies most directly to a teller who totally ignores it at his own peril. The fall of Simon the Magician adds to this relationship between teller and tale, for the narrative pattern developed in both the tale and its frame is analogous to a rise followed by a rapid fall. Within the tale, the finding of the bushels of gold fixes the moment of reversal, when there is a change from a rise to a fall. The grimly ironic "no lenger thanne after death they soughte" is the structural fulcrum of the tale, fixing the moment at which fortune changes drastically for the three rioters: no longer three carefree drunks off to find death, they are now deadly serious brutes ready to cheat and even kill each other to become sole owner of the gold. The change in tone signals the rapid denouement. As we have already observed, they no longer seek death because they have found it, and their quick and gruesome end is testimony both to the urgency of their greed and to the economy of Chaucer's methods. They see themselves at the end of a successful quest; we see them in death's grasp, having achieved that other now-forgotten quest to find death at the very moment when they no longer give it any thought. To read the tale then as structured according to a rise and a fall is to do no more than to follow the rioters to the tree under which the gold is hidden.[69]

Within the frame, the Pardoner experiences the same pattern of a rise and a fall. As he confesses his fraud and greed, his sense of confidence and mastery of his audience grows to such an extent that he woefully misconstrues his effect on the pilgrim audience. He attempts a flight of imagination, a flight no less dazzling and audacious in its way than the two physical flights that are central to the apocalyptic imagination: the flight of Simon Magus, attempted in order to deceive the early Church; and the flight that Antichrist will attempt at the end of his long career of deception. At the very moment when the Pardoner attempts his "flight," he is abruptly and rapidly brought back to earth by the Host's threat to enshrine his testicles in a hog's turd. Here too a rise in the Pardoner's self-estimation and presumed status among the pilgrims is followed by a rapid fall that provides the structural symmetry for the frame. In the Prologue, his greed is so self-consuming that he loses sight of any other reality. In the Epilogue he comes crashing back to earth. We hardly need to remind ourselves that the fall of Simon the Magician is a warning against the sin of simony and that the fall of Antichrist is a promise that at the end of time even the great hypocrite's deceit will be revealed and punished. Thus the Pardoner's pattern of rising and falling is energized by the same apocalyptic tradition. As the structural skeleton of both the tale and the frame, it encourages the reader to make the very connection that the Pardoner ignores: that the tale with its warning that greed leads to death applies to his own life. The blindness that leads to death and damnation within the tale just as surely leads to the spiritual death of its teller, and the analogies with the falls of Simon Magus and Antichrist provide subtle yet precise ways of keeping the audience aware of that connection.

One final way in which the critical awareness of the apocalyptic imagination can enhance our understanding of the Pardoner and his position among the pilgrims in *The Canterbury Tales* remains to be discussed. The spiritual association of the Pardoner with simony and Antichrist provides a parallel for another much-discussed aspect of his character: his physical relationship as the companion and implied homosexual partner of the Summoner as described in the General Prologue (I.669–73).[70] Medieval exegetes often described simony as "spiritual sodomy." To quote one treatise, "For as the sin of Sodom was the greatest against nature and thus the greatest sin in the old law, so is simony as doctors say the greatest sin against grace and the law of grace."[71] Thus, as is characteristic of Chaucer, the Pardoner's outward physical situation (the signs implying sodomy) reflects his inner spiritual condition (as evidenced by his simony), just as often the individual character manifests the general spiritual condition of the universal Church.

The associations, moreover, continue to build on one another, as is clear from a brief analysis of the Pardoner's partner, the Summoner. The General Prologue characterizes him by means of outward and inward signs: his leprous physical condition (I.624–25) and his avaricious spiritual condition, particularly suggested by the juxtapositioning of "soule" and "purs" (I.656). Both characteristics, furthermore, associate the Summoner with the Old Testament simoniac, Gehazi, the servant of Elisha (2 Kings 5).[72] For accepting payment from Naaman, the Syrian who was miraculously cleansed of leprosy after washing in the Jordan, Gehazi was himself cursed with leprosy and, in medieval exegesis, identified as a simoniac. This identification led many theologians, from Caesarius of Arles to Bernard of Clairvaux and Thomas Aquinas, to equate simony with leprosy and to compare simoniac prelates to Gehazi.[73] The equation became commonplace, as is evident in the following stanzas from Walter of Chatillon's lyric, "Licet eger cum egrotis":

> Si privata degens vita
> vel sacerdos vel levita
> sibi dari vult petita,
> hac incedit via trita:
>   previa fit pactio
>   Simonis officio
>   cui succedit datio,
>   sic fit Giezita.

> [If any man of mean estate,
> Deacon or priest, would now obtain
> A boon he long has hoped to gain,
> A well-worn path leads to it straight:
>   Make firm the agreement
>   With Simon Magus,
>   Then like Gehazi
>   Take reward.][74]

The leprous and simoniac Gehazi—an Old Testament type of Simon Magus—can thus be understood as a model for the Summoner. In this complex typological relationship, therefore, the Pardoner, through his physical and spiritual kinship with the Summoner, who himself is a contemporary antitype of Gehazi and Simon Magus, is further associated with Simon Magus and thus ultimately with Antichrist.

The presence of the Pardoner amidst the pilgrims on the road to Canterbury is Chaucer's most extended commentary on the Church *in novissimis diebus* and on the sharp division between its ideals and its practices. But the Pardoner is not simply an ordinary evil ecclesiastic, a "portrait" of the typical fourteenth-century pardoner, however subtly drawn. As we have seen, without departing from his realistic mode, Chaucer charges his portrayal of the Pardoner with allusions to the well-known traditions of the two great false spiritual leaders, Simon Magus and Antichrist. He provides thereby an apocalyptic urgency to his portrayal of this vivid band of men and women approaching the end of their pilgrimage and to his understanding of the Church at this point in the pilgrimage of history. In comparison with Langland's *Piers Plowman*, Chaucer's portrayal of his complex contemporary world is more subtle. The dangers faced by the pilgrims are not manifest in the frontal attack of Antichrist, Pride, and other explicit personifications of the deadly sins, but arise from the Antichrist-like simoniac in their midst. Nevertheless, Chaucer's portrayal clearly reflects the concerns of the rich apocalyptic imagination evident in a wide range of medieval literature. The general structure and specific allusions developed in this masterpiece point beyond the particular to the universal and suggest the many critical possibilities made possible by reading *The Canterbury Tales* in eschatological perspective.

Abbreviations

Bible	*Bibliorum sacrorum iuxta vulgatam Clementinam, nova editio.* Ed. Aloisius Gramatica. Rome: Vatican, 1959. Douay-Rheims trans. from the Vulgate. Turnhout: Brepols, 1938.
Bonaventure	S. Bonaventura. *Legenda Maior S. Francisci Assisiensis et eiusdem Legenda Minor.* Ed. Collegii S. Bonaventurae. Florence: Quaracchi, 1941. Trans. Ewert Cousins. *Bonaventure: The Soul's Journey into God, The Tree of Life, The Life of Francis.* New York: Paulist Press, 1978.
CCCM	Corpus Christianorum: Continuatio mediaevalis.
CCSL	Corpus Christianorum: Series Latina.
"Census"	Richard Kenneth Emmerson and Suzanne Lewis. "Census and Bibliography of Medieval Manuscripts Containing Apocalypse Illustrations, ca. 800-1500." *Traditio* 40 (1984): 337–79; 41 (1985): 367–409; 42 (1986): 443–72.
Chaucer	Larry D. Benson, gen. ed. *The Riverside Chaucer.* 3rd ed. Boston: Houghton Mifflin, 1987.
CSEL	Corpus scriptorum ecclesiasticorum Latinorum.
Dante	Dante Alighieri. *The Divine Comedy.* Ed. and trans. Charles S. Singleton. 3 vols. Bollingen Series 80. Princeton, NJ: Princeton University Press, 1970.
EETS	Early English Text Society. Original series.

EETS ES   Early English Text Society. Extra series.

EETS SS   Early English Text Society. Supplementary series.

Emmerson, *Antichrist*   Richard Kenneth Emmerson. *Antichrist in the Middle Ages: A Study of Medieval Apocalypticism, Art, and Literature.* Seattle: University of Washington Press, 1981.

Glossa   *Glossa ordinaria: Biblia sacra cum glossis interlineari, et ordinaria, Nicolai Lyrani postilla, ac moralitalibus, Burgensis additionibus et Thoringi replicis.* Venice, 1588.

McGinn, *Joachim*   Bernard McGinn. *The Calabrian Abbot: Joachim of Fiore in the History of Western Thought.* New York: Macmillan, 1985.

McGinn, *Visions*   Bernard McGinn, ed. *Visions of the End: Apocalyptic Traditions in the Middle Ages.* Records of Civilization, Sources and Studies 96. New York: Columbia University Press, 1979.

PL   Patrologia cursus completus: Series Latina. Ed. J. P. Migne. Paris, 1844–64.

Reeves, *Prophecy*   Marjorie Reeves. *The Influence of Prophecy in the Later Middle Ages: A Study in Joachimism.* Oxford: Clarendon, 1969.

Roman de la Rose   Felix Lecoy, ed. *Le Roman de la Rose.* Classiques français du moyen âge 92, 95, 98. Paris: Librairie Honoré Champion, 1965–70. Trans. Charles Dahlberg. *The Romance of the Rose.* 1971; rpt. Hanover, NH: University Press of New England, 1983.

SC   Sources Chretiennes.

Notes

Chapter 1: The Apocalypse and Joachim of Fiore

1. By the mid-thirteenth century, the beguines, religious women living in urban convents without any standardized rule, were being accused of heresy and sexual immorality. See R. E. Lerner, *The Heresy of the Free Spirit in the Later Middle Ages* (Berkeley: University of California Press, 1972).

2. Augustine, *De civitate Dei* 20.8, trans. Henry Bettenson and ed. David Knowles, *The City of God* (Baltimore: Penguin, 1972), p. 911. In the high Middle Ages the understanding of the Apocalypse as encompassing all Church history coexisted with the earlier view that John's prophecy dealt with the end of history. For example, Joachim of Fiore described the Apocalypse as encompassing "totidem tempora ab adventu salvatoris usque ad extremum iudicium" ["all the periods (*tempora*) from the advent of the Savior to the Last Judgment"]. See *Expositio in Apocalypsim* (Venice, 1527; rpt. Frankfurt: Minerva, 1964), fol. 16^r. On the other hand Thomas Aquinas noted that the Apocalypse is a prophecy "de fine Ecclesiae" ["concerning the end of the Church"]. See *Summa theologiae* 2a.2ae.174.6, ed. Roland Potter (New York: McGraw Hill, 1970), p. 92. Unless otherwise noted, all translations from the Latin are ours.

3. Augustine concludes the *City of God* (22.30, p. 1091) with a brief outline of the ages of history, which is based on the six days of Creation. It became the standard organizing scheme of universal history throughout the Middle Ages. See, for example, Robert Grosseteste's explanation, "De sex mundi aetatibus," *Hexaëmeron* 8.30, ed. Richard C. Dales and Servus Gieben, British Academy, Auctores Britannici Medii Aevi 6 (London: Oxford University Press, 1982), pp. 253–55.

4. Augustine, *City of God* 20.17, p. 929. Augustine's approach to the Apocalypse follows Tyconius, who emphasized the symbolic recapitulations found in Scripture. Augustine discussed Tyconius and his rule of "recapitulation" in *De doctrina Christiana* 3.36: "Some things are so described as though they follow each other in the order of time, or as if they narrate a continuous sequence of events, when the narrative covertly refers to previous events which had been omitted; and unless this situation is understood in accordance with this rule, the reader will err" (trans. D. W. Robertson, Jr., *On Christian Doctrine* [Indianapolis: Bobbs-Merrill, 1958], p. 113). For Tyconius, see F. C. Burkitt, *The Book of Rules of Tyconius*, Texts and Studies: Contributions to Biblical and Patristic Literature 3.1 (Cambridge: Cambridge University Press, 1894); and Pamela Bright, *The Book of Rules of Tyconius: Its Purpose and Inner Logic* (Notre Dame, IN: University of Notre Dame Press, 1988).

5. Bernard McGinn has argued that it is a mistake to make expectation of the imminent end "the sole touchstone of apocalypticism" and discusses several dominant themes in early Christian apocalyptic eschatology. As is evident in the *City of God* and elsewhere, and as McGinn acknowledges, Augustine was concerned with all of these themes. See McGinn, "Early Apocalypticism: The Ongoing Debate," in *The Apocalypse in English Renaissance Thought and Literature*, ed. C. A. Patrides and Joseph Wittreich (Ithaca, NY: Cornell University Press, 1984), pp. 23–31. Rather than labeling Augustine as anti-apocalyptic, we believe he is best understood as antimillenarian.

6. *City of God* 18.53, p. 838; see also 20.9, pp. 914–15; 20.11, pp. 919–20.

7. M.-D. Chenu, "Theology and the New Awareness of History," in *Nature, Man, and Society in the Twelfth Century: Essays on New Theological Perspectives in the Latin West*, trans. Jerome Taylor and Lester K. Little (Chicago: University of Chicago Press, 1968), p. 191. On the development of schemes delineating stages or periods of Church history, see Henri de Lubac, *Exégèse médiévale: les quatre sens de l'Ecriture*, II, i (Paris: Aubier, 1961), pp. 504–27.

8. Bede, *Explanatio Apocalypsis* 1.6.1; trans. Edw. Marshall (Oxford: James Parker, 1878), p. 38.

9. On the influence of Bede's approach, see Robert Lerner, "Joachim of Fiore's Breakthrough to Chiliasm," *Cristianesimo nella storia* 6 (1985): 500–507. For early medieval exegesis of the Apocalypse, see Wilhelm Kamlah, *Apokalypse und Geschichtstheologie: Die mittelalterliche Auslegung der Apokalypse vor Joachim von Fiore*, Historische Studien 285 (Berlin: Emil Ebering, 1935); and the essays by Paula Frederiksen and E. Ann Matter in the forthcoming volume, *The Apocalypse in the Middle Ages*, ed. Richard Emmerson and Bernard McGinn (Ithaca, NY: Cornell University Press, 1992).

10. Augustine, *City of God* 22.30, p. 1091.

11. Anselm of Havelberg, *Dialogues* 1.7, ed. G. Salet, SC 118 (Paris, 1966), p. 68; trans. McGinn, *Visions*, p. 114. On Anselm's view of history and his significance in the development of the twelfth-century understanding of the *status* of the Church, see W. Edyvean, *Anselm of Havelberg and the Theology of History* (Rome: Catholic Book Agency, 1972); and Guntram Bischoff, "Early Premonstratensian Eschatology: The Apocalyptic Myth," in *The Spirituality of Western Christendom*, ed. E. Rozanne Elder (Kalamazoo, MI: Medieval Institute Publications, 1976), pp. 56–61.

12. Anselm, *Dialogues* 1.10, p. 84; trans. McGinn, *Visions*, p. 115.

13. *Dialogues* 1.12, p. 110; trans. McGinn, *Visions*, p. 116. Similar interpretations of the opening of the seven seals were developed by Richard of Saint Victor and other twelfth-century commentators and became a commonplace in the comprehensive exegetical compilations of the High Middle Ages. See, for example, Richard of Saint Victor, *In Apocalypsim Ioannis* 2.3–10, PL 196:754–76; *Glossa*, vol. 6, fols. 248ᵛ-252ʳ; and the commentary traditionally attributed to Hugh of Saint Cher, *Opera omnia in universum Vetus et Novum Testamentum* (Lyon, 1645), vol. 7, fols. 385ʳ-390ʳ. See also Robert Lerner, "Poverty, Preaching, and Eschatology in the Revelation Commentaries of 'Hugh of St. Cher,'" in *The Bible in the Medieval World: Essays in Memory of Beryl Smalley*, ed. Katherine Walsh and Diana Wood (Oxford: Blackwells, 1985), pp. 157–89.

14. On Antichrist's role as concluding the sixth age of world history, see Emmerson, *Antichrist*, pp. 17–19. See also the extensive discussions and charts in Guy Lobrichon, "L'Ordre de ce temps et les désordres de la fin: Apocalypse et société, du IXᶜ à la fin du XIᶜ siècle," in *The Use and Abuse of Eschatology in the Middle Ages*, ed. Verbeke, Verhelst, Welkenhuysen, pp. 221–41. To identify one of the seven Augustinian divisions of history ranging from Creation to Doomsday, we will use the term "age" or *aetas*; to identify one of the seven divisions of Church history ranging from the Incarnation to Doomsday, we will use the term "period" or *tempus*.

15. Virtually every aspect of Joachim's life, thought, and canon is problematic. A good starting point is Morton W. Bloomfield, "Joachim of Flora: A Critical Survey of his Canon, Teachings, Sources, Bibliography and Influence," *Traditio* 13 (1957): 249–311. During the past twenty years, scholarship on Joachim of Fiore has multiplied tremendously. See Morton Bloomfield, "Recent Scholarship on Joachim of Fiore and His Influence," in *Prophecy and Millenarianism*, ed. Williams, pp. 21–52; and Valeria de Fraja, "Gioacchino da Fiore: bibliografia 1969–1988," *Florensia* 2 (1988): 7–59 (*Florensia* is the journal of the Centro internazionale di Studi Gioachimiti). For the most useful current evaluation of Joachim and his approach to the Apocalypse, see McGinn, *Joachim*, pp. 25–30 and pp. 145–60; and McGinn, "Symbolism in the Thought of Joachim of Fiore," in *Prophecy and Millenarianism*, ed. Williams, pp. 143–64. For Joachim's canon, see Kurt-Victor Selge, *L'origine delle opere di Gioacchino da Fiore*, in *L'attesa della fine dei tempi nel Medioevo*, ed. Ovidio Capitani and Jürgen Miethke (Bologna: Il Mulino, 1990), pp. 87–131. On Joachim's influence, see Marjorie Reeves, *Prophecy*; Reeves, "The Originality and Influence of Joachim of Fiore," *Traditio* 36 (1980): 269–313; and Henri de Lubac, *La Postérité spirituelle de Joachim de Flore*, 2 vols. (Paris: Editions Lethielleux, 1979–81).

16. Joachim of Fiore, *Enchiridion super Apocalypsim*, ed. Edward K. Burger, Studies and Texts 78 (Toronto: Pontifical Institute of Mediaeval Studies, 1986), p. 88.

17. Joachim of Fiore, *Enchiridion super Apocalypsim*, p. 88.

18. On the four creatures, see Martin of Leon, *Expositio libri Apocalypsis*, PL 209:327. On the four beasts of Dan. 7:2–7, see Jerome, *De Antichristo in Danielem*, ed. François Glorie, CCSL 75A; trans. Gleason L. Archer, Jr., *Jerome's Commentary on Daniel* (1958; Grand Rapids, MI: Baker Book House, 1977), pp. 71–77.

19. "In primo tempore conflixit ordo apostolicus assimilatus leoni, cum synagoga Judaeorum quam designat leaena. In secundo, ordo martyrum designatus in vitulo, cum imperio Romano quod significat ursus. In tertio, ordo doctorum designatus in Joanne, cum populo Ariano, quem significat pardus. In quarto, ordo virginum designatus in aquila, cum gente Saracenorum designata in bestia illa terribili, occupante Africam et Aegyptum, Syriam simul et Asiam, in quibus maxime partibus sacrae virgines et heremitae crebruisse leguntur" ["In the first period (*tempus*), the apostolic order signified by the lion fought against the synagogue of the Jews, which the lioness signifies. In the second, the order of martyrs signified by the bull fought against the Roman empire, which the bear signifies. In the third, the order of doctors signified by John fought against the Arians, whom the leopard

signifies. In the fourth, the order of virgins signified by the eagle fought against the Saracen nation signified by that terrible fourth beast which occupies Africa and Egypt, Syria and Asia together, in which regions holy virgins and hermits are read to have most increased"] (Joachim of Fiore, *Enchiridion super Apocalypsim*, p. 89). For Joachim's interpretations of the opening of the seven seals, see Marjorie Reeves and Beatrice Hirsch-Reich, "The Seven Seals in the Writings of Joachim of Fiore," *Recherches de théologie ancienne et médiévale* 21 (1954): 211–47.

20. *Enchiridion super Apocalypsim*, p. 89.

21. Joachim similarly identifies the Woman with the Church: "Mulier ista generaliter matrem designat ecclesiam que in verbo predicationis clamando et parturiendo laborabat" ["This woman generally signifies mother church who labored in proclaiming and delivering the word of preaching"] (*Expositio in Apocalypsim*, fol. 154ʳ).

22. Compare Joachim, *Expositio in Apocalypsim*, fol. 10ʳ: "Quintum caput draconis fuit vnus de regibus babylonis noue qui volens sedere super montem testamenti et apparere similis altissimo multas propter hoc ecclesie persecutiones ingessit" ["The fifth head of the dragon was one of the kings of the new Babylon who, wishing to sit himself on the mount of the covenant and to appear similar to the Most High poured forth many persecutions of the Church"], with fol. 196ᵛ: "Quintus is qui primus in partibus occiduis cepit fatigare ecclesiam pro investitura ecclesiarum ob quam causam multa scismata et tribulationes orta sunt ex eo tempore in ecclesia dei" ["The fifth is he who first began to weary the Church in the western regions about the investiture in the churches, because of which many schisms and tribulations arose from that time in the Church of God"]. In the *figura* of the seven-headed Dragon, however, Joachim identifies the fifth head as Mesemothus. For an explanation, see Marjorie Reeves and Beatrice Hirsch-Reich, *The Figurae of Joachim of Fiore*, Oxford-Warburg Studies (Oxford: Clarendon, 1972), pp. 87–88. As is evident from this example, it is essential in studying Joachim's interpretation of apocalyptic imagery to keep the following in mind: "Now one of the most obvious characteristics of Joachim's thought is the way in which his fecund imagination played constant variations on his basic themes" (Reeves and Hirsch-Reich, p. 88).

23. On Joachim's ambivalent expectations concerning the crusades, see E. Randolph Daniel, "Apocalyptic Conversion: The Joachite Alternative to the Crusades," *Traditio* 25 (1969): 127–39, esp. pp. 132–35 on Saladin.

24. All our quotations from this *figura* are from Leone Tondelli, Marjorie Reeves, and Beatrice Hirsch-Reich, eds., *Il Libro delle figure dell'abate Gioachino da Fiore*, 2nd ed. (Turin: Società Editrice Internazionale, 1953), vol. 2, which provides both a facsimile and a transcription of the figure (pl. XIV). In collaboration with the Centro internazionale di Studi Gioachimiti, Roberto Rusconi has recently reedited this facsimile and edition (Turin: Società Editrice Internazionale, 1990); since we were unable to secure a copy of the new edition, we cite the second edition. For the manuscript and its provenance, see Fabio Troncarelli and Elena B. di Gioia, "Scrittura, testo, immagine in un manoscritto gioachimita," *Scrittura e civiltà* 5 (1981): 149–85. For a discussion of the figure of the Dragon, see Reeves and Hirsch-Reich, *Figurae*, pp. 146–52. For a translation of its captions and notes,

see Bernard McGinn, *Apocalyptic Spirituality*, Classics of Western Spirituality (New York: Paulist, 1979), pp. 135–41.

25. *Figura*, 2, XIV; trans. McGinn, *Apocalyptic Spirituality*, p. 136.

26. The gloss continues: "quamvis sit alius similis, nec minor eo in malitia designatus in cauda" ["Although there will be another like him, no less evil, symbolized by the tail"]. The reference, of course, is to the tail of the Dragon, which is inscribed: "Gog. iste est ultimus Antichristus" ["Gog. He is the final Antichrist"]. See *Figura*, 2, XIV; trans. McGinn, *Apocalyptic Spirituality*, p. 136. For a detailed analysis of Joachim's understanding of the two final Antichrists, see Robert E. Lerner's excellent study, "Antichrists and Antichrist in Joachim of Fiore," *Speculum* 60 (1985): 553–70. We agree with Lerner's conclusion that "the Antichrist of the seventh head—'he who is properly called Antichrist'—was undoubtedly for Joachim the 'real and true' one" (p. 566), not only for the reasons argued by Lerner, but also, as we will show below, because Joachim clearly presents the persecutor designated by the seventh head as the traditional Antichrist. For the traditional Antichrist, see Wilhelm Bousset, *The Antichrist Legend*, trans. A. H. Keane (London: Hutchinson, 1896); Horst Dieter Rauh, *Das Bild des Antichrist im Mittelalter: von Tyconius zum deutschen Symbolismus*, Beiträge zur Geschichte der Philosophie und Theologie des Mittelalters, n.s. 9 (Münster: Aschendorff, 1973); and Emmerson, *Antichrist*.

27. *Figura*, 2, XIV; trans. McGinn, *Apocalyptic Spirituality*, p. 138. The length of Antichrist's rule is based on the apocalyptic time prophecies of Daniel and the Apocalypse; they are sometimes given in "times" ($3\frac{1}{2}$ years), in months (42 months), or in days (1,260 days). For an interpretation that similarly interprets God's "shortening of the days" by calling on the apocalyptic time prophecies, see Nicholas of Lyra's *Postilla* in *Glossa*, vol. 5, fol. 74^r.

28. *Figura*, 2, XIV; trans. McGinn, *Apocalyptic Spirituality*, p. 139. Note that we have been translating Joachim's term, *tempus*, as "period," as in the periods of the Church described by Anselm of Havelberg.

29. *Figura*, 2, XIV; trans. McGinn, *Apocalyptic Spirituality*, p. 140.

30. Lerner, "Antichrists and Antichrist," p. 566: "we may define Joachim's innovation in the realm of Antichrist periodization as consisting of a doctrine of multiple Antichrists in which the two most evil Antichrists in the Devil's arsenal were still to arrive—one before and one after an earthly Sabbath. . . . The Antichrist of the tail was Joachim's greatest novelty, for no one hitherto had posited a final Antichristian persecution coming after an ultimate earthly Sabbath."

31. Augustine, *City of God* 20.11–13, pp. 919–23.

32. McGinn, *Joachim*, p. 154, for example, states that "no single part" of Joachim's *Expositio in Apocalypsin* shows his "break with 700 years of Latin exegetical tradition more decisively than his treatment of the Apocalypse's description of the thousand-year reign of Christ and the saints upon earth." See also McGinn, "Joachim of Fiore's *Tertius Status*: Some Theological Appraisals," in *L'età dello Spirito e la fine dei tempi in Gioacchino da Fiore e nel gioachimismo medievale*, ed. Antonio Crocco, pp. 219–36. Lerner, "Breakthrough to Chiliasm," p. 490, also argues that Joachim's "attempt to fathom the meaning of the Book of Revelation" is what "led him to become a chiliast."

33. *Figura*, 2, XIV; trans. McGinn, *Apocalyptic Spirituality*, p. 141.

34. *Figura*, 2, XIV; trans. McGinn, *Apocalyptic Spirituality*, p. 141.

35. Joachim does not, however, deal with Antichrist's birth and Jewish parentage, but understands Antichrist as a persecutor arising from the West. For the parodic nature of Antichrist's life, see Emmerson, *Antichrist*, pp. 74–107. On the *Libellus* as modelled upon a traditional hagiographic *vita*, see Richard Kenneth Emmerson, "Antichrist as Anti-Saint: The Significance of Abbot Adso's *Libellus de Antichristo*," *American Benedictine Review* 30 (1979): 175–90. For an edition of the *Libellus*, see *Adso Dervensis, De ortu et tempore Antichristi*, ed. Daniel Verhelst, CCCM 45 (1976).

36. Joachim of Fiore, *Liber concordie Novi ac Veteris Testamenti* (Venice, 1519; rpt. Frankfurt: Minerva, 1964), fol. 133ʳ.

37. *Figura*, 2, XIV; trans. McGinn, *Apocalyptic Spirituality*, p. 140.

38. In his *figurae* of the Trinitarian Circles, Joachim associates the "E" of the Tetragrammaton (IEVE) with both the Holy Spirit and Elijah. See *Figura* 2, XIa-b. For a discussion of these *figurae*, see Reeves and Hirsch-Reich, *Figurae*, pp. 192–98. For the importance of Joachim's Trinitarian theology to his vision of history, see E. Randolph Daniel, "The Double Procession of the Holy Spirit in Joachim of Fiore's Understanding of History," *Speculum* 55 (1980): 469–83. In his discussion of the Tetragrammaton Daniel notes that "The emergence of the *spirituales viri* with Elijah in the Old Testament *tempus* and of the Benedictine monks in the New Testament period as well as the parallel development of the *spiritualis intellectus* are the historical manifestation of the double procession of the Holy Spirit" (p. 479). He fails to note, however, that the *spirituales viri* associated with the procession of the Holy Spirit from the Son is identified in the *figura* with Elijah. The connection between Trinitarian theology and philosophy of history may have been suggested to Joachim by his elucidation of a key passage in Apoc. 1:8: "Ego sum Alpha and Omega." Certainly the symbols of Alpha and Omega reappear repeatedly in these discussions. See Harold Lee, "The Anti-Lombard Figures of Joachim of Fiore: A Reinterpretation," in *Prophecy and Millenarianism*, ed. Williams, pp. 129–33.

39. Joachim draws on these texts in other discussions as well—to explain, for example, how John the Baptist begins the seventh *aetas*, whereas the return of Elias represents its *clarificatio*. See E. Randolph Daniel, "Abbot Joachim of Fiore: The *De Ultimis Tribulationibus*," in *Prophecy and Millenarianism*, ed. Williams, p. 170. Interestingly, Joachim himself became a figure of *renovatio* associated with these and other biblical types. His prophetic status among the Cistercians—his former order—and the Florensians—the order he founded—is evident not only in the miracles attributed to him shortly after his death, but also in his being associated with Moses, Elijah, and John the Revelator. See Stephen E. Wessley, *Joachim of Fiore and Monastic Reform* (New York: Peter Lang, 1990), pp. 88–92.

40. On the traditional interpretations of the Two Witnesses as Enoch and Elijah, see Emmerson, *Antichrist*, pp. 41; 95–101. Joachim knows the tradition that identifies Enoch with the second Witness of Apoc. 11, but he prefers to cite only Elias based on the authority of Malachi 4:5–6: "Non quia solus Helias predicaturus sit et docturus Iudeos, et non etiam ceteri perfecti uiri qui erunt in diebus

eius, sed quia ipse erit precipuus ueritatis predicatio; etsi secundum Apocalipsim alius sit futurus cum eo ueritatis predicatio quem magni ualde doctores arbitrantur Enoch. Verum, ideo tibi occurrit occasio ut de hoc fiat sermo, de solo Helia facimus mentionem, quia de sola eius missione locutus est Malachias; et de solo eo locutus est dominus dicens: 'Helias quidem ueniet et restituet omnia'" ["Not because Elijah alone will preach to the Jews and teach them, and not the other perfect men who will be in his days, but because he himself will be the especial preacher of truth, although according to the Apocalypse there will be another preacher of truth together with him, whom very distinguished doctors believe to be Enoch. But because the opportunity is given to speak to you of this, we make mention of Elijah alone, because Malachi spoke of his mission alone; and of him alone did the Lord speak, saying 'Certainly Elijah will come and he will restore all things'"] (Joachim, *De Ultimus Tribulationibus*, ed. Daniel; in *Prophecy and Millenarianism*, ed. Williams, p. 186).

41. Jerome argued the principle of a parallel typology to identify the evil king of Daniel 11:24 with Antiochus Epiphanes and ultimately with Antichrist: "Sicut igitur Saluator habet et Salomonem et ceteros sanctos in typum aduentus sui, sic et Antichristus pessimum regem Antiochum, qui sanctos persecutus est templumque uiolauit, recte typum sui habuisse credendus est" ["And so, just as the Savior had Solomon and the other saints as types of His Advent, so also we should believe that the Antichrist very properly had as the type of himself the utterly wicked king Antiochus who persecuted the saints and defiled the temple"] (Jerome, *De Antichristo in Danielem* 4.11, CCSL 75A:915; trans. Archer, *Jerome's Commentary on Daniel*, p. 130). Adso extended the argument: "Hic itaque Antichristus multos habet sue malignitatis ministros, ex quibus iam multi in mundo precesserunt, qualis fuit Antiochus, Nero, Domicianus. Nunc quoque, nostro tempore, Antichristos multos nouimus esse. Quicumque enim, siue laicus, siue canonicus, siue etiam monachus, contra iusticiam uiuit et ordinis sui regulam impugnat et quod bonum est blasphemat, Antichristus est, minister satane est" ["Furthermore, Antichrist has many servants of evil here, many of whom have already preceded him in the world, such as Antiochus, Nero, and Domitian. In our own time also we know that there are many Antichrists. For whatever man—layman, cleric, or monk—lives contrary to justice and opposes the rule of his station in life and blasphemes the good, he is Antichrist and the servant of Satan"] (Adso of Montier-en-Der, *De ortu et tempore Antichristi*, CCCM 45:22; trans. John Wright, in *The Play of Antichrist* [Toronto: Pontifical Institute of Mediaeval Studies, 1967], p. 102). On the types of Antichrist, see Emmerson, *Antichrist*, pp. 24–30.

42. *Figura*, 2, XIV; trans. McGinn, *Apocalyptic Spirituality*, p. 139.

43. On Antichrist's double nature, see Emmerson, *Antichrist*, pp. 90–95.

44. Lerner, "Antichrists and Antichrist," p. 569.

45. On the demonic trinity, see Emmerson, *Antichrist*, pp. 22–24.

46. Haimo of Auxerre, *Expositio in Apocalypsin*, PL 117:1000. Migne misattributes the *Expositio* to Haimo of Halberstadt. See also Martin of Leon, *Expositio libri Apocalypsis*, PL 209:370: "Ita ut etiam ignem de coelo descendere faciat, id est spiritum malignum quasi spiritum sanctum descendere in terram" ["Thus shall he also make a fire descend from heaven, that is he will cause an evil spirit to descend

to earth as if it were the holy spirit"]. The fourteenth-century Velislav Bible pictures small winged devils hovering over the heads of Antichrist's followers as fire and stones descend from the sky. The explanatory rubric states: "Faciet et ignem de celo descendere in terram et lapides de celo cadere et malignum spiritum super suos descendere ut loquuntur variis linguis" ["He will also cause a fire to descend from heaven onto earth and stones fall from heaven and an evil spirit descend on his people so that he will speak in various tongues"]. See Karel Stejskal, ed., *Velislai Biblia picta*, Editio Cimelia Bohemica 12 (Prague: Progopress, 1970), fol. 133ᵛ. The rubric is based upon Hugh of Strassburg, *Compendium theologiae veritatis*, 7.9, ed. S. A. Borgnet, *B. Alberti Magni Opera omnia* 34 (Paris, 1896), p. 242. For the Velislav Bible, see "Census," 42 (1986): 454–55, no. 141.

47. British Library Harley 1527, fol. 136ᵛ. See *Bible Moralisée. Consèrvé á Oxford, Paris et Londres*, ed. Alexandre de Laborde, vol. 4 (Paris: Société française de reproductions de manuscrits à peintures, 1921), pl. 607. For a description of the manuscript and a bibliography, see "Census," 42 (1986): 461–62, no. 154.

48. For the legend of Simon Magus see *Actus Petri cum Simone*, ed. R. A. Lipsius and M. Bonnet, *Acta apostolorum apocrypha post Constantinum* (Leipzig, 1891), 1:45–103; *Pseudo-Clementine Homily* 2.17–22, ed. B. Rehm, GCS 42.40–43; Gregory, *Moralia* 29.7.15, PL 76:484; Berengaudus, *Expositio super septem visiones libri Apocalypsis*, PL 17:970–71; *Glossa*, vol. 6, fol. 115ʳ; and Jacobus de Voragine, *The Golden Legend*, trans. Granger Ryan and Helmut Ripperger (1941; rpt. New York: Arno Press, 1969), pp. 332–36.

49. "Ecce sonat in aperto," lines 17–36, ed. and trans. George F. Whicher, *The Goliard Poets: Medieval Latin Songs and Satires* (New York: New Directions, 1949), pp. 150–51. Although the translation is loose, it provides a good sense of the original's tone.

50. On Simon Magus as a type of Antichrist, see Emmerson, *Antichrist*, pp. 26–28; on the development of the legend and its iconography in medieval art, see pp. 122–24. See also Ronald B. Herzman and William R. Cook, "Simon the Magician and the Medieval Tradition," *Journal of Magic History* 2 (1980): 28–43.

51. Bonaventure, *Collationes in Hexaemeron* 15.8, ed. A. Parma, *Opera omnia* 5: *Opuscula Varia Theologica* (Florence: Quaracchi, 1896), 399; trans. José de Vinck, *Works of Bonaventure*, vol. 5 (Paterson, NJ: St. Anthony Guild Press, 1970), p. 220.

52. Chaucer, The Parson's Tale, *The Canterbury Tales* X.787.

53. *Figura*, 2, XIV; trans. McGinn, *Apocalyptic Spirituality*, p. 138.

54. Here we disagree with Reeves and Hirsch-Reich, who interpret the figure's notes to mean that the pagan king will work signs to aid Antichrist: "He [Antichrist] will be a king from the Occident, but to aid him will arise a 'caput paganorum' who will do great signs 'sicut Simon magus (fecit) in conspectu Neronis'" (*Figurae*, p. 150). But the Latin clearly states that Antichrist is the Simon-like wonder-worker.

55. Joachim, *Expositio in Apocalypsim*, fol. 168ʳ.

56. Bernard McGinn notes that "Outside of John of Revelation [Joachim] has no rival in the apocalyptic tradition. Even in comparison with his illustrious forebear, the combination of author and iconographer we find in the person of the

Abbot of Fiore provides us with an insight into the genesis and development of apocalyptic symbols that is unique." See "Symbolism in the Thought of Joachim of Fiore," p. 157.

57. See E. Randolph Daniel's excellent introduction to his *Abbot Joachim of Fiore: Liber de Concordia Noui ac Veteris Testamenti, Transactions of the American Philosophical Society* 73.8 (Philadelphia: American Philosophical Society, 1983), esp. pp. xxii–xlii. See also the fourth chapter, "The Trinity and History," of Delno C. West and Sandra Zimdars-Swartz, *Joachim of Fiore: A Study in Spiritual Perception and History* (Bloomington: Indiana University Press, 1983), pp. 41–77, which concludes with a helpful outline of Joachim's four major commentaries: *Liber Concordie novi ac veteris Testamenti, Tractatus super Quatuor Evangelia, Psalterium decem chordarum,* and *Expositio in Apocalypsim.*

58. McGinn has noted this tendency in our own time no less than in the Middle Ages. See "Joachim of Fiore's *Tertius Status,*" pp. 219–36. For the later medieval understanding of Joachim, see Morton W. Bloomfield and Marjorie Reeves, "The Penetration of Joachism into Northern Europe," *Speculum* 29 (1954): 772–93.

59. Several studies have attempted to trace the Joachimist influence on Dante's *Commedia.* See Herbert Grundmann, "Dante und Joachim von Fiore zu Paradiso X–XI," *Deutsches Dante-Jahrbuch* 14 (1932): 210–56; Raoul Manselli, "A proposito del Cristianesimo di Dante: Gioacchino da Fiore, gioachimismo, Spiritualismo francescano," in *Letteratura e critica: Studi in onore di Natalino Sapegno* (Rome: Bulzoni, 1975), 2:163–92; Marjorie Reeves, "Dante and the Prophetic View of History," in *The World of Dante: Essays on Dante and His Times,* ed. Cecil Grayson (Oxford: Clarendon, 1980), pp. 44–60; and Reeves, "The Third Age: Dante's Debt to Gioacchino da Fiore," in *L'età dello Spirito,* ed. Crocco, pp. 125–39.

60. *On Christian Doctrine,* trans. Robertson, p. 104. For Tyconius, see note 4.

61. Jacopone da Todi, *The Lauds,* trans. Serge and Elizabeth Hughes, Classics of Western Spirituality (New York: Paulist, 1982), p. 166.

62. The beautifully illuminated *Bedford Book of Hours* (British Library MS Add. 18,850) exemplifies the continuing influence of both approaches to apocalyptic symbolism in the fifteenth century. The glosses that accompany its 310 Apocalypse illustrations include both allegorized and historical interpretations. See "Census," 42 (1986): 469, no. 169.

63. *Hortus Deliciarum,* fols. 258ʳ, 258ᵛ, 261ʳ, 263ᵛ. Rosalie Green, ed., *Herrad of Hohenbourg: Hortus Deliciarum,* Studies of the Warburg Institute 36 (London: Warburg Institute, 1979), 1: 221–22, 224–25; 2: scenes 340–41, 343–44, pls. 148–49, 151–52. See also "Census," 42 (1986): 470–72, no. 172. The original manuscript was destroyed during the bombing of Strasbourg in 1870; the extant drawings are based upon an early nineteenth-century copy.

64. Joachim of Fiore, *Enchiridion super Apocalypsim,* ed. Burger, p. 21.

65. Gulbenkian Apocalypse, Lisbon, Museu Calouste Gulbenkian MS L.A. 139, fol. 39ᵛ. See "Census," 41 (1985): 383, no. 62; and Suzanne Lewis, "*Tractatus adversus Judaeos* in the Gulbenkian Apocalypse," *Art Bulletin* 68 (1986): 543–66, esp. pp. 557–58, fig. 19.

66. Lewis, "Gulbenkian Apocalypse," p. 557, n. 82.

67. McGinn, "Symbolism in Joachim," p. 148. McGinn suggests the need to relearn how to read symbolism more generally in his chapter "Joachim the Symbolist," in *Joachim*, pp. 115–16.

68. Peter John Olivi states in *Expositio super regulam*: "Sic per Christi uitam et regulam in suis membris passuram 'plenitudo gentium intret et omnis Israel saluus fiat' [Rom. 11.26], expresse predicetur in Apocalipsi sub apertione sexti signaculi et sub sexto angelo tuba canente [Apoc. 7.1–2; 9.13–14]. Vnde et angelus sexti signaculi, Franciscus scilicet, 'habens in se signum' et stigmata 'dei uiri,' in huius misterium sexto sue conuersionis anno transire ad Saracenos disposuit" (quoted by Daniel, "Apocalyptic Conversion," p. 145, n. 81). We translate the passage as follows: "It is expressly predicted in the Apocalypse by the opening of the sixth seal and by the sixth angel sounding the trumpet that through the life of Christ and the rule that will be revealed in his members 'the fullness of the gentiles will come in and all Israel will be saved.' Whence also the angel of the sixth seal, namely Francis, 'having in himself' the sign and stigmata 'of the God-man,' in the allegory of this [rule] in the sixth year of his conversion was disposed to pass over to the Saracens." For the significance and originality of Olivi's exegesis, see David Burr, "Olivi, the *Lectura super Apocalypsim*, and Franciscan Exegetical Tradition," in *Francescanesimo e Cultura Universitaria*, Atti del XVI Convegno internazionale (1988), pp. 115–35.

69. McGinn, *Joachim*, pp. 150–51.

70. See McGinn, *Visions*, pp. 173–76. For a fascinating, and entertaining, account of one aspect of these polemics, which draw upon Joachim's *figura* of the Dragon, see Robert E. Lerner, "Frederick II, Alive, Aloft and Allayed in Franciscan-Joachite Eschatology," in *The Use and Abuse of Eschatology in the Middle Ages*, ed. Verbeke, Verhelst, Welkenhuysen, pp. 359–84.

71. Letter XVIII, trans. Robert Coogan, *Babylon on the Rhône: A Translation of Letters by Dante, Petrarch, and Catherine of Siena on the Avignon Papacy*, Studia Humanitatis (Madrid: Jose Porrua Turanzas, 1983), pp. 89–97.

72. For analyses of some of these works within one strain of the apocalyptic imagination, that reflecting the Antichrist tradition, see Emmerson, *Antichrist*, pp. 146–203; and Emmerson, "'Nowe Ys Common This Daye': Enoch and Elias, Antichrist, and the Structure of the Chester Cycle," in *"Homo, Memento Finis": The Iconography of Just Judgment in Medieval Art and Drama*, ed. David Bevington, et al., Early Drama, Art and Music Monograph Series 6 (Kalamazoo, MI: Medieval Institute Publications, 1985), pp. 89–120. Although we disagree with their understanding of "apocalyptic," other studies dealing with a variety of "apocalyptic" literary works include Forrest S. Smith, *Secular and Sacred Visionaries in the Late Middle Ages* (New York: Garland, 1986); and Michael D. Cherniss, *Boethian Apocalypse: Studies in Middle English Vision Poetry* (Norman, OK: Pilgrim Books, 1987).

73. Richard Landes argues that our modern difficulty in studying medieval apocalypticism results partly from our periodization of history, and adds that historiographic terminology encourages historians to "overlook or trivialize the fact that those 'medieval' men were living not in the Middle Ages, in their own minds at least, but at the very end of the Last one." See Landes, "Lest the Millennium be

Fulfilled: Apocalyptic Expectations and the Pattern of Western Chronography 100–800 CE," in *The Use and Abuse of Eschatology in the Middle Ages*, ed. Verbeke, Verhelst, and Welkenhuysen, pp. 204–5.

Chapter 2: The Legenda Maior

1. For a concise summary of the circumstances surrounding publication, see Ewert Cousins's introduction to *Bonaventure*, his edition of the *Legenda Maior* in the Classics of Western Spirituality series, esp. pp. 40–41. Regis J. Armstrong, "The Spiritual Theology of the *Legenda Major* of St. Bonaventure" (Ph.D. diss. Fordham Univ., 1978), passim, provides a more detailed account.

2. As the Quaracchi edition points out, the reference is also to Acts 2:17, which would connect the introduction to Pentecost and the Holy Spirit as well (p. 4).

3. On this identification, see S. Bihel, "S. Franciscus fuitne Angelus sexti sigilli?" *Antonianum* 2 (1927): 29–70.

4. Detailed analysis of this pattern is to be found in Austin Farrer, *A Rebirth of Images: The Making of St. John's Apocalypse* (1949; rpt. Albany: State University of New York Press, 1986).

5. John V. Fleming, *From Bonaventure to Bellini* (Princeton, NJ: Princeton University Press, 1982), p. 152.

6. On Anselm of Havelberg and other interpretations of the apocalyptic seals, see Chapter 1, esp. notes 11–13.

7. See Chapter 1, n. 4.

8. The history of the anti-fraternal tradition and its influence on important literary texts has been expertly traced by Penn Szittya, *The Antifraternal Tradition in Medieval Literature* (Princeton, NJ: Princeton University Press, 1986).

9. For a more detailed discussion of the place of the *Defense* in the order, see John V. Fleming, *An Introduction to the Franciscan Literature of the Middle Ages* (Chicago: Franciscan Herald Press, 1977), pp. 83ff.

10. Fleming, *From Bonaventure to Bellini*, p. 18.

11. For a good overview of scholarship, see Cousins's introduction to *Bonaventure*. For an analysis of the *Legenda* in terms of spirituality, see Armstrong's dissertation, "The Spiritual Theology of the *Legenda Major*." Armstrong's more recent study of the structure and spirituality of the *Legenda* remains unpublished: "Towards an Unfolding of the Structure of Bonaventure's *Legenda Major*."

12. John Moorman, *A History of the Franciscan Order From Its Origins to the Year 1517* (Oxford: Clarendon, 1968), p. 287: "But when we compare it [the *Legenda*] with the writings of Celano—or even more with the writings of Brother Leo and his companions—we see how inadequate it is." Moorman had earlier claimed that Bonaventure "never really understood the Franciscan ideal." A. G. Little stated that the *Legenda* "adds little that is new, and its chief historical value lies in its omissions and in its subsequent influence." See "Guide to Franciscan Studies," *Études franciscaines* 40 (1928): 517–33; 41 (1929): 64–78. Anthony Mockler

has characterized the *Legenda* as biased, misleading, and almost worthless. A. Mockler, *Francis of Assisi: The Wandering Years* (London: Phaidon Press, 1940), pp. 7–8, as quoted in Armstrong, diss., p. 3. For an account of the modern reputation of the *Legenda*, see Armstrong, diss., p. 3ff. See also the comments of Fleming, *Franciscan Literature*, p. 48.

13. The completed manuscript of *I Celano* was presented to the pope in 1228 and received his approbation seven months later, on February 25, 1229. *II Celano* was written between August 1246 and July 1247, the date of the general chapter held at Lyons. For the details surrounding the publication of Celano's two lives of Francis, see Marion A. Habig, ed., *St. Francis of Assisi: Writings and Early Biographies, English Omnibus of the Sources for the Life of St. Francis* (Chicago: Franciscan Herald Press, 1973), pp. 179–212.

14. Daniel, "St. Bonaventure a Faithful Disciple of St. Francis? A Reexamination of the Question," in *S. Bonaventura 1274–1974*, ed. Jacques Guy Bougerol (Grottaferrata: Collegio S. Bonaventura, 1974), 2:171–87.

15. In addition to the studies of Regis Armstrong mentioned above (n. 11), see John V. Fleming, "The Iconographic Unity of the Blessing for Brother Leo," *Franziskanische Studien* 63 (1981): 204; Sophronius Clasen, "Einteilung und Anliegen der Legenda maior s. Francisci Bonaventuras," *Franciscan Studies* 27 (1967): 115–62; and William R. Cook, "Tradition and Perfection: Monastic Typology in Bonaventure's *Life of St. Francis*," *American Benedictine Review* 33 (1982): 1–20.

16. *Die Opuscula des Hl. Franziscus von Assisi*, ed. Kajetan Esser (Grottaferrata: Collegium S. Bonaventurae, 1976).

17. For an astute evaluation of the inadequacies of this critical point of view, see Armstrong, diss., pp. 40ff.

18. As Ewert Cousins has argued, Christology is one of the major *foci* in Bonaventure's thought. See "The Coincidence of Opposites in the Christology of Saint Bonaventure," *Franciscan Studies* 28 (1968): 27–45; and *Bonaventure and the Coincidence of Opposites* (Chicago: Franciscan Herald Press, 1978), ch. 5, "Christ the Center," pp. 131–59. Although Cousins discusses the Christology of Bonaventure in comprehensive terms, the texts that he analyzes in detail are the *Itinerarium* and *Collationes*.

19. McGinn notes that scholastic philosophers "had been tending to lose contact both with the historical dimensions of the Christian faith and with the historical order of the Scriptures, the *ordo historiae*." See McGinn, *Joachim*, p. 222. See also Cousins, *Bonaventure and the Coincidence of Opposites*, pp. 210–14, for a comparison between Bonaventure and Thomas which reinforces the historical dimension of Bonaventure's thought.

20. McGinn, *Joachim*, p. 222. McGinn suggests that the *Collations* deserves comparison with Augustine's *City of God*; see p. 224.

21. Joseph Ratzinger, *The Theology of History in St. Bonaventure*, trans. Zachary Hayes (Chicago: Franciscan Herald Press, 1971), pp. 33–35. Ratzinger notes that Bonaventure first makes the identification in his *Quaestiones disputatae* concerning evangelical perfection (from 1255 or 1256).

22. Bonaventure, *Collationes in Hexaemeron* 16.16, ed. A. Parma, *Opera omnia* 5: *Opuscula Varia Theologica* (Florence: Quaracchi, 1896), p. 405. Translated José de

Vinck, *Collations on the Six Days*, The Works of Bonaventure 5 (Paterson, NJ: St. Anthony Guild Press, 1970), p. 238. The "he" in the last sentence refers to Bonaventure himself. The text of the work includes both first and third person narration, since it is a reporting of what Bonaventure said, presumably by those students who were his original audience.

23. McGinn, *Joachim*, p. 218.

24. de Vinck, trans., *Collations*, p. 238, note.

25. Fleming, "Blessing for Brother Leo," p. 205. See this study for a detailed analysis of this document. For detailed discussions of the Tau sign, see Fleming, *From Bonaventure to Bellini*, p. 113 ff., and Ratzinger, *Theology*, p. 34.

26. Ratzinger, *Theology*, p. 35, points out that this association was already made in antiquity.

27. Fleming, *From Bonaventure to Bellini*, p. 116.

28. Cousins makes this point in the notes of his translation of the *Legenda*, p. 182, n. 27.

29. Daniel, "St. Bonaventure's Debt to Joachim," p. 69. Daniel has also pointed out in another study that the opening of the seven seals, as described in the third book of the *Liber de Concordia*, is an integral part of Joachim's vision. See Daniel's "The Double Procession of the Holy Spirit in Joachim of Fiore's Understanding of History," *Speculum* 55 (1980): 402. See also McGinn, *Joachim*, pp. 173, 223, 218.

30. Joachim, *Liber de Concordia Noui ac Veteris Testamenti* 3.2.6, ed. E. Randolph Daniel, *Transactions of the American Philosophical Society* 73.8 (Philadelphia: American Philosophical Society, 1983), p. 303.

31. E. Randolph Daniel, "St. Bonaventure's Debt to Joachim," *Medievalia et Humanistica* n.s. 11 (1982): 69.

32. See Emmerson, *Antichrist*, pp. 41, 95–101. The identification of the Two Witnesses is often taken for granted, as when Lotario dei Segni (Innocent III) simply juxtaposes Mal. 4 and Apoc. 11: "Mittetur, autem, 'Helyas propheta priusquam veniat dies Domini magnus et horribilis, et convertet corda patrum in filios et corda filiorum ad patres.' Cum quo veniet Enoch, 'et prophetabunt diebus mille ducentis sexaginta amicti saccis' " ["'Elias the prophet,' however, 'will be sent 'before the great and dreadful day of the Lord cometh, and he shall turn the hearts of the fathers to the children and the hearts of the children to the fathers.' With him will come Enoch, 'and they shall prophesy a thousand two hundred sixty days clothed in sackcloth' "] (ed. and trans. Robert E. Lewis, *De miseria condicionis humane* 3.12, the Chaucer Library [Athens: University of Georgia Press, 1978], pp. 223–25).

33. *Collationes* 15.28, *Opera omnia* 5, p. 402; trans. de Vinck, p. 230.

34. The connection between Francis and Elijah continued to be made by later Franciscan commentators. For example, in his survey of Bonaventure's influence on Franciscan Apocalypse commentaries, David Burr notes that one exegete, whom he identifies as Vital du Four, "offers an extended parallel between Elijah and Francis . . . . Francis' animals are compared with Elijah's raven; Francis's witness before the sultan with Elijah's firmness in the face of a hostile king; and Francis' ride in a fiery chariot with Elijah's own." See Burr, "Franciscan Exegesis and

Francis as Apocalyptic Figure," in *Monks, Nuns, and Friars in Mediaeval Society*, ed. Edward B. King, Jacqueline T. Schaefer, and William B. Wadley (Sewanee, TN: The Press of the University of the South, 1989), p. 61.

35. For an extended discussion of the eschatological significance of the Transfiguration, see Jeffrey T. Schnapp, *The Transfiguration of History at the Center of Dante's Paradiso* (Princeton, NJ: Princeton University Press, 1986), pp. 70–169.

36. Augustine, *City of God*, 22.30, trans. Henry Bettenson, ed. David Knowles (Baltimore: Penguin, 1972), p. 1091.

37. See Farrer, *A Rebirth of Images*, pp. 42, 49, 53, 57, 63. The importance of the sevenfold pattern in later Franciscan Apocalypse exegesis is noted by Burr, "Franciscan Exegesis and Francis as Apocalyptic Figure," pp. 55–57.

38. Anselm of Havelberg, *Dialogues* 1.12, ed. G. Salet, SC 118 (Paris, 1966), p. 110.

39. See Farrer, *Rebirth of Images*, p. 53. Burr, "Franciscan Exegesis and Francis as Apocalyptic Figure," notes that later Franciscan exegesis understands the seven visions of the Apocalypse to be similarly divided: "the first four visions are said to deal with the *status generalis* or *status universalis* of the church, the last three with its *status finalis*" (p. 55, n. 16).

40. McGinn, *Joachim*, p. 113. For a fuller discussion of the new spiritual men, see also Reeves, *Prophecy*, pp. 133–392, esp. 175–241; and Daniel, "The Double Procession of the Holy Spirit," pp. 478–79.

41. E. Randolph Daniel, "St. Bonaventure: Defender of Franciscan Eschatology," in *S.Bonaventura 1274–1974*, ed. Jacques Guy Bougerol (Grottaferrata: Collegio S. Bonaventura, 1974), 4: 796. Or again, "The eschatology of Bonaventure in the *Legenda* is unmistakenly Augustinian, both in its structure of history and its emphasis on *renovatio*" (4: 801).

42. That later Franciscan exegetes understood the various ways in which Francis as "book" is symbolized by the apocalyptic book with the seven seals and related to other "books" is evident in the *Expositio super Apocalypsim* (Assisi MS 66), which David Burr ascribes to Vital du Four. According to Burr, "Vital suggests that the book with seven seals (Rev. 5:1) 'can be said to be the divine plan, Christ's life, the church militant, the church triumphant, the blessed virgin, the Apocalypse, Christ in the sacrament, and the blessed Francis.' Francis is such because he 'is a book written inside spiritually through compassion and outside physically through the stigmata of Christ's passion, the seven seals of which the lion of the tribe of Judah opened'" (Burr, "Franciscan Exegesis and Francis as Apocalyptic Figure," p. 58, citing *Expositio super Apocalypsim*, fol. 50ᵛ).

43. Moreover, as Schnapp has convincingly argued, the Transfiguration was itself connected to the cross, in that it was through an understanding of the Transfiguration that the cross too changed from an instrument of torture to the eschatological sign of Christ's victory and second coming. See Schnapp, *Transfiguration*, pp. 84–85. Thus for Francis the reception of the stigmata, linked with the Transfiguration, is at once a sign of suffering and triumph and in this way too an apocalyptically significant event.

44. See also Cook, "Monastic Typology," pp. 7–8.

45. Francis and Dominic, or the new orders generally, *become* the two witnesses in some later exegesis, especially among the Spiritual Franciscans. See Richard K. Emmerson and Ronald B. Herzman, "Antichrist, Simon Magus, and Dante's *Inferno XIX*," *Traditio* 36 (1980): 374, n.4; and 386. In later medieval illuminated manuscripts, the Two Witnesses are often portrayed as friars. Once again Bonaventure is asserting the apocalyptic significance of Francis without assuming the apocalyptic extravagances of the Spirituals.

Chapter 3: *The* Roman de la Rose

1. David F. Hult, *Self-fulfilling Prophecies: Readership and Authority in the First Roman de la Rose* (Cambridge: Cambridge University Press, 1986), p. 4.

2. In the *Liber introductorius* Gerard argued that with the arrival of the age of the Holy Ghost, the Eternal Evangel (comprising Joachim of Fiore's *Expositio in Apocalypsim, Psalterium decem chordarum,* and *Liber concordie Novi ac Veteris Testamenti*) had replaced the Old and New Testaments. See H. Denifle, "Das Evangelium aeternum und die Commission zu Anagni," *Archiv für Literatur und Kirchengeschichte des Mittelalters* 1 (1885): 49–142; and Bernhard Töpfer, "Eine Handschrift des Evangelium aeternum des Gerardino von Borgo San Donnino," *Zeitschrift für Geschichtswissenschaft* 7 (1960): 156–63. On the "scandal of the eternal evangel," see Marjorie Reeves, *The Influence of Prophecy in the Later Middle Ages: A Study in Joachimism* (Oxford: Clarendon, 1969), pp. 59–70.

3. For the dispute between the secular masters and the mendicants, the most complete account is that of Michel-Marie Dufeil, *Guillaume de Saint-Amour et la polémique universitaire parisienne, 1250–1259* (Paris: Picard, 1972). See also P. Glorieux, "Le conflit de 1252–1257 à la lumière du mémoire de Guillaume de Saint-Amour," *Recherches de théologie ancienne et médiévale* 24 (1957): 354–72; and Penn R. Szittya, *The Antifraternal Tradition in Medieval Literature* (Princeton, NJ: Princeton University Press, 1986), pp. 11–61.

4. See Peter R. McKeon, "The Status of the University of Paris as *Parens scientiarum*: An Episode in the Development of Its Autonomy," *Speculum* 39 (1964): 670, who argues that Guillaume's apocalyptic imagery "appears to be only a rhetorical device, from which one may properly draw no conclusions as to the beliefs of the authors, for the *De periculis* is a parody on Joachim and on the Joachites." See also Joseph Ratzinger, *The Theology of History in St. Bonaventure*, trans. Zachary Hayes (Chicago: Franciscan Herald Press, 1971), pp. 111–13, who similarly dismisses Guillaume's expectation of the imminent end as polemical. It is a mistake, however, to assume that institutional polemics are incompatible with sincere apocalyptic fervor.

5. Szittya, *Antifraternal Tradition*, p. 20.

6. Bibliothèque nationale MS fr. 1569, fol. 28ʳ: "Ci dit l'aucteur comment mestre Jehan de Meun parfist cest romans a la requeste mestre Guillaume de Saint Amor, qui le commencement en fist, si ne le pot parfaire." Quoted by Hult, *Self-*

fulfilling Prophecies, pp. 88–89. Hult (p. 78) notes that Guillaume de Lorris is identified as Guillaume de Saint-Amour in other manuscripts as well.

7. See Rutebeuf, "Complainte de Guillaume," line 86, ed. Edmond Faral and Julia Bastin, *Oeuvres complètes de Rutebeuf* (Paris: Picard, 1969), 1:262; and Arié Serper, "L'influence de Guillaume de Saint-Amour sur Rutebeuf," *Romance Philology* 17 (1963–64): 391–402.

8. Guillaume de Saint-Amour, *De periculis novissimorum temporum* 3, in *Opera omnia* (Constance [Paris], 1632), p. 29.

9. See, for example, Charles Dahlberg, trans., *The Romance of the Rose* (1971; rpt. Hanover, NH: University Press of New England, 1983), note to line 11,293, pp. 395–96.

10. William W. Ryding, "Faus Semblant: Hero or Hypocrite?" *Romanic Review* 60 (1969): 163. It is likely that the impetus for this line of interpretation comes from C. S. Lewis, whose assumptions about the digressiveness of Jean de Meun are evident throughout *The Allegory of Love*. One example can stand for many: "The meandering in Jean de Meun's work is therefore a fault, and a fault fatal to the poem" (*The Allegory of Love* [Oxford: Oxford University Press, 1936], p. 142). See also Sister M. Faith McKean, R.S.M., "The Role of Faux Semblant and Astenance Constrainte in the *Roman de la Rose*," in *Romance Studies in Memory of E. Ham*, ed. U. T. Holmes (Hayward, CA., 1967), pp. 103–7. Sister McKean argues that many of the elements in this episode are best explained by going outside the allegory to history, that is, to the quarrel at the University of Paris. Where she differs from Ryding is in her assessment that if this is a fault, it is not a fatal one: "The interruption in the thought of the allegory, once it is seen as such, does not seriously mar Jean's work, which after all did retain its popularity even after the appearance of an allegory in which Dante's personal antagonisms were flawlessly woven into his plot structure" (p. 107).

11. *Apocalypsis Goliae*, ed. Karl Strecker, *Die Apokalypse des Golias*, Texte zur Kulturgeschichte des Mittelalters 5 (Rome: W. Regenberg, 1928); trans. F. X. Newman, in *The Literature of Medieval England*, ed. D. W. Robertson, Jr. (New York: McGraw-Hill, 1970), pp. 253–61.

12. Charles Dahlberg, *The Literature of Unlikeness* (Hanover, NH: University Press of New England, 1988), p. 112. Dahlberg, who does not argue for "any direct influence," is primarily concerned with the ways both poems develop the first-person narrator.

13. Augustine, *City of God* 20.8, p. 911.

14. "Satire contre les differents états" (ca. 1173), ed. Edelstand du Meril, *Poésies inédites du moyen âge* (Paris, 1854), p. 321. On the medieval expectation that in the last days the vices will become ubiquitous and all powerful, see Joseph R. Keller, "The Topoi of Virtue and Vice: A Study of Some Features of Social Complaint in the Middle Ages" (Ph.D. diss., Columbia University, 1958), pp. 42–49.

15. Jerome, *De Antichristo in Danielem* 4.11, CCSL 75A:915. See also Chapter 1, note 41.

16. Augustine, *Tractatus in epistolam Ioannis ad Parthos* 3.9, PL 35:2001-2002.

17. See Berengier, *De l'avenement Antecrist*, lines 34–35, ed. E. Walberg,

Deux versions inédites de la légende de l'antéchrist en vers français du xiiie siècle (Lund: C. W. K. Gleerup, 1928); and *Le Jour du Jugement: Mystère français sur le Grand Schisme*, ed. Emile Roy, Études sur le théatre français au xive siècle (Paris: Emile Bouillon, 1902), lines 193–455. The exegetical tradition is more circumspect. It identifies the parents of Antichrist as human, but emphasizes that even as a child he is possessed by devils. On Antichrist's parentage see Emmerson, *Antichrist*, pp. 81–83; and "Wynkyn de Worde's *Byrthe and Lyfe of Antechryst* and Popular Eschatology on the Eve of the English Reformation," *Medievalia* 14 (1991, for 1988): 288–95.

18. Adso, *De ortu et tempore Antichristi*, ed. Verhelst, CCCM 45, p. 22; trans. John Wright, *The Play of Antichrist* (Toronto: Pontifical Institute of Mediaeval Studies, 1967), p. 102. On the *Libellus* as a *vita* see Richard Kenneth Emmerson, "Antichrist as Anti-Saint: The Significance of Abbot Adso's *Libellus de Antichristo*," *American Benedictine Review* 30 (1979): 175–90.

19. Dahlberg, *The Literature of Unlikeness*, p. 121.

20. *Der Antichrist: Der staufische Ludus de Antichristo*, ed. Gerhard Günther (Hamburg: Friedrich Wittig, 1970), rubrics after lines 150 and 186. For a translation see Wright, *Play of Antichrist*. Note that the *Ludus de Antichristo* also places Antichrist into a historical scheme that resembles the schemes based on the Apocalypse. The play first traces salvation history to the time of the apostolic Church by staging the songs of the three religions (Gentilitas, Synagoga, Ecclesia) and then introduces Antichrist, who is preceded by Heresy and Hypocrisy. These two allegorical figures not only characterize Antichrist and his followers, but also suggest that historically the time of the third and fourth seals (i.e., the time of the heretics and hypocrites) has passed and that the time of Antichrist (i.e., the sixth seal) is imminent.

21. Emmerson, *Antichrist*, pp. 91–95.

22. Emmerson, *Antichrist*, pp. 22–24.

23. Augustine, *City of God* 20.9, p. 917. The vicious life of Faus Semblant also connects him to the Beast that rises from the sea, whose seven heads, according to Berengaudus, represent the seven deadly sins. See Berengaudus, *Expositio super septem visiones libri Apocalypsis*, PL 17:965.

24. Haimo of Auxerre, *Expositio in Apocalypsin*, PL 117:1098.

25. We are grateful to Professor Michael Twomey of Ithaca College for pointing out this allusion.

26. See Emmerson, *Antichrist*, p. 76.

27. Arnold of Villanova, *Tractatus de tempore adventus Antichristi*, ed. Heinrich Finke, *Aus den Tagen Bonifaz VIII: Funde und Forschungen*, Vorreformationsgeschichtliche Forschungen 2 (Münster: Aschendorff, 1902), p. cxxxvii.

28. On the *viri spirituales*, see McGinn, *Joachim*, pp. 112–15.

29. See Emmerson, *Antichrist*, pp. 101–3.

30. Augustine, *In epistolam Ioannis ad Parthos* 1.7, PL 35:1977; trans. Mary T. Clark, "Homily on the First Epistle of St. John," *Augustine* (New York: Paulist Press, 1984), p. 300. Jerome repeatedly refers to the "cooling of charity" as a sign of Antichrist and the end. See, for example, *De Antichristo in Danielem* 4.11, p. 922; and *Commentariorum in Esaiam*, ed. Marcus Adriaen, CCSL 73, 6.13.12, p. 231.

31. Robert Grosseteste, *Hexaëmeron* 8.30.7, ed. Richard C. Dales and Servus Gieben, British Academy, Auctores Britannici Medii Aevi 6 (London: Oxford University Press, 1982), p. 255.

32. Adso, *De ortu et tempore Antichristi*, p. 25; trans. Wright, *Play of Antichrist*, p. 104.

33. A. C. Spearing, *Medieval Dream-Poetry* (Cambridge: Cambridge University Press, 1976), p. 39.

34. Szittya further comments that "the parallel between the two pilgrims and their respective assaults suggests that their worlds—the world of hypocrisy and of cupidinous love—are not unconnected." *Antifraternal Tradition*, p. 189.

35. Bernard of Clairvaux, *On the Song of Songs* 33.15; trans. Kilian Walsh, Works of Bernard of Clairvaux 3 (Kalamazoo, MI: Cistercian Publications, 1976), 2:157.

36. John V. Fleming, *The "Roman de la Rose": A Study in Allegory and Iconography* (Princeton, NJ: Princeton University Press, 1969), pp. 166–67.

37. Marta Powell Hartley, "Narcissus, Hermaphroditus, and Attis: Ovidian Lovers at the Fontaine d'Amors in Guillaume de Lorris's *Roman de la Rose,*" *PMLA* 101 (1986): 335. Explicating another passage drawing on classical mythology—Reason's description of the dream of Croesus—Eric Jager has also emphasized Amant's self-love: "In both Croesus and the Lover, the weakness for literal readings and for worldly goods stems ultimately from a narcissistic self-love. Looking into the Well of Narcissus at the stone crystals, the Lover figuratively sees his own eyes. Similarly, Croesus sees a flattering reflection of himself in his dream. The vision of himself enjoyed by each dreamer betrays the self-love that is the root of his error." See Eric Jager, "Reading the *Roman* Inside Out: The Dream of Croesus as a *Caveat Lector,*" *Medium Aevum* 57 (1988): 71.

38. On Amant's idolatry see Maureen Quilligan, "Allegory, Allegoresis, and the Deallegorization of Language: The *Roman de la Rose*, the *De planctu Naturae*, and the *Parlement of Foules,*" in *Allegory, Myth, and Symbol*, ed. Morton W. Bloomfield, Harvard English Studies 9 (Cambridge, MA: Harvard University Press, 1981), esp. pp. 166–69. Quilligan concludes that Jean's treatment of Amant's final assault on the Rose "warns the reader that to translate the real facts of physical sexuality into metaphoric terms is a form of idolatry" (p. 185).

39. For a differing view of Amant's "progress," see René Louis, *Le roman de la Rose: Essai d'interprétation de l'allegorisme érotique* (Paris: Honoré Champion, 1974). Louis argues that Jean de Meun radically transformed Guillaume's young, naive, and idealistic Lover, making him older, experienced, and "un véritable gourmet" of the pleasures of love (p. 138).

40. Spearing, *Medieval Dream-Poetry*, p. 37. For the debate concerning the status of Nature, especially in relation to Reason, see George D. Economou, *The Goddess Natura in Medieval Literature* (Cambridge, MA: Harvard University Press, 1972), pp. 104–24; and John V. Fleming, *Reason and the Lover* (Princeton, NJ: Princeton University Press, 1984).

41. Rosemond Tuve argues that the poem's "frankly sensual, or rather lustful, final metaphor" prevents the reader from reading the plucking of the Rose "as a defense of honest, healthy, generative 'Love' with Nature and Venus as twin pre-

siding goddesses. Jean takes care to make the image exceedingly narrow; there is very little 'love' in it, especially in the sense the writers of the Middle Ages used that complicated word. We are intended to have a hard time finding even Venus as a cosmological principle lurking in any image" (*Allegorical Imagery: Some Mediaeval Books and Their Posterity* [Princeton, NJ: Princeton University Press, 1966], p. 279).

42. Winthrop Wetherbee, *Platonism and Poetry in the Twelfth Century: The Literary Influence of the School of Chartres* (Princeton, NJ: Princeton University Press, 1972), p. 257. See also Paul Piehler, *The Visionary Landscape: A Study in Medieval Allegory* (Montreal: McGill-Queen's University Press, 1971): "While the dreamer experiences a certain psychic shock when he first encounters the arrows of the God of Love, he never undergoes anything comparable in depth to the spiritual crises of the heroes of the Chartrian allegories, and thus never feels the urgency of their desire for a vision of the ultimate truth concerning their spiritual condition" (pp. 109–10).

43. Carolyn Van Dyke, *The Fiction of Truth: Structures of Meaning in Narrative and Dramatic Allegory* (Ithaca, NY: Cornell University Press, 1985), p. 93.

44. Ugo Foscolo and Francesco de Sanctis are two critics who exemplify the romantic reading. For useful summaries of the criticism of this episode, see Renato Poggioli, "Tragedy or Romance? A Reading of the Paolo and Francesca Episode in Dante's *Inferno*," *PMLA* 72 (1957): 313–58; and Lawrence V. Ryan, "*Stornei, Gru, Columbe*: The Bird Images in *Inferno* V," *Dante Studies* 94 (1976): 25–27. Recently critics have recognized the parallel between the lovers in *Inferno* 5 and Amant and described their respective situations in the more negative terms that we are suggesting. See, for example, Jesse M. Gellrich, *The Idea of the Book in the Middle Ages: Language Theory, Mythology, and Fiction* (Ithaca, NY: Cornell University Press, 1985), p. 46: "As Paolo and Francesca are seduced by the Book, Amant in the *Roman* is so enthralled by his dream of a rosy maiden that he knows not lady from flower until he embraces both as a stone statue in a castle wall. For one whose assent to the power of illusions is so absolute, a palinode offers little salvation."

45. For the "Ithacan Heresy" see Fleming, *Reason and the Lover*, pp. 3–24; and Hill's response in *Speculum* 60 (1985): 973–77. Hill argues that "although the *Roman* was widely read and cited in the Middle Ages, it was not thought a particularly Christian work" (p. 976). For the original "Querelle" see Maxwell Luria, *A Reader's Guide to the Roman de la Rose* (Hamden, CN: Archon, 1982), pp. 68–74, 183–202, 252–53; Fleming, *Roman de la Rose*, p. vi; and Pierre-Yves Badel, *Le Roman de la Rose au XIVᵉ siècle: Étude de la réception de l'oeuvre* (Geneva: Droz, 1980).

Chapter 4: The Commedia

1. Jonathan B. Riess, "Luca Signorelli's Frescoes in the Chapel of San Brizio as Reflections of their Time and Place," in *Renaissance Studies in Honor of Craig Hugh Smyth*, ed. Andrew Morrogh, et al. (Florence: Giunti Barbera, 1985), 2: 383.

2. See, for example, Enzo Carli, *Il Duomo di Orvieto* (Rome: Instituto Po-

ligrafico della Stato, 1965), pp. 106–11; Carli, *Luca Signorelli: Gli Affreschi nel Duomo di Orvieto* (Bergamo: Instituto Italiano d'Arti Grafiche, 1946); Luitpold Dussler, *Signorelli des Meisters Gemälde* (Stuttgart: Deutsche Verlags-Anstalt, 1927), pp. xxxii–xxxvii; Pietro Scarpellini, *Luca Signorelli*, Collana d'Arte 10 (Florence: G. Barbera Editore, 1964), pp. 40–45; Jonathan B. Riess, "La genesi degli affreschi del Signorelli per la Cappella Nuova," in *Il duomo di Orvieto*, ed. Lucio Riccetti (Rome: Laterza, 1988), pp. 247–83.

3. The portraits are identified by, among others, Mario Salmi, *Luca Signorelli* (Novara: Instituto Geografico de Agostini, 1953), pp. 24–25.

4. On the portrayal of John in illuminated Apocalypses, see Barbara Nolan, *The Gothic Visionary Perspective* (Princeton, NJ: Princeton University Press, 1977), pp. 59–67.

5. Typical of the traditional interpretation of the Two Witnesses is Tertullian, *De Anima* 50, *PL* 2:780; Gregory, *Moralia* 15.58.69, *PL* 75:1117; and *Glossa*, vol. 6, fols. 256^r-256^v.

6. For the later identification of the witnesses with Francis and Dominic, see Ubertino da Casale, *Arbor vite crucifixe Jesu* 5.8 (Venice, 1485), fol. 229^r. The Spiritual Franciscans particularly claimed to fulfill the role of the Two Witnesses, whom they identified with the spiritual men prophesied by Joachim of Fiore. See Marjorie Reeves, *The Influence of Prophecy in the Later Middle Ages* (Oxford: Clarendon, 1969), pp. 148, 176, 180–81, 198–99.

7. See, for example, the portrayal of the Two Witnesses in the Douce Apocalypse, Oxford, Bodleian Library MS Douce 180, fol. 30^r–31^v. For a facsimile, see Peter Klein, ed. *Apokalypse, MS. Douce 180, Bodleian Library, Oxford*, Codices Selecti 72 (Graz: Akademische Druck-u. Verlagsanstalt, 1981); and Klein's study of the manuscript, *Endzeiterwartung und Ritterideologie: Die englischen Bilderapokalypsen der Fruhgotik und MS Douce 180* (Graz: Akademische Druck-u. Verlagsanstalt, 1983). For other studies, see "Census," *Traditio* 41 (1985): 400–401, no. 98.

8. See, for example, Bernardino of Siena, "De mercationibus et vitiis mercatorum," sermon 34, *Opera omnia*, vol. 4 (Florence: Typographia Colegii S. Bonaventurae, 1956). On Bernardino, see Roberto Rusconi, "Apocalittica ed escatologia nella predicazione di Bernardino da Siena," *Studi Medievali* 3rd ser., 22 (1981): 85–128.

9. Quoted by Louis Green, *Chronicle Into History: An Essay on the Interpretation of History in Florentine Fourteenth-Century Chronicles* (Cambridge: Cambridge University Press, 1972), p. 38. Green notes that the late fifteenth century witnessed a great revival of "apocalyptic prediction" (p. 146). For a study of the apocalyptic dimensions of the great plague, see Robert E. Lerner, "The Black Death and Western European Eschatological Mentalities," *American Historical Review* 86 (1981): 533–52; for the effect of such attitudes on art, see Millard Meiss, *Painting in Florence and Siena after the Black Death* (Princeton, NJ: Princeton University Press, 1951; rpt. in paperback 1978), p. 78.

10. Quoted by Pauline Moffitt Watts, "Prophecy and Discovery: On the Spiritual Origins of Christopher Columbus's 'Enterprise of the Indies,'" *American Historical Review* 90 (1985): 73. Arguing that Columbus's apocalypticism corresponds to the more conservative eschatology of Pierre d'Ailly, Watts disputes John

Leddy Phelan's view that Columbus "consciously sought to surround himself with the magic aura that over the centuries had enveloped the name of Joachim by proclaiming himself the Joachimite Messiah." For Phelan's arguments, see *The Millennial Kingdom of the Franciscans in the New World: A Study of the Writings of Geronimo de Mendieta (1525–1604)*, University of California Publications in History 42 (Berkeley: University of California Press, 1956), p. 22.

11. See M. Gaster, "The Letter of Toledo," *Folk-Lore* 13 (1902): 126–29. On the importance of the Sibylline tradition, see Bernard McGinn, "'Teste David cum Sibylla': The Significance of the Sibylline Tradition in the Middle Ages," in *Women of the Medieval World*, ed. J. Kirshner and S. Wemple (New York: Oxford University Press, 1985), pp. 7–35; and, more specifically, McGinn, "Joachim and the Sibyl," *Citeaux* 24 (1973): 97–138.

12. See the thorough and fascinating account of the various permutations of this vision in Robert E. Lerner, *The Powers of Prophecy: The Cedar of Lebanon Vision from the Mongol Onslaught to the Dawn of the Enlightenment* (Berkeley: University of California Press, 1983).

13. André Chastel, "L'Antéchrist à la Renaissance," in *L'Umanesimo e li demonico, Atti del II Congresso Internazionale di Studi Umanistici*, ed. Enrico Castelli (Roma: Fratelli Bocca Editori, 1952), pp. 177–86. Reeves also describes the general anxiety of the 1480s and 1490s in *The Influence of Prophecy*, pp. 430–40.

14. André Chastel, "L'Apocalypse en 1500: La fresque de l'Antéchrist à la Chapelle Saint-Brice d'Orvieto," *Bibliothèque d'humanisme et renaissance* 14 (1952): 124–40. For a critique of Chastel, see R. de Maio, "Savonarola, Alessandro VI e il mito dell'Anticristo," *Rivista storica italiana* 82 (1970): 533–59; and Jonathan B. Riess, "Republicanism and Tyranny in Signorelli's *Rule of the Antichrist*," in *Art and Politics in Late Medieval and Renaissance Italy*, ed. Charles Rosenberg (Notre Dame, IN: University of Notre Dame Press, 1990), pp. 157–86.

15. On "the dreadful trials that Orvieto itself endured" in the closing years of the fifteenth century and their influence on contemporary apocalypticism, see Riess, "Luca Signorelli's Frescoes in San Brizio," p. 384.

16. During the fifteenth century, several block-books were printed that traced the *vita* of Antichrist from his birth to his death. These usually also included the Fifteen Signs of Doomsday and the Last Judgment. See, for example, Ernst Kelchner, ed., *Der Enndkrist der Stadt-Bibliothek zu Frankfurt am Main* (Frankfurt: Frankfurter Lichdruckanstalt Wiesbaden, 1891); Kurt Pfister, ed., *Das Buch von dem Entkrist* (Leipzig: Insel Verlag, 1925); H. Th. Musper, ed., *Der Antichrist und die fünfzehn Zeichen*, 2 vols. (Munich: Prestel Verlag, 1970); and Karin Boveland, Christoph Peter Burger, and Ruth Steffen, eds., *Der Antichrist und die fünfzehn Zeichen vor dem Jüngsten Gericht*, 2 vols. (Hamburg: Friedrich Wittig, 1979). For an early sixteenth-century English example, see Richard K. Emmerson, "Wynkyn de Worde's *Byrthe and Lyfe of Antechryst* and Popular Eschatology on the Eve of the English Reformation," *Medievalia* 14 (1991, for 1988): 281–311.

17. For an introduction to Savonarola as an apocalyptic thinker and for a selection from *Compendio de Rivelazioni e Dialogus de veritate prophetica*, see Bernard McGinn, ed., *Apocalyptic Spirituality* (New York: Paulist Press, 1979), pp. 183–274. McGinn considers Chastel's interpretation of the Signorelli fresco to

be "plausible" (p. 183), whereas Riess, "Republicanism and Tyranny," suggesting that such an interpretation reduces "the mural to something that verges on mere poster art," persuasively argues that Chastel "misses the larger political and ecclesiastical significance of the work" (p. 158). There are other problems with Chastel's interpretation in addition to the fact that it is topically reductionist: for example, Antichrist in the fresco is not a Dominican. It seems more likely that the Dominicans in the background assume the traditional role of the Two Witnesses (often Enoch and Elijah) in opposition to Antichrist; if so, the fresco may be a Dominican version of the Franciscan claim to represent the prophets of the last days. In "Republicanism and Tyranny" Riess argues, in fact, that the aged Dominican who stands behind Antichrist may be a portrait of St. Vincent Ferrer, whose popular sermons on Antichrist led to his being designated as the "Angel of the Apocalypse" (p. 162).

18. Riess, "Republicanism and Tyranny," passim.

19. Antichrist is devil-inspired throughout the Velislav Bible's *vita* of Antichrist, for example. See Karel Stejskal, *Velislai Biblia picta*, Editio Cimelia Bohemica 12 (Prague: Progopress, 1970), fols. 130ᵛ-135ᵛ; and "Census," *Traditio* 42 (1986): 454–55, no. 141. See also the block-book *vitae* cited in note 14. For portrayals of Antichrist's career, see Emmerson, *Antichrist*, pp. 108–45; Bernard McGinn, "Portraying Antichrist in the Middle Ages," in *The Use and Abuse of Eschatology in the Middle Ages*, ed. Verbeke, Verhelst, and Welkenhuysen, pp. 1–48; and Renate Blumenfeld-Kosinski, "Illustration as Commentary in Late Medieval Images of Antichrist's Birth," *Deutsche Vierteljahrsschrift für Literaturwissenschaft und Geistesgeschichte* 63 (1989): 589–607.

20. For Adso's *Libellus de Antichristo*, see D. Verhelst, *Adso Dervensis, De Ortu et tempore Antichristi*, CCCM 45. In addition to the illustrations described from the Morgan Library Apocalypse, Antichrist's methods of gaining power are also illustrated in the Velislav Bible and the block-book *vitae*. See also the *Hortus Deliciarum*, ed. R. Green, M. Evans, C. Bischoff, and M. Curschmann, *Herrad of Hohenbourg: Hortus Deliciarum*, Studies of the Warburg Institute 3 (London: Warburg Institute, 1979), fol. 241ᵛ. For the *Hortus Deliciarum*, see "Census," *Traditio* 42 (1986): 470–72, no. 172.

21. For New York, Pierpont Morgan Library MS M. 524, see "Census," *Traditio* 41 (1985): 397, no. 90.

22. For Antichrist's miracles, see Thomas Aquinas, *Summa theologiae* 1.114.4; and Nicholas of Lyra, *Postilla*, in *Glossa*, vol. 6, fol. 114ᵛ.

23. On Antichrist's death, see Jerome, *In Esaiam* 8.25.6–8, ed. M. Adriaen, CCSL 73:327; Bede, "De temporibus Antichristi," *De temporum ratione*, PL 90:574; Adso, *Libellus de Antichristo*, ed. Verhelst, pp. 28–29; *Glossa*, vol. 6, fol. 270ᵛ; and Jacobus da Voragine, *Legenda aurea*, ed. Th. Graesse (1890; rpt. Osnabruck: Otto Zeller, 1969), p. 642.

24. Hartmann Schedel, *Liber chronicarum* (Nuremberg, 1493), fol. 262ᵛ; and Adrian Wilson, *The Making of the Nuremberg Chronicle*, 2nd ed. (Amsterdam: Nico Israel, 1978), pl. 10. On the chronicle's possible influence on Signorelli, see Scarpellini, *Luca Sgnorelli*, p. 133.

25. The Apocalypse of London, Wellcome Historical Medical Library, MS 49 (fol. 13ʳ), for example, pictures Antichrist's fall from the hands of devils. At-

tempting to rise from the Mount of Olives, he has been struck down by an angel, who watches from above. For this manuscript, see "Census," *Traditio* 42 (1986): 448, no. 128. The block-book *vitae* similarly emphasize the final events of Antichrist's life by showing, in full-page pictures rather than the more usual half-page illustrations, Antichrist's rise into the heavens and fall after being struck down by an angel.

26. See Fabio Bisogni, "Problemi Iconografici Riminesi: Le storie dell' Anticristo in S. Maria in Porto Fuori," *Paragone* 305 (July 1975): 13–23.

27. In addition to Morgan Library MS M. 524, fols. 19^r and 20^r, see Paris, Bibliothèque nationale, fr. 403, fols. 39^v–40^r; "Census," *Traditio* 41 (1985): 405–6, no. 107. See also the Moralized Bible, British Library, Harley MS 1527, fol. 148^r; "Census," *Traditio* 42 (1986): 461–62, no. 154.

28. See Richard Kenneth Emmerson, "Antichrist as Anti-Saint: The Significance of Abbot Adso's *Libellus de Antichristo*," *American Benedictine Review* 30 (1979): 175–90.

29. For the *Biblia Pauperum*, see the fifteenth-century manuscript, Vatican Library Pal. Lat. 871, ed. Karl-August Wirth (Zurich: Belser Verlag, 1982); for the *Speculum Humanae Salvationis*, see Adrian Wilson and Joyce Lancaster Wilson, *A Medieval Mirror: Speculum Humanae Salvationis, 1324–1500* (Berkeley: University of California Press, 1984), "Casus Luciferi," p. 142. For the significance of the Fall of Lucifer in the cycle plays, see Robert W. Hanning, "'You Have Begun a Parlous Pleye': The Nature and Limits of Dramatic Mimesis as a Theme in Four Middle English 'Fall of Lucifer' Cycle Plays," *Comparative Drama* 7 (1973): 22–50.

30. For the Simon Magus legend, see the references in Chapter 1, n. 41; and the *Acts of Peter*, ed. Edgar Hennecke and Wilhelm Schneemelcher, *New Testament Apocrypha* (Philadelphia: Westminster Press, 1963), 1:282–322. For the continuity of the tradition in art and literature, see Ronald B. Herzman and William R. Cook, "Simon the Magician and the Medieval Tradition," *Journal of Magic History* 2 (1980): 28–43.

31. *Legenda aurea* 89, ed. Graesse; trans. Granger Ryan and Helmut Ripperger, *The Golden Legend of Jacobus de Voragine* (1941; rpt. New York: Arno, 1969), pp. 335–36.

32. Suzanne Lewis, "*Tractatus adversus Judaeos* in the Gulbenkian Apocalypse," *Art Bulletin* 68 (1986), comments that in the thirteenth century "the architrave of the portico of Old St. Peter's in Rome was painted with a fresco cycle that included the dispute of Peter with Simon Magus, his fall, and the death of Nero" (559), and adds in a note that "the oldest representation of Simon Magus is known in a 17th-century copy from the Oratory of John VII (705–707) in Old St. Peter's, showing his flight and fall next to the dispute before Nero" (559, n. 90). See Vatican Library, MS Barb. lat. 2732, fol. 75^v, which is reproduced in Luba Eleen, *The Illustration of the Pauline Epistles in French and English Bibles of the Twelfth and Thirteenth Centuries* (Oxford: Clarendon, 1982), fig. 30. Emile Mâle, *Les saints: compagnons du Christ* (Paris: Paul Hartmann, 1958), comments that "Le miracle de saint Pierre qui a été représenté le plus souvent en Italie est celui de la chute de Simon le Magicien" (pp. 105–6).

33. See Herzman and Cook, "Simon the Magician," fig. 6. See also the twelfth-century mosaics portraying the meeting of Nero and Simon Magus in

Monreale Cathedral and in the Palatine Chapel at Palermo. For early manuscript representations of Simon Magus, see F. Bucher, ed., *The Pamplona Bibles* (New Haven, CN: Yale University Press, 1970), fol. 206^r; and Eleen, *Illustrations of Pauline Epistles*, fig. 33 (Antiphonary of Prüm, Paris, Bibl. nat. MS lat. 9448, fol. 54^v), and fig. 35 (Fulda Sacramentary, Göttingen, Univ. Bibl., MS Theol. 232, fol. 93). For the representation of Simon Magus in English art at Peterborough Cathedral and Bury St. Edmunds, see George Henderson, "The Damnation of Nero and Related Themes," in *The Vanishing Past: Studies in Medieval Art, Liturgy and Metrology Presented to Christopher Hohler*, ed. A. Borg and A. Martindale (Oxford: Oxford University Press, 1981), 39–44. For the representation of Simon Magus in stained glass windows at Chartres, Bourges, Angers, and Tours, see Emile Mâle, *The Gothic Image: Religious Art in France of the Thirteenth Century*, trans. D. Nussey (New York: Harper and Row, 1972), pp. 296–98. For a later version, see the north aisle window of Cologne Cathedral (early 16th c.), which portrays a cycle including Christ's calling of Peter, his coronation, his cursing Simon Magus, his trial, and his upside-down crucifixion; reproduced in Herbert Rode, *Die Mittelalterlichen Glasmalereien des Kölner Domes*, Corpus vitrearum medii aevi, Deutschland 4.1 (Berlin: Deutscher Verlag für Kunstwissenschaft, 1974), pl. 223, and for detail, pl. 225.

34. Charles S. Singleton, "Inferno XIX: 'O Simon Mago!'" *Modern Language Notes* 80 (1965): 92–99. Singleton includes two depictions of Simon's fall in twelfth-century cathedral sculpture.

35. For comparisons of Antichrist and Simon Magus, see Pseudo-Clementine Homily 2.17–22, ed. and trans. Hennecke and Schneemelcher, *New Testament Apocrypha*, 2:545–47; Gregory, *Moralia* 29.7.15, PL 76:484; Berengaudus, *Expositio super septem visiones libri Apocalypsis*, PL 17:970–71; Bruno of Segni, *Commentaria in Matthaeum* 4.99, PL 165:269–70; and *Glossa*, vol. 6, fol. 115^r. In his commentary on the Apocalypse, Peter John Olivi identifies both Simon Magus and Nero as types of the great Antichrist: "Magnus . . . antichristus assimilatur Neroni pagano imperanti toti orbi et Simoni Mago dicenti se deum et filium dei" ["The great Antichrist is similar to the pagan Nero who gives commands to the whole world, and to Simon Magus who claims to be a god and a son of God"] (quoted by David Burr, "Olivi's Apocalyptic Timetable," *Journal of Medieval and Renaissance Studies* 11 [1981]: 242, n. 16). The translation is ours.

36. Bonaventure, *Collationes in Hexaemeron* 15.8; trans. José de Vinck, *Works of Bonaventure*, vol. 5 (Paterson, NJ: St. Anthony Guild Press, 1970), p. 220. Bonaventure's identification of Antichrist and Simon Magus may be the source for Dante's association of the two deceivers, even as the entire *Collationes* is a source for Dante's conception of history.

37. See, for example, Haimo of Auxerre, *Expositio in Apocalypsin*, PL 117:1100; see also the discussion below, and the references in notes 75–77.

38. Lisbon, Museu Calouste Gulbenkian MS L.A. 139; on Apoc. 13, see fol. 39^v; on Apoc. 8, see fol. 16^r. Both are discussed and illustrated in Lewis, "*Tractatus adversus Judaeos*," 557–59, figs. 19–20. For this Apocalypse manuscript, see "Census," *Traditio* 41 (1985): 383, no. 62.

39. See, for example, the gloss on Apoc. 8:1 in Paris, Bibl. nat., fr. 403 (facsimile ed. L. Delisle and P. Meyer, *L'Apocalypse en Français au xiiie siècle* vol. 2

[Paris: Firmin Didot, 1901]), fol. 11ᵛ. On the period of peace following the death of Antichrist, see Robert E. Lerner, "Refreshment of the Saints: The Time After Antichrist as a Station for Earthly Progress in Medieval Thought," *Traditio* 32 (1976): 97–144.

40. Most biblical scholars believe that the description in 2 Thes. 2:3–10, an important source for the medieval Antichrist tradition, refers to Nero. Certainly in much early Christian literature Nero is portrayed as Antichrist. See Emmerson, *Antichrist*, pp. 26–30.

41. See Ronald B. Herzman and William A. Stephany, "'O miseri seguaci': Sacramental Inversion in *Inferno* XIX," *Dante Studies* 96 (1978): 39–65. The notes document the range of sources used by Dante in the canto.

42. Herzman and Stephany, "'O miseri seguaci,'" 44 and 63, n. 8.

43. Although the accounts in the *Acts of Peter* and the *Legenda aurea* are quite similar, they differ in one key respect. In the earlier version, Simon Magus is not killed by his fall: "And Peter, seeing this incredible sight, cried out to the Lord Jesus Christ, 'Let this man do what he understood, and all who have believed on thee shall now be overthrown, and the signs and wonders which thou gavest them through me shall be disbelieved. Make haste, Lord, with thy grace; and let him fall down from (this) height, and be crippled, but not die; but let him be disabled and break his leg in three places!' And he fell down from that height and broke his leg in three places. Then they stoned him and went to their own homes; but from that time they all believed in Peter." See *Acts of Peter* 32.3, in Hennecke and Schneemelcher, *New Testament Apocrypha*, 2:316.

44. For traditional features of Peter's legend cited in hymns, see J. Szoverffy, "The Legends of St. Peter in Medieval Latin Hymns," *Traditio* 10 (1954): 275–322.

45. See Herzman and Stephany, "'O miseri seguaci,'" 63–64.

46. See Herzman and Stephany, "'O miseri seguaci,'" 54.

47. John Block Friedman, "Antichrist and the Iconography of Dante's Geryon," *Journal of the Warburg and Courtauld Institutes* 35 (1972): 120; see also 118–19.

48. See Herzman and Stephany, "'O miseri seguaci,'" 47.

49. Charles T. Davis, *Dante and the Idea of Rome* (Oxford: Oxford University Press, 1957), p. 197. Davis discusses the perceived affinities between Dante and Joachimist writers in a useful appendix (see note B, pp. 239–43). Some exegetes also identified the Whore with Antichrist. See the French gloss accompanying many of the thirteenth-century illuminated Apocalypses, for example in Bibl. nat., fr. 403, ed. L. Delisle and P. Meyer, *L'Apocalypse en Français*, 2:89.

50. Robert E. Kaske, "Dante's 'DXV' and 'Veltro,'" *Traditio* 17 (1961): 202–203. For bibliography and some cautions about Kaske's conclusions, see Albert L. Rossi, "'A l'ultimo suo': *Paradiso* XXX and Its Vergilian Context," *Studies in Medieval and Renaissance History* 2 (1982): 43–44.

51. In the third chapter of *Dante and the Idea of Rome*, "Dante and the Papal City" (pp. 195–235), Davis provides extensive documentation of Dante's knowledge of these writers. See also Kaske, "'DXV' and 'Veltro'"; and Friedman, "Dante's Geryon," especially pp. 113, 118.

52. For the complex relationship between these writers and Spiritual Franciscanism, see John V. Fleming, *An Introduction to the Franciscan Literature of the Middle Ages* (Chicago: Franciscan Herald Press, 1977), pp. 98–104.

53. On the question of Peter John Olivi's influence on Dante, for example, Davis writes: "Like the Spiritual Franciscans of his day, and in particular the famous teacher Pier Giovanni Olivi, who lectured at Santa Croce between 1287 and 1289, he lamented the perversion of the Roman destiny revealed in the corruption of the Church, even more deeply than in the weakness of the Empire." Davis further compares the language of Olivi's commentary on Apoc. 17 with the apocalyptic language of *Inferno* 19. See *Dante and the Idea of Rome*, p. 226. In his "Education in Dante's Florence," Davis also argues that it is likely that Dante "heard some of Olivi's and Ubertino's sermons and felt the force of the strong Spiritual movement in Florence before 1290." See *Dante's Italy and Other Essays* (Philadelphia: University of Pennsylvania Press, 1984), p. 153. As with Joachim himself, the extent of deviation from orthodoxy among the three Spirituals is the subject of much scholarly debate. To take one example, David Burr has shown Olivi's indebtedness to Bonaventure in "The Apocalyptic Element in Olivi's Critique of Aristotle," *Church History* 40 (1971): 15–29.

54. Reeves, *Prophecy*, pp. 191–94, 395–415; see also Bernard McGinn, "Angel Pope and Papal Antichrist," *Church History* 47 (1978): 155–73. For a comprehensive treatment of the poverty issue, see David Burr, *Olivi and Franciscan Poverty* (Philadelphia: University of Pennsylvania Press, 1989).

55. Robert E. Lerner, "On the Origins of the Earliest Latin Pope Prophecies: A Reconsideration," *Fälschungen im Mittelalter*, Monumenta Germaniae Historica Schriften 33 (Hanover, 1988), 5:628–29. Lerner further ventures (p. 632) that the Rabano whom Dante placed in the circle of the sun (*Paradiso* 12.139) is to be identified with Rabanus Anglicus—the putative author of the *Vaticinia*—rather than with Rabanus Maurus as is usually thought. For the conventional understanding of the origins of the prophecies, and for a discussion of their images, see Herbert Grundmann, "Die Papstprophetien des Mittelalters," *Archiv für Kulturgeschichte* 19 (1929): 77–138; rpt. *Joachim von Fiore*, Monumenta Germaniae Historica Schriften 25 (Hanover, 1977), 2:1–57.

56. Reeves, *Prophecy*, p. 193.

57. Herbert Grundmann made this connection in "Dante und Joachim von Fiore zu Paradiso X–XI," *Deutsches Dante-Jahrbuch* 14 (1932): 252. Friedman suggests that through their portrayal of Antichrist these same prophecies may have influenced the iconography of Geryon in *Inferno* 16. See Friedman, "Geryon," pp. 115ff.

58. Ubertino da Casale, *Arbor vite crucifixe Jesu* 5.12, fol. 240ʳ–40ᵛ; see also 5.8, fols. 228ᵛ–33ᵛ. On Ubertino, see Marino Damiata, *Pietà e Storia nell'Arbor Vitae di Ubertino da Casale* (Florence: Edizioni 'Studi Francescani,' 1988).

59. Davis, *Dante and the Idea of Rome*, p. 226. See also Davis's "Education," in *Dante's Italy*, pp. 152–54.

60. The connection is made by Davis, *Dante and the Idea of Rome*, p. 217; and Friedman, "Dante's Geryon," 133. See also Erich Auerbach's seminal analysis, "St. Francis of Assisi in Dante's *Commedia*," *Italica* 22 (1945): 166–79. Fleming, describ-

ing Ubertino's influence on Dante, says that "the poet paid homage to the friar in deed if not word, however, for he borrowed from him details of his own Franciscan poetic myth" (*Franciscan Literature*, p. 230).

61. For an extended analysis of the language of matrimony in *Inferno* 19, its connection with sacramental inversion as part of the canto's *contrapasso*, and its figural relevance to *Paradiso* 11, see Herzman and Stephany, "'O miseri seguaci,'" 55–59.

62. Kenelm Foster, "The Canto of the Damned Popes: *Inferno* XIX," *Dante Studies* 87 (1969): 57, states that "unlike Ubertino, Dante never identifies Boniface with Antichrist." This is surely true. But our point is not that Boniface and the other popes *are* Antichrist (or that they *are* Simon Magus). Boniface and the others are forerunners or predecessors of Antichrist in the last days and represent the working of Antichrist in the Church, just as they are the *seguaci* of Simon Magus.

63. Reeves, *Prophecy*, p. 196. Lerner, "Origins" (p. 627), leaves the dating of the earliest Latin prophecies somewhat undetermined, somewhere between 1277 and 1305.

64. Not surprisingly, in *Dante and the Idea of Rome*, Davis emphasizes the influence of the opposition between Rome and Babylon on the *Commedia*. See, esp. ch. 3, "Dante and the Papal City." See also Ernst Kantorowicz's review of Davis, in *Speculum* 34 (1959): 103–9. The identification of the corrupt church with Babylon, of course, preceded the move to Avignon. Peter John Olivi, for example, notes in his commentary on the Apocalypse that the contemporary church "is infected from head to toe and turned into a new Babylon as it were." Quoted by Burr, "Olivi's Apocalyptic Timetable," 238.

65. *Rime* 114, ed. Ferdinando Neri, Francesco Petrarca, *Rime, Trionfi, e Poesie Latine*, La Letteratura Italiana Storia e Testi 6 (Milan: Riccardo Ricciardi Editore, 1951), p. 156. Trans. Joseph Auslander, *The Sonnets of Petrarch* (London: Longmans, Green, 1931), p. 91.

66. Benvenuto da Imola, *Commentum super Dantis Aldigherij Comoediam*, ed. Giamcomo Filippo Lacaita (Florence: G. Barbera, 1887), 2:54.

67. *De Antichristo in Danielem* 4.11.21, ed. F. Glorie, CCSL 75A:915; trans. Gleason L. Archer, Jr., *Jerome's Commentary on Daniel* (1958; rpt. Grand Rapids: Baker Book House, 1977), p. 130. A text of equal importance immediately precedes it: "cumque multa, quae postea lecturi et exposituri summus, super Antiochi persona conueniant, typum eum uolunt fuisse Antichristi, et quae in illo ex parte praecesserint, in Antichristo ex toto esse complenda" ["Those of our school insist also that since many of the details which we are subsequently to read and explain are appropriate to the person of Antiochus, he is to be regarded as a type of the Antichrist, and those things which happened to him in a preliminary way are to be completely fulfilled in the case of the Antichrist"] (CCSL 75A:913; trans. Archer, p. 129). See also Rabanus Maurus, *Commentaria in libros Machabaeorum*, PL 109:1134. For Antiochus Epiphanes as one of the most widely discussed types of Antichrist in the Middle Ages, see Emmerson, *Antichrist*, p. 28.

68. William Langland, *Piers Plowman*, B.15.555–59, ed. A. V. C. Schmidt, *The Vision of Piers Plowman: A Complete Edition of the B-Text* (London: J. M. Dent, 1978).

69. Mark Musa has made the valuable point that the initial apostrophe ("O Simon Mago!") is that of Dante the poet, whereas the final apostrophe ("Ahi Constantin") is spoken by the pilgrim, thus reflecting how his insight in the canto has grown to equal the poet's. See Musa, *Advent at the Gates* (Bloomington: Indiana University Press, 1974), ch. 3, "From Measurement to Meaning: Simony," pp. 52ff.

70. Bernard, *De Consideratione* 4.3.6; trans. John D. Anderson and Elizabeth T. Kennan, *Five Books On Consideration: Advice to a Pope*, The Works of Bernard of Clairvaux 13 (Kalamazoo: Cistercian Publications, 1976), p. 117. Given the all-pervasive opposition between Simon Magus and Simon Peter in the canto, this opposition supports Musa's argument that these two apostrophes are central to the canto's structure. See also Herzman and Stephany, "'O miseri seguaci,'" 64, n. 28.

71. Guido da Pisa, *Expositiones et Glose super Comediam Dantis*, ed. Vincenzo Cioffari (Albany: State University of New York Press, 1974), p. 368.

72. Heretics and reformers from the twelfth through the sixteenth century, identifying Antichrist with the papacy, attacked the Donation of Constantine as the origin of Antichrist's power. See, for example, on the Catharist heretics, Walter L. Wakefield and Austin P. Evans, eds., *Heresies of the High Middle Ages*, Records of Civilization: Sources and Studies 81 (New York: Columbia University Press, 1969), p. 173. However, as Davis, *Dante and the Idea of Rome*, has shown, the disapproval of the Donation was so widespread in Dante's time that it is not necessary to turn to "the works of heretics and extremists" for possible sources (p. 85).

73. See Herzman and Stephany, "'O miseri seguaci,'" 40–41.

74. See Herzman and Stephany, "'O miseri seguaci,'" 41. Nicholas's speech at the beginning of the canto is balanced by Dante's rebuke at the end. Although Nicholas is no prophet (or rather he is a false prophet), Dante becomes one at this point in the *Commedia*. Not only does he cry out, as the Old Testament prophets cried out against the terrible evils of their times, but Dante does so invoking apocalyptic language that links present and future in prophetic fashion (as the conclusion of this chapter explains in more detail).

75. Martin of Leon, *Expositio libri Apocalypsis*, PL 209:370, comments: "Ita ut etiam ignes de coelo descendere faciat, id est spiritum malignum quasi spiritum sanctum descendere in terram" ["Thus he shall also cause a fire to descend from heaven, that is an evil spirit to descend on earth as if it were the Holy Spirit"].

76. Velislav Bible, fol. 133^v. The rubric is based on Hugh of Strassburg's explanation in the *Compendium*. For a facsimile, see Stejskal, ed., *Velislai Biblia picta*.

77. *The Coming of Antichrist*, lines 193–204; ed. R. M. Lumiansky and David Mills, *The Chester Mystery Cycle*, EETS SS 3 (1974), p. 416.

78. Kaske, "Dante's 'DXV,'" 202.

79. Herzman and Stephany, "'O miseri seguaci,'" 62.

80. See Musa, *Advent at the Gates*, pp. 52–61.

81. For analysis of the apocalyptic symbolism of the final cantos of the *Purgatorio*, see Robert E. Kaske's articles: "Dante's *Purgatorio* XXXII and XXXIII: A Survey of Christian History," *University of Toronto Quarterly* 43 (1974): 193–214; and "The Seven *Status Ecclesiae* in *Purgatorio* XXXII and XXXIII," in *Dante, Petrarch, Boccaccio: Studies in the Italian Trecento in Honor of Charles S. Singleton*, ed.

Aldo S. Bernardo and Anthony L. Pellegrini, Medieval and Renaissance Texts and Studies 22 (Binghamton: State University of New York Press, 1983), pp. 89–113.

82. Very instructive in this regard is the work of Peter Dronke. In *Dante and Medieval Latin Traditions* (Cambridge: Cambridge University Press, 1986), he argues that the personal meanings of these final chapters of the *Purgatorio* must supercede the allegorical (pp. 55 and 81). Dronke fails to consider the possibility that the allegorical and the personal work together, however; this is unfortunate, for despite Dronke's intention of providing a "medieval reading" of the poem, the split between the allegorical and the personal—just as the split between the universal and the individual—is a modern one. See Ronald Herzman's review of *Dante and Medieval Latin Traditions* in *Studies in the Age of Chaucer* 9 (1987): 209–12.

83. Jeffrey Schnapp, *The Transfiguration of History at the Center of Dante's Paradiso* (Princeton, NJ: Princeton University Press, 1986), p. 11.

84. Davis, "Education," notes that before he was twenty Dante had probably read both the *Actus b. Francisci et sociorum eius* and Bonaventure's *Legenda maior* at Santa Croce. See *Dante's Italy*, pp. 152–53. For an excellent recent study of Dante's treatment of Bonaventure and Thomas in the circle of the Sun, see Teodolinda Barolini, "Dante's Heaven of the Sun as a Meditation on Narrative," *Lettere Italiane* 40 (1988): 3–36.

85. The apocalyptic concerns of the circle of the Sun and the Circle of Mars are examined in more detail in Ronald B. Herzman, "Dante and the Apocalypse," in *The Apocalypse in the Middle Ages*, ed. Emmerson and McGinn. See also Ronald Herzman, "Dante and Francis," *Franciscan Studies* 42 (1982): 96–114.

Chapter 5: The Canterbury Tales

1. Morton Bloomfield, *Piers Plowman as a Fourteenth-century Apocalypse* (New Brunswick, NJ: Rutgers University Press, 1961). See also, for example, Barbara Nolan, *The Gothic Visionary Perspective* (Princeton, NJ: Princeton University Press, 1977), pp. 205–58; Mary J. Carruthers, "Time, Apocalypse, and the Plot of *Piers Plowman*," in *Acts of Interpretation*, ed. Mary J. Carruthers and Elizabeth D. Kirk (Norman, OK: Pilgrim Books, 1982), pp. 175–88; Douglas Bertz, "Prophecy and Apocalypse in Langland's *Piers Plowman*, B-Text, Passus XVI–XIX," *Journal of English and Germanic Philology* 84 (1985): 313–27; and, most recently and thoroughly, Kathryn Kerby-Fulton, *Reformist Apocalypticism and Piers Plowman* (Cambridge: Cambridge University Press, 1990).

2. The reference to the "Pocalips" during the banquet scene (B.13.90) is usually identified as an allusion to the *Apocalypsis Goliae*; but see Richard K. Emmerson, "'Coveitise to Konne,' 'Goddes Privetee,' and Will's Ambiguous Visionary Experience in *Piers Plowman*," in *Visions of Piers Plowman: Essays in Honor of David C. Fowler*, ed. Míċeál F. Vaughan (East Lansing, MI: Colleagues Press, forthcoming). Kerby-Fulton, *Reformist Apocalypticism*, has once again refurbished Bloomfield's identification of the poem as an apocalypse, arguing that "the apocalypse, as

the mode of fully developed visionary narrative within the religious tradition, is perhaps the best term we have for describing these qualities and tendencies in *Piers Plowman*" (96). But, as Emmerson argues in "The Apocalypse in Medieval Culture: An Overview," in *The Apocalypse in the Middle Ages*, ed. Emmerson and McGinn, the existence of an apocalypse genre in the Middle Ages is doubtful. For more typical identifications of the poem as a dream vision, see Elizabeth Kirk, *The Dream Thought of Piers Plowman* (New Haven, CN: Yale University Press, 1972); George Economou, "The Vision's Aftermath in *Piers Plowman*: The Poetics of the Middle English Dream-Vision," *Genre* 18 (1985): 313–21; and James F. G. Weldon, "The Structure of Dream Visions in *Piers Plowman*," *Mediaeval Studies* 49 (1987): 254–81. In "The Subject of *Piers Plowman*," *The Yearbook of Langland Studies* 1 (1987): 3, David Lawton, however, warns against a simple identification of the poem as a dream vision.

3. On the poem's prophecies, see Richard Kenneth Emmerson, "The Prophetic, the Apocalyptic, and the Study of Medieval Literature," in *Poetic Prophecy in Western Literature*, ed. Jan Wojcik and Raymond-Jean Frontain (Rutherford, NJ: Fairleigh Dickinson University Press, 1984), pp. 40–54. On its portrayal of the friars, see Penn R. Szittya, *The Antifraternal Tradition in Medieval Literature* (Princeton, NJ: Princeton University Press, 1986), pp. 247–87. On the arguments of Need, see Robert Adams, "The Nature of Need in 'Piers Plowman' XX," *Traditio* 34 (1978): 273–301. For an excellent discussion of the poem's apocalyptic outlook, see Robert Adams, "Some Versions of Apocalypse: Learned and Popular Eschatology in *Piers Plowman*," in *The Popular Literature of Medieval England*, ed. Thomas J. Heffernan, Tennessee Studies in Literature 28 (Knoxville: University of Tennessee Press, 1985), 194–236.

4. Emmerson, *Antichrist*, pp. 193–203.

5. *Piers Plowman* Prol.11–16. All references to the B-text are from A. V. C. Schmidt, ed., *The Vision of Piers Plowman: A Complete Edition of the B-Text*, rev. ed. (London: Dent, 1984). The C-text makes the apocalyptic dualism even more explicit:

> Estward y beheld aftir þe sonne
> And say a tour—as y trowed, Treuthe was there-ynne.
> Westward y waytede in a while aftir
> And seigh a depe dale—Deth, as y leue,
> Woned in tho wones, and wikkede spiritus.

Derek Pearsall, ed., *Piers Plowman by William Langland: An Edition of the C-text* (Berkeley: University of California Press, 1979), Prol. 14–18.

6. *Piers Plowman* 20.121–28. We emend line 127 following E. T. Donaldson and George Kane, eds., *Piers Plowman, the B Version* (London: Athlone Press, 1975), p. 667: "And [pressed on] þe [pope] and prelates þei maden." The emendation is supported by the C-text, 20.127 (Pearsall, ed., p. 367). Those B-text manuscripts that depict the agents of Antichrist preaching to the people (followed by Schmidt, p. 253) do not significantly alter our argument, which depends

on the close association of Simony and Antichrist during the apocalyptic age of hypocrisy.

7. Pearsall, "Introduction," *Piers Plowman*, pp. 13–14; Carruthers, in *Acts of Interpretation*, p. 186.

8. Adams, "Versions of Apocalypse," p. 209. Throughout *Reformist Apocalypticism* Kerby-Fulton argues that the apocalypticism of *Piers Plowman* is closer to that reflected in high medieval reformist traditions, such as those of Hildegard of Bingen and Joachim of Fiore, than to the traditional eschatological apocalypticism which we trace to Augustine. Nevertheless, she agrees that the poem's apocalypticism is non-revolutionary. On these distinctions, see Emmerson's review of Kerby-Fulton forthcoming in *Modern Philology* 90 (Nov. 1992).

9. Other literary works developing orthodox apocalyptic resonances are studied in Valerie M. Lagorio, "The Apocalyptic Mode in the Vulgate Cycle of Arthurian Romances," *Philological Quarterly* 57 (1978): 1–22; Nolan, *Gothic Visionary Perspective*, esp. on *Pearl*, pp. 156–204; Muriel A. Whitaker, "Pearl and Some Illustrated Apocalypse Manuscripts," *Viator* 12 (1981): 183–96; and Emmerson, *Antichrist*, pp. 146–93. For an example of the pitfalls awaiting those who link apocalypticism and revolutionary movements, see Thomas J. J. Altizer, *History as Apocalypse* (Albany: State University of New York Press, 1985); and the comments in Richard K. Emmerson, "Apocalypse Now and Then," *Modern Language Quarterly* 46 (1985): 437–39.

10. For helpful studies of eschatological features in specific tales, see Míċeál F. Vaughan, "Chaucer's Imaginative One-Day Flood," *Philological Quarterly* 60 (1981): 117–23; and Bruce A. Rosenberg, "Swindling Alchemist, Antichrist," *Centennial Review* 6 (1962): 566–80. Joseph Anthony Wittreich, Jr., *Visionary Poetics: Milton's Tradition and His Legacy* (San Marino, CA: Huntington Library, 1979), has suggested that the structure of the Apocalypse is "analogous" to that of *The Canterbury Tales*, "where each panel of story adds to what precedes it, introducing a new perspective and yielding a new perception" (p. 6).

11. Thomas Wimbledon, "Redde rationem villicationis tue," ed. Ione Kemp Knight, *Wimbledon's Sermon, Redde Rationem Villicationis Tue: A Middle English Sermon of the Fourteenth Century*, Duquesne Studies, Philological Series 9 (Pittsburgh: Duquesne University Press, 1967), p. 98. All references to Wimbledon are to this edition and will be cited in the text by page number. The sermon, extant in several Middle English and Latin manuscripts, is considered one of the most important sermons delivered at Paul's Cross. See Knight's introduction, p. 1.

12. See Emmerson, *Antichrist*, pp. 42–43.

13. According to Philip Ziegler, "Contemporary chronicles abound in accusations that the years which followed the Black Death were stamped with decadence and rich in every kind of vice. The crime rate soared; blasphemy and sacrilege was a commonplace; the rules of sexual morality were flouted; the pursuit of money became the be-all and end-all of people's lives." *The Black Death* (Harmondsworth: Pelican Books, 1970), p. 279. For a contemporary (ca. 1391) complaint, see "On the Pestilence," ed. Thomas Wright, *Political Poems and Songs Relating to English History, From the Ascension of Edward III to Richard III*, Rolls Series 14 (London: Longman, 1859), I.279–81.

14. David F. Marshall, "Unmasking the Last Pilgrim: How and Why Chaucer Used the Retraction to Close *The Tales of Canterbury*," *Christianity and Literature* 31 (1982): 69.

15. For the astrological and theological significance of Libra in this passage, see Chaucey Wood, *Chaucer and the Country of the Stars: Poetic Uses of Astrological Imagery* (Princeton, NJ: Princeton University Press, 1970), pp. 275–97. Wood notes that in medieval reckoning the Parson's Tale is told "at the eleventh hour" (p. 297).

16. David Aers, *Chaucer, Langland and the Creative Imagination* (London: Routledge & Kegan Paul, 1980), p. 114. For a helpful review of early critical commentary on the "Retraction," see James D. Gordon, "Chaucer's Retraction: A Review of Opinion," in *Studies in Medieval Literature*, ed. MacEdward Leach (Philadelphia: University of Pennsylvania Press, 1961), pp. 81–96. More recent and sympathetic studies include Olive Sayce, "Chaucer's 'Retractions': The Conclusion of the *Canterbury Tales* and Its Place in Literary Tradition," *Medium Ævum* 40 (1971): 230–48; Marshall, "Unmasking the Last Pilgrim," 55–74; and Robert S. Knapp, "Penance, Irony, and Chaucer's Retraction," *Assays* 2 (1983), who argues that the Retraction is both ironic and "a religious act of penance" (p. 48). John Wall, "Penance as Poetry in the Late Fourteenth Century," in *Medieval English Religious and Ethical Literature: Essays in Honour of G. H. Russell*, ed. Gregory Kratzmann and James Simpson (Cambridge: D. S. Brewer, 1986), describes the Retraction as "a serious parody of the Pardoner's sinful exhortation to his several audiences which was followed by the approach to individuals; for the Parson's 'predicacioun' bears fruit in the individual poet's formal act of penitence" (p. 191).

17. See, for example, Edmund Reiss, "The Pilgrimage Narrative and the *Canterbury Tales*," *Studies in Philology* 67 (1970): 295–305. On the relationship of pilgrimage to other structures in *The Canterbury Tales*, see Donald R. Howard, *The Idea of the Canterbury Tales* (Berkeley: University of California Press, 1976). On the relationship between pilgrimage narratives and *The Canterbury Tales*, see Howard, *Writers and Pilgrims: Medieval Pilgrimage Narratives and their Posterity* (Berkeley: University of California Press, 1980). For the ideals of Christian pilgrimage, see F. S. Gardiner, *The Pilgrimage of Desire: A Study of Theme and Genre in Medieval Literature* (Leiden: Brill, 1971).

18. The classic statement of such an approach is R. M. Lumiansky, *Of Sondry Folk: The Dramatic Principle of the Canterbury Tales* (Austin: University of Texas Press, 1955). For a critique, see H. Marshall Leicester, Jr., *The Disenchanted Self: Representing the Subject in the Canterbury Tales* (Berkeley: University of California Press, 1990), esp. pp. 7–9.

19. Jonathan Sumption, *Pilgrimage: An Image of Mediaeval Religion* (Totowa, NJ: Rowman and Littlefield, 1975), p. 262.

20. Howard, *Writers and Pilgrims*, p. 121.

21. D. W. Robertson, Jr., *Preface to Chaucer: Studies in Medieval Perspectives* (Princeton, NJ: Princeton University Press, 1962), p. 373.

22. Augustine, *The City of God* 15.1, trans. Henry Bettenson, ed. David Knowles (Baltimore: Penguin, 1972), p. 596.

23. "Truth," 18–21, ed. in Benson, *Chaucer*, p. 653.

24. See Leonard J. Bowman, "*Itinerarium*: The Shape of the Metaphor," in *Itinerarium: The Idea of Journey*, ed. Leonard J. Bowman, Salzburg Studies in English Literature (Salzburg: Institut für Anglistik und Amerikanistik, 1983), pp. 30–31. The connection between pilgrimage and the Exodus is a critical commonplace in Dante scholarship. We include these reminders from Scripture, Augustine, and Chaucer because Chaucer scholarship usually has not considered the implications of the connection.

25. *City of God*, 18.51, ed. Knowles, p. 835.

26. Critics have repeatedly pointed to other examples of Harry Bailey's inadequacy as a leader and judge of literary merit. John V. Fleming, "Chaucer and Erasmus on the Pilgrimage to Canterbury: An Iconographical Speculation," in *The Popular Literature of Medieval England*, ed. Thomas J. Heffernan, Tennessee Studies in Literature 28 (Knoxville: University of Tennessee Press, 1985), describes the Host as "the worst interpreter of Chaucerian text to be born before the year 1800" (p. 159).

27. Howard, *Writers and Pilgrims*, p. 97. For a radically different reading of the *Canterbury Tales*, see Aers, *Creative Imagination*, who describes the pilgrimage as a "holy journey from pub to pub via Canterbury Cathedral" (p. 100).

28. Howard, *Writers and Pilgrims*, p. 97.

29. *City of God* I.35, ed. Knowles, pp. 45, 46.

30. Wall, "Penance as Poetry," in *Medieval English Religious and Ethical Literature*, p. 189.

31. The warning is V. A. Kolve's, in *Chaucer and the Imagery of Narrative: The First Five Canterbury Tales* (Stanford, CA: Stanford University Press, 1984), p. 82.

32. For a survey of the manuscript evidence, see Larry D. Benson, "The Order of *The Canterbury Tales*," *Studies in the Age of Chaucer* 3 (1981): 77–120. Benson argues that the order of the tales in the Ellesmere manuscript is "Chaucer's own final arrangement" (p. 79). For an alternate arrangement making use of the "Bradshaw Shift," see Robert A. Pratt, "The Order of the *Canterbury Tales*," *PMLA* 66 (1951): 1141–67. See also Helen Cooper's chapter on "The Ordering of the *Canterbury Tales*" in *The Structure of the Canterbury Tales* (Athens: University of Georgia Press, 1984), pp. 56–71. Although in the following discussion the order of tales corresponds roughly to that of the Ellesmere manuscript, our purpose is not to discuss the arrangment of the individual tales, but to suggest how the comic tales—perhaps even more than the overtly didactic tales—share a moral seriousness based on a common eschatological perspective.

33. Leicester, *Disenchanted Self*, p. 281, argues that the Knight's rather dark view of the human tendency toward destruction and inability to achieve order suggests "a kind of apocalyptic despair at the violent ruin human life is exposed to," a giving in to "the apocalyptic impulse to load all human misfortune into the here and now . . . ." John M. Ganim, *Chaucerian Theatricality* (Princeton: Princeton University Press, 1990), also associates the disorder of the *Knight's Tale* with "apocalyptic images" (p. 116).

34. Although we see the *Knight's Tale* as less subversive than does Joseph Westlund, we agree that this first tale provides a kind of fictional impetus for pil-

grimage. See "The *Knight's Tale* as an Impetus for Pilgrimage," *Philological Quarterly* 43 (1964): 526–37.

35. Pursuing a basically Bakhtinian reading, Ganim has recently stressed the role of parody in the *Canterbury Tales*, describing the tales "as a parody of medieval literary forms" (*Chaucerian Theatricality*, p. 106). We agree that parody is "central" to Chaucer, just as it is to the medieval apocalyptic imagination.

36. It would be rash to rely very much on evidence from dating the individual tales, but it is worth noting that many of the noble and allegorical tales were written earlier in Chaucer's career and fitted into the Canterbury framework at some later point. The comic tales, written later, represent Chaucer's final statement, his "*Paradiso.*"

37. Gail McMurray Gibson, "Resurrection as Dramatic Icon in The Shipman's Tale," *Signs and Symbols in Chaucer's Poetry*, ed. J. P. Hermann and J. J. Burke, Jr. (University: University of Alabama Press, 1981), p. 104.

38. Kolve, *Chaucer and the Imagery of Narrative*, p. 206.

39. Kolve, *Chaucer and the Imagery of Narrative*, p. 159. Kolve's repeated insistence on this point seems to be based on two unsupported assumptions: that the "cherles tale" automatically excludes interpreting "the action 'under the aspect of eternity,' in terms of good and evil, heaven or hell" (p. 160); and that Chaucer intended to limit the tale's central image to "the boundaries of the game itself" (p. 191). As numerous studies of the Miller's Tale and Chaucer's other fabliaux have shown, however, the comic and the realistic do not exclude the moral and the anagogic; furthermore, whatever the author "intended," the meaning of an iconographic image is rarely restricted to narrow boundaries. For a critique of Kolve's *Chaucer and the Imagery of Narrative*, see our review in *Studies in the Age of Chaucer* 7 (1985): 212–18.

40. Kelsie B. Harder, "Chaucer's Use of the Mystery Play Tradition in the *Miller's Tale*," *Modern Language Notes* 17 (1956): 193–98, although citing the parodic affinities between the tale and the story of Noah as comically staged in the cycle plays, fails to note their larger implications. Many critics have shown how parody and inversion are consistently woven into the poem for serious purposes. See, for example, Paul E. Beichner, C.S.C., "Absolon's Hair," *Mediaeval Studies* 12 (1950): 222–33; John J. O'Connor, "The Astrological Background of the *Miller's Tale*," *Speculum* 31 (1956): 120–25; and Jesse M. Gellrich, "The Parody of Medieval Music in the *Miller's Tale*," *JEGP* 23 (1974): 176–88. In his study of Chaucer's parodic use of the *Canticum Canticorum*, Robert E. Kaske sets forth a principle that we believe applies to the poet's parody of other biblical language, events, and characters: "A medieval poet, alluding to what is perhaps the most consistently allegorized work in the Middle Ages would be alluding clumsily indeed if he did not either permit the implications following from its extra literal significance, or take postive steps to mute them." See "The *Canticum Canticorum* in the *Miller's Tale*," *Studies in Philology* 59 (1962): 449.

41. Vaughan, "Chaucer's Imaginative One-Day Flood," *Philological Quarterly* 60 (1981): 117–23.

42. See Ronald B. Herzman, "Millstones: An Approach to the *Miller's Tale* and the *Reeve's Tale*," *English Record* 18 (1977): 18–21, 26. For a systematic review

of the exegetical tradition connected with the "Mystic Mill," see Anthony K. Cassell's discussion and notes in *Dante's Fearful Art of Justice* (Toronto: University of Toronto Press, 1984), pp. 100 ff. In his discussion of the visual imagery of the Reeve's Tale, Kolve considers the Mill as a "subordinate" image (p. 363). This view seems more a consequence of rejecting the tale's theological resonances than of accurately assessing the mill's importance.

43. Fisher, *The Complete Poetry and Prose of Geoffrey Chaucer*, 2nd ed. (New York: Holt, Rinehart, Winston, 1989), p. 71, note to line 3941.

44. See also Ronald B. Herzman, "The *Reeve's Tale*, Symkyn, and Simon the Magician," *The American Benedictine Review* 33 (1982): 325–33.

45. Gibson, "Resurrection as Dramatic Icon in *The Shipman's Tale*," p. 109.

46. Mary's experience was consistently glossed in the Middle Ages as a conversion story. See William A. Stephany, "Biblical Allusions to Conversion in *Purgatorio XXI*," *Stanford Italian Review* 3 (1983): 149–51.

47. F. C. Gardiner, *Pilgrimage of Desire*, p. 39. See also Stephany, "Biblical Allusions to Conversion," pp. 148–49.

48. Compare Luke 24:30 ("Et factum est, dum recumberet eum eis, accepit panem, et benedixit, ac fregit et porrigebat illis") with the account of the establishment of the Eucharist in Matt. 26:26 ("Coenantibus autem eis, accepit Jesus panem, et benedexit, ac fregit, deditque discipulis suis . . . ").

49. This point was suggested indirectly in an article that traces connections between the tale and the final cantos of the *Inferno*, a section of the *Commedia* with rich Eucharistic resonances. See Ronald B. Herzman, "The *Friar's Tale*: Chaucer, Dante, and the *Translatio Studii*," *ACTA* 9 (1985): 1–17.

50. The phrase is Szittya's, *Antifraternal Tradition*, p. 32; see also pp. 232–38. For earlier studies, see John V. Fleming, "The Summoner's Prologue: An Iconographic Adjustment," *Chaucer Review* 2 (1967): 95–107; and Alan Levitan, "The Parody of Pentecost in Chaucer's *Summoner's Tale*," *University of Toronto Quarterly* 40 (1971): 236–46.

51. On the eschatological dimension of the parodic Pentecost, see Emmerson, *Antichrist*, pp. 24, 132–33, 141, 285; and Szittya, *Antifraternal Tradition*, pp. 245–46.

52. Fleming, "Summoner's Prologue," p. 106.

53. In "Swindling Alchemist, Antichrist," Bruce Rosenberg describes the Canon as "the spirit of the antichrist stalking fourteenth-century England" (p. 580).

54. See Malcolm Pittock, "The Pardoner's Tale and the Quest of Death," *Essays in Criticism* 24 (1974): 107–23.

55. Peter G. Beidler has recently pointed to several allusions to the plague in the Pardoner's Tale; see "The Plague and Chaucer's Pardoner," *Chaucer Review* 16 (1982): 257–69.

56. See, for example, the extended discussion of the relationship of the Pardoner to Faus Semblant in P. M. Kean, *Chaucer and the Making of English Poetry* (London: Routledge and Kegan Paul, 1972), 2:96–109. The identification was first made by Dean S. Fansler, *Chaucer and the Roman de la Rose*, Columbia University Studies in English and Comparative Literature 7 (New York: Columbia University

Press, 1914; rpt. Gloucester, MA: Peter Smith, 1965), pp. 162–66. See also James L. Calderwood, "Parody in the *Pardoner's Tale*," *English Studies* 45 (1964): 302; Felicity Currie, "Chaucer's Pardoner Again," *Leeds Studies in English* 4 (1971): 11–22; and Jane Chance, "'Disfigured is thy Face': Chaucer's Pardoner and the Protean Shape-Shifter Fals-Semblant," *Philological Quarterly* 67 (1988): 423–35.

57. Leicester, *Disenchanted Self*, p. 55.

58. For the rivalry between the Pardoner and Host, see Stephen A. Khinoy, "Inside Chaucer's Pardoner?" *Chaucer Review* 6 (1972): 255–67; Robert E. Jungman, "The Pardoner's Quarrel with the Host," *Philological Quarterly* 55 (1976): 279–81; and Marc Glasser, "The Pardoner and the Host: Chaucer's Analysis of the Canterbury Game," *CEA Critic* 46 (1983–84): 37–45.

59. "Of Prelates," 5, ed. F. D. Matthew, *The English Works of Wyclif, Hitherto Unprinted* EETS 74 (1880), pp. 66–67.

60. For an extented discussion of the opposition between Pardoner and Parson, see Howard, *Idea of Canterbury Tales*, pp. 333–87.

61. For the Pardoner as showman, see Howard, *Idea of Canterbury Tales*, pp. 345–49.

62. Lawrence Besserman notes that "throughout the Prologue and Tale, the Bible serves the Pardoner as a disguise; it is the cloak behind which he goes about his work as a self-proclaimed apostle of Antichrist." See "Chaucer and the Bible: Parody and Authority in the *Pardoner's Tale*," in David H. Hirsch and Nehama Aschkenasy, eds., *Biblical Patterns in Modern Literature*, Brown Judaic Studies 77 (Chico, CA: Scholars Press, 1984), p. 48.

63. See Raymond E. Brown and John P. Meier, *Antioch and Rome: New Testament Cradles of Catholic Christianity* (New York: Paulist Press, 1983), pp. 205–8.

64. See Emmerson, *Antichrist*, pp. 90–91.

65. Of the ME forms of *bull*—"bole, bule, bulle"—"bole" and "bule" (from OE "bula") usually refer to the animal, and "bulle" (from Latin "bulla") usually refers to the papal documents. The plural form, "bulles," is the same for both terms.

66. We are not suggesting that these psychological readings are invalid or even secondary, but rather that Chaucer has it both ways. As we saw in chapter 4, Nicholas III, Dante's simoniac pope, likewise boasts of his sins in his inverted confession in *Inferno* 19. Such similarities suggest that the conjuction between simony, false confession, and boasting is more than simply Chaucer's own variation on a theme.

67. See Thomas Aquinas, *Summa Theologiae* 3a.65.3 and 3a.73.3 for a discussion of the meaning and importance of the Eucharist which emphasizes these aspects. For Thomas the Eucharist is the crown and culmination of the sacraments.

68. "Chaucer's Pardoner and the Mass," *Chaucer Review* 6 (1972): 183. Miller and Bosse point out that a line spoken by one of the rioters ("Now let us sitte and drink and make us merry" [VI.883]) is a paraphrase of Paul's account of the chosen people feasting and worshipping the Golden Calf (Ex. 32:4) and a warning against idolatry: "Neque idololatrae efficiamini, sicut quidam ex ipsis, quemadmodum scriptum est: 'Sedit populus manducare et bibere, et surrexerunt ludere'" (1 Cor. 10:7). The echo of Exodus 32:4 supports our reading of the Golden Calf story as

crucially important in the tale. See also Joseph R. Millichap, "Transubstantiation in the *Pardoner's Tale*," *Bulletin of the Rocky Mountain Modern Language Association* 28 (1974): 104–8; and Rodney Delasanta, "Sacrament and Sacrifice in the Pardoner's Tale," *Annuale Mediaevale* 14 (1973): 43–52.

69. Although not relating it to the Simon Magus tradition, Charles A. Owen stressed the importance of this passage to the Pardoner's life in "The Crucial Passages in Five of *The Canterbury Tales*: A Study of Irony and Symbol," *JEGP* 52 (1953): 294–311.

70. See Monica E. McAlpine, "The Pardoner's Homosexuality and How It Matters," *PMLA* 95 (1980): 8–22.

71. "Of Prelates," *English Works of Wyclif*, p. 68. See Jill Mann, *Chaucer and Medieval Estates Satire: The Literature of Social Classes and the General Prologue to the Canterbury Tales* (Cambridge: Cambridge University Press, 1973), pp. 145–47; and Terrence A. McVeigh, "Chaucer's Portraits of the Pardoner and Summoner and Wyclif's *Tractatus de Simonia*," *Classical Folia* 20 (1974): 54–58.

72. There is some scholarly debate concerning the Summoner's leprosy. See Walter Clyde Curry, *Chaucer and the Medieval Sciences*, rev. ed. (New York: Barnes & Noble, 1960), pp. 37–47; and Saul Nathaniel Brody, *The Disease of the Soul: Leprosy in Medieval Literature* (Ithaca: Cornell University Press, 1974), p. 12. The Summoner's simony, of course, is clearly evident in his portrait in the General Prologue. That this portrait "owes a good deal to Jean de Meun, and in particular to Jean's most brilliant creation, Faussemblant . . . ," further connects him to the Pardoner. See John V. Fleming, "Chaucer and the Visual Arts of His Time," in *New Perspectives in Chaucer Criticism*, ed. Donald M. Rose (Norman, OK: Pilgrim Books, 1981), p. 135. The link between the Summoner and Pardoner, together with the link between the Summoner and Friar that is instrumental to their respective tales, suggests that the Pardoner's Tale should not be read in isolation. In their comic tales these pilgrims represent a unified treatment of the key themes of penance and pilgrimage. The fact that the Friar is the other character in *The Canterbury Tales* whose literary origins can be traced to Faus Semblant further links him to the Pardoner.

73. See Hans-Jurgen Horn, "Giezie und Simonie," *Jahrbuch für Antike und Christentum* 8/9 (1965/66): 189–202.

74. "Licet eger cum egrotis," lines 9–16, ed. and trans. George F. Whicher, *The Goliard Poets: Medieval Latin Songs and Satires* (New York: New Directions, 1949), pp. 132–33. For a similar coupling of Simon Magus and Gehezi, see John Lydgate's translation of Deguileville's *Pèlerinage*, *The Pilgrimage of the Life of Man*, line 17,940, ed. F. J. Furnivall, EETS es 77, 83, 92 (London: Kegan Paul, 1899–1904), p. 480.

Bibliography

Primary Sources

Actus Petri cum Simone. Ed. R. A. Lipsius and M. Bonnet. *Acta apostolorum apocrypha post Constantinum*. Leipzig, 1891. 1:45–103.

Adso of Montier-en-Der. *Libellus de Antichristo*. Ed. Daniel Verhelst. *Adso Dervensis, De ortu et tempore Antichristi*. CCCM 45. 1976.

———. Trans. John Wright. *The Play of Antichrist*. Toronto: Pontifical Institute of Mediaeval Studies, 1967. Pp. 100–110.

Anselm of Havelberg. *Dialogues*. Ed. G. Salet. SC 118. Paris, 1966.

Der Antichrist und die fünfzehn Zeichen. Ed. H. Th. Musper. 2 vols. Munich: Prestel Verlag, 1970.

Der Antichrist und die fünfzehn Zeichen vor dem Jüngsten Gericht. Ed. Karin Boveland, Christoph Peter Burger, Ruth Steffen. 2 vols. Hamburg: Friedrich Wittig, 1979.

L'Apocalypse en Français au xiiiᵉ siècle. Ed. L. Delisle and P. Meyer. Société des anciens textes français 44. 2 vols. Paris: Firmin Didot, 1900–1901.

Apocalypsis Goliae. Ed. Karl Strecker. *Die Apokalypse des Golias*. Texte zur Kulturgeschichte des Mittelalters 5. Rome: W. Regenberg, 1928.

———. Trans. F. X. Newman. In *The Literature of Medieval England*. Ed. D. W. Robertson, Jr. New York: McGraw-Hill, 1970. Pp. 253–61.

Apokalypse, MS. Douce 180, Bodleian Library, Oxford. Ed. Peter Klein. Codices Selecti 72. Graz: Akademische Druck-u. Verlagsanstalt, 1981.

Arnold of Villanova. *Tractatus de tempore adventus Antichristi*. Ed. Heinrich Finke. *Aus den Tagen Bonifaz VIII: Funde und Forschungen*. Vorreformationsgeschichtliche Forschungen 2. Münster: Aschendorff, 1902.

Augustine. *De civitate Dei*. CCSL 48.

———. *De civitate Dei*. Trans. Henry Bettenson, ed. David Knowles. *The City of God*. Baltimore: Penguin, 1972.

———. *De doctrina Christiana*. Trans. D. W. Robertson, Jr. *On Christian Doctrine*. Indianapolis: Bobbs-Merrill, 1958.

———. "Homily on the First Epistle of St. John." *Augustine*. Ed. Mary T. Clark. Classics of Western Spirituality. New York: Paulist Press, 1984.

———. *Tractatus in epistolam Ioannis ad Parthos*. PL 35: 1977–2062.

Bede. *Explanatio Apocalypsis*. PL 93:129–206.

———. *Explanatio Apocalypsis*. Trans. Edw. Marshall. Oxford: James Parker, 1878.

———. *De temporum ratione*. PL 90:295–578.

Benvenuto da Imola. *Commentum super Dantis Aldigherij Comoediam.* Ed. Giacomo Filippo Lacaita. 2 vols. Florence: G. Barbera, 1887.

Berengaudus. *Expositio super septem visiones libri Apocalypsis.* PL 17:843–1058.

Berengier. *De l'avenement Antecrist.* Ed. E. Walberg. *Deux versions inédites de la légende de l'Antéchrist en vers français du xiii⁰ siècle.* Lund: C. W. K. Gleerup, 1928.

Bernard of Clairvaux. *De Consideratione.* Trans. John D. Anderson and Elizabeth T. Kennan. *Five Books On Consideration: Advice to a Pope.* The Works of Bernard of Clairvaux 13. Kalamazoo, MI: Cistercian Publications, 1976.

———. *On the Song of Songs.* Trans. Kilian Walsh. Works of Bernard of Clairvaux 3. Kalamazoo, MI: Cistercian Publication, 1976.

Bernardino of Siena. *Opera omnia.* 4 vols. Florence: Typographia Collegii S. Bonaventurae, 1950–56.

Bible. *Bibliorum sacrorum iuxta Vulgatum Clementinam, nova editio.* Ed. Aloisius Gramatica. Rome: Vatican City, 1959.

Bible Moralisée. Consèrvé á Oxford, Paris et Londres. Ed. Alexandre de Laborde. Paris: Société française de reproductions de manuscrits à peintures, 1911–27.

Biblia Pauperum: Vatican Library Pal. Lat. 871. Ed. Karl-August Wirth. Zurich: Belser Verlag, 1982.

Bonaventure. *Collationes in Hexaemeron.* Ed. A. Parma. *Opera omnia.* Vol. 5. *Opuscula Varia Theologica.* Florence: Quaracchi, 1896.

———. *Collations on the Six Days.* Trans. José de Vinck. *The Works of Bonaventure.* Vol. 5. Paterson, NJ: St. Anthony Guild Press, 1970.

———. *Legenda Maior S. Francisci Assisiensis et eiusdem Legenda Minor.* Ed. Collegii S. Bonaventurae. Florence: Quaracchi, 1941.

———. *Legenda Maior.* Trans. Ewert Cousins. Classics of Western Spirituality. New York: Paulist Press, 1978.

Bruno of Segni. *Commentaria in Matthaeum.* PL 165:65–314.

Das Buch von dem Entkrist. Ed. Kurt Pfister. Leipzig: Insel Verlag, 1925.

Chaucer, Geoffrey. *The Complete Poetry and Prose of Geoffrey Chaucer.* 2nd ed. Ed. John H. Fisher. New York: Holt, Rinehart, Winston, 1989.

———. *The Riverside Chaucer.* 3rd ed. Larry D. Benson, gen. ed. Boston: Houghton Mifflin, 1987.

The Chester Mystery Cycle. Ed. R. M. Lumiansky and David Mills. EETS SS 3 (1974).

Dante Alighieri. *The Divine Comedy.* Ed. and trans. Charles S. Singleton. 3 vols. Bollingen Series 80. Princeton: Princeton University Press, 1970.

Der Enndkrist der Stadt-Bibliothek zu Frankfurt am Main. Ed. Ernst Kelchner. Frankfurt: Frankfurter Lichdruckanstalt Wiesbaden, 1891.

Francis of Assisi. *St. Francis of Assisi: Writings and Early Biographies, English Omnibus of the Sources for the Life of St. Francis.* Ed. Marion A. Habig. Chicago: Franciscan Herald Press, 1973.

———. *Die Opuscula des Hl. Franziscus von Assisi.* Ed. Kajetan Esser. Grottaferrata: Collegium S. Bonaventurae, 1976.

Glossa ordinaria: Biblia sacra cum glossis interlineari, et ordinaria, Nicolai Lyrani postilla, ac moralitalibus, Burgensis additionibus et Thoringi replicis. 7 vols. Venice, 1588.

The Goliard Poets: Medieval Latin Songs and Satires. Ed. George F. Whicher. New York: New Directions, 1949.

Gregory the Great. *Moralia*. PL 75:509–76:782.

Grosseteste, Robert. *Hexaëmeron*. Ed. Richard C. Dales and Servus Gieben. British Academy, Auctores Britannici Medii Aevi 6. London: Oxford University Press, 1982.

Guido da Pisa. *Expositiones et Glose super Comediam Dantis*. Ed. Vincenzo Cioffari. Albany: State University of New York Press, 1974.

Guillaume de Lorris and Jean de Meun. *Le Roman de la rose*. Ed. Félix Lecoy. Les Classiques Français du Moyen Age, 92, 95, 98. 3 vols. Paris: Librairie Honoré Champion, 1966–82.

———. *The Romance of the Rose*. Trans. Charles Dahlberg. 1971; rpt. Hanover, NH: University Press of New England, 1983.

Guillaume de Saint-Amour. *De periculis novissimorum temporum. Opera omnia*. Constance (Paris), 1632.

Haimo of Auxerre. *Expositio in Apocalypsin*. PL 117:937–1220.

Hennecke, Edgar, and Wilhelm Schneemelcher, eds. *New Testament Apocrypha*. 2 vols. Philadelphia: Westminster Press, 1963.

Herrad of Hohenbourg. *Hortus Deliciarum*. Ed. R. Green, M. Evans, C. Bischoff, and M. Curschmann. *Herrad of Hohenbourg: Hortus Deliciarum*. Studies of the Warburg Institute 36. 2 vols. London: Warburg Institute, 1979.

Hugh of Saint Cher. *Opera omnia in universum Vetus et Novum Testamentum*. Lyon, 1645.

Hugh of Strassburg. *Compendium theologicae veritatis*. Ed. S. A. Borgnet. *B. Alberti Magni . . . Opera omnia*. Vol. 34. Paris, 1896.

Jacobus da Voragine. *Legenda aurea*. Ed. Th. Graesse. 1890; rpt. Osnabruck: Otto Zeller, 1969.

———. Trans. Granger Ryan and Helmut Ripperger. *The Golden Legend*. 1941; rpt. New York: Arno Press, 1969.

Jacopone da Todi. *The Lauds*. Trans. Serge and Elizabeth Hughes. Classics of Western Spirituality. New York: Paulist Press, 1982.

Jerome. *De Antichristo in Danielem*. Ed. François Glorie. CCSL 75A.

———. Trans. Gleason L. Archer, Jr. *Jerome's Commentary on Daniel*. 1958; rpt. Grand Rapids: Baker Book House, 1977.

———. *Commentariorum in Esaiam*. Ed. Marcus Adriaen. CCSL 73.

Joachim of Fiore. *De Ultimis Tribulationibus*. Ed. E. Randolph Daniel. "Abbot Joachim of Fiore: The *De Ultimis Tribulationibus*." In *Prophecy and Millenarianism: Essays in Honour of Marjorie Reeves*. Ed. Ann Williams. London: Longman, 1980. Pp. 165–89.

———. *Enchiridion super Apocalypsim*. Ed. Edward K. Burger. Studies and Texts 78. Toronto: Pontifical Institute of Mediaeval Studies, 1986.

———. *Expositio in Apocalypsim*. Venice, 1527; repr. Frankfurt: Minerva, 1964.

———. *Liber concordie Novi ac Veteris Testamenti*. Venice, 1519; rpt. Frankfurt: Minerva, 1964.

———. *Liber de Concordia Noui ac Veteris Testamenti*. Ed. E. Randolph Daniel. *Abbot Joachim of Fiore: Liber de Concordia Noui ac Veteris Testamenti. Transac-*

tions of the American Philosophical Society. Vol. 73.8. Philadelphia: American Philosophical Society, 1983.

————. *Il Libro delle figure dell'abate Gioachino da Fiore*. Ed. Leone Tondelli, Marjorie Reeves, and Beatrice Hirsch-Reich. 2nd ed. Turin: Società Editrice Internazionale, 1953.

Le Jour du Jugement: Mystère français sur le Grand Schisme. Ed. Emile Roy. Études sur le théatre français au xiv⁴ siècle. Paris: Emile Bouillon, 1902.

Langland, William. *Piers Plowman, the B Version*. Ed. E. T. Donaldson and George Kane. London: Athlone Press, 1975.

————. *Piers Plowman by William Langland: An Edition of the C-text* Ed. Derek Pearsall. Berkeley: University of California Press, 1979.

————. *The Vision of Piers Plowman: A Complete Edition of the B-Text*. Ed. A. V. C. Schmidt. Rev. ed. London: J. M. Dent, 1984.

Lotario dei Segni (Innocent III). *De miseria condicionis humane*. Ed. Robert E. Lewis. The Chaucer Library. Athens: University of Georgia Press, 1978.

Ludus de Antichristo. Ed. Gerhard Günther. *Der Antichrist: Der staufische Ludus de Antichristo*. Hamburg: Friedrich Wittig, 1970.

————. Trans. John Wright. *The Play of Antichrist*. Toronto: Pontifical Institute of Mediaeval Studies, 1967.

Lydgate, John. *The Pilgrimage of the Life of Man*. Ed. F. J. Furnivall. EETS ES 77, 83, 92.

Martin of Leon. *Expositio libri Apocalypsis*. PL 209 : 299–420.

McGinn, Bernard, ed. *Apocalyptic Spirituality*. Classics of Western Spirituality. New York: Paulist, 1979.

————. *Visions of the End: Apocalyptic Traditions in the Middle Ages*. Records of Civilization: Sources and Studies 96. New York: Columbia University Press, 1979.

Nicholas of Lyra. *Postilla*. In *Glossa ordinaria*.

Olivi, Peter John. *Expositio super regulam*. Ed. David Flood. *Olivi's Rule Commentary*. Wiesbaden, 1972.

The Pamplona Bibles. Ed. F. Bucher. New Haven, CN: Yale University Press, 1970.

Petrarch, Francis. Letter XVIII. Trans. Robert Coogan. *Babylon on the Rhone: A Translation of Letters by Dante, Petrarch, and Catherine of Siena on the Avignon Papacy*. Studia Humanitatis. Madrid: Jose Porrua Turanzas, 1983.

————. *Rime, Trionfi, e Poesie Latine*. Ed. Ferdinando Neri. La Letteratura Italiana Storia e Testi 6. Milan: Riccardo Ricciardi Editore, 1951.

————. *The Sonnets of Petrarch*. Trans. Joseph Auslander. London: Longmans, Green, 1931.

Pseudo-Clementine Homily. Ed. B. Rehm. Die griechischen christlichen Schriftsteller der ersten drei Jahrhunderte 42.

Rabanus Maurus. *Commentaria in libros Machabaeorum*. PL 109 : 1125–1256.

Richard of Saint Victor. *In Apocalypsim Ioannis*. PL 196 : 683–888.

Rutebeuf. *Oeuvres complètes de Rutebeuf*. Ed. Edmond Faral and Julia Bastin. Paris: Picard, 1969.

"Satire contre les differents états." Ed. Edelstand du Meril. *Poésies inédites du moyen âge*. Paris, 1854.

Schedel, Hartmann. *Liber chronicarum*. Nuremberg, 1493.

Tertullian. *De Anima*. PL 2:681–798.

Thomas Aquinas. *Summa theologiae*. Ed. and trans. Roland Potter. New York: McGraw Hill, 1970.

Tyconius. *The Book of Rules of Tyconius*. Ed. F. C. Burkitt. Texts and Studies: Contributions to Biblical and Patristic Literature 3.1. Cambridge: Cambridge University Press, 1894.

Ubertino da Casale. *Arbor vite crucifixe Jesu*. Venice, 1485.

Velislav Bible. *Velislai Biblia picta*. Ed. Karel Stejskal. Editio Cimelia Bohemica 12. Prague: Progopress, 1970.

Wakefield, Walter L. and Austin P. Evans, eds. *Heresies of the High Middle Ages*. Records of Civilization: Sources and Studies 81. New York: Columbia University Press, 1969.

Wimbledon, Thomas. "Redde rationem villicationis tue." Ed. Ione Kemp Knight. *Wimbledon's Sermon, Redde Rationem Villicationis Tue: A Middle English Sermon of the Fourteenth Century*. Duquesne Studies, Philological Series 9. Pittsburgh: Duquesne University Press, 1967.

Wright, Thomas, ed. *Political Poems and Songs Relating to English History, From the Ascension of Edward III to Richard III*. 2 vols. Rolls Series 14. London: Longman, 1859.

Wyclif, John. *The English Works of Wyclif, Hitherto Unprinted*. Ed. F. D. Matthew. EETS 74 (1880).

SECONDARY SOURCES

Adams, Robert. "The Nature of Need in 'Piers Plowman' XX." *Traditio* 34 (1978): 273–301.

———. "Some Versions of Apocalypse: Learned and Popular Eschatology in *Piers Plowman*." In *The Popular Literature of Medieval England*. Ed. Thomas J. Heffernan. Tennessee Studies in Literature 28. Knoxville: University of Tennessee Press, 1985. Pp. 194–236.

Aers, David. *Chaucer, Langland and the Creative Imagination*. London: Routledge & Kegan Paul, 1980.

Altizer, Thomas J. J. *History as Apocalypse*. Albany: State University of New York Press, 1985.

Armstrong, Regis J. "The Spiritual Theology of the *Legenda Major* of St. Bonaventure." Dissertation, Fordham University, 1978.

Auerbach, Erich. "St. Francis of Assisi in Dante's *Commedia*." *Italica* 22 (1945): 166–79.

Badel, Pierre-Yves. *Le Roman de la Rose au XIVᵉ siècle: Étude de la réception de l'oeuvre*. Geneva: Droz, 1980.

Barolini, Teodolinda. "Dante's Heaven of the Sun as a Meditation on Narrative." *Lettere Italiane* 40 (1988): 3–36.

Beichner, Paul E., C.S.C. "Absolon's Hair." *Mediaeval Studies* 12 (1950): 222–33.

Beidler, Peter G. "The Plague and Chaucer's Pardoner." *Chaucer Review* 16 (1982): 257–69.

Benson, Larry D. "The Order of *The Canterbury Tales*." *Studies in the Age of Chaucer* 3 (1981): 77–120.

Bertz, Douglas. "Prophecy and Apocalypse in Langland's *Piers Plowman*, B-Text, Passus XVI-XIX." *Journal of English and Germanic Philology* 84 (1985): 313–27.

Besserman, Lawrence. "Chaucer and the Bible: Parody and Authority in the *Pardoner's Tale*." In *Biblical Patterns in Modern Literature*. Ed. David H. Hirsch and Nehama Aschkenasy. Brown Judaic Studies 77. Chico, CA: Scholars Press, 1984. Pp. 43–50.

Bihel, S. "S. Franciscus fuitne Angelus sexti sigilli?" *Antonianum* 2 (1927): 29–70.

Bisogni, Fabio. "Problemi Iconografici Riminesi: Le storie dell' Anticristo in S. Maria in Porto Fuori." *Paragone* 305 (July 1975): 13–23.

Bischoff, Guntram. "Early Premonstratensian Eschatology: The Apocalyptic Myth." In *The Spirituality of Western Christendom*. Ed. E. Rozanne Elder. Kalamazoo, MI: Medieval Institute Publications, 1976. Pp. 41–71.

Bloomfield, Morton W. "Joachim of Flora: A Critical Survey of his Canon, Teachings, Sources, Bibliography and Influence." *Traditio* 13 (1957): 249–311.

———. *Piers Plowman as a Fourteenth-century Apocalypse*. New Brunswick: Rutgers University Press, 1961.

———. "Recent Scholarship on Joachim of Fiore and His Influence." In *Prophecy and Millenarianism*. Ed. Williams. Pp. 21–52.

Bloomfield, Morton W., and Marjorie Reeves. "The Penetration of Joachism into Northern Europe." *Speculum* 29 (1954): 772–93.

Blumenfeld-Kosinski, Renate. "Illustration as Commentary in Late Medieval Images of Antichrist's Birth." *Deutsche Vierteljahrsschrift für Literaturwissenschaft und Geistesgeschichte* 63 (1989): 589–607.

Bousset, Wilhelm. *The Antichrist Legend*. Trans. A. H. Keane. London: Hutchinson, 1896.

Bowman, Leonard J. "*Itinerarium*: The Shape of the Metaphor." In *Itinerarium: The Idea of Journey*. Ed. Leonard J. Bowman. Salzburg Studies in English Literature. Salzburg: Institut für Anglistik und Amerikanistik, 1983. Pp. 3–33.

Bright, Pamela. *The Book of Rules of Tyconius: Its Purpose and Inner Logic*. Notre Dame, IN: University of Notre Dame Press, 1988.

Brody, Saul Nathaniel. *The Disease of the Soul: Leprosy in Medieval Literature*. Ithaca, NY: Cornell University Press, 1974.

Brown, Raymond E., and John P. Meier. *Antioch and Rome: New Testament Cradles of Catholic Christianity*. New York: Paulist Press, 1983.

Burr, David. "The Apocalyptic Element in Olivi's Critique of Aristotle." *Church History* 40 (1971): 15–29.

———. "Bonaventure, Olivi and Franciscan Eschatology." *Collectanea Franciscana* 53 (1983): 23–40.

———. "Franciscan Exegesis and Francis as Apocalyptic Figure." In *Monks, Nuns, and Friars in Mediaeval Society*. Ed. Edward B. King, Jacqueline T. Schaefer, and William B. Wadley. Sewanee, TN: The Press of the University of the South, 1989. Pp. 51–62.

————. *Olivi and Franciscan Poverty*. Philadelphia: University of Pennsylvania Press, 1989.

————. "Olivi, Apocalyptic Expectation, and Visionary Experience." *Traditio* 41 (1985): 273–88.

————. "Olivi, the *Lectura super Apocalypsim*, and Franciscan Exegetical Tradition." In *Francescanesimo e Cultura Universitaria*. Atti del XVI Convegno internazionale , Assisi, 13–15 ottobre 1988. Pp. 115–35.

————. "Olivi's Apocalyptic Timetable." *Journal of Medieval and Renaissance Studies* 11 (1981): 237–60.

Calderwood, James L. "Parody in the *Pardoner's Tale*." *English Studies* 45 (1964): 302–9.

Carli, Enzo. *Il Duomo di Orvieto*. Rome: Instituto Poligrafico della Stato, 1965.

————. *Luca Signorelli: Gli Affreschi nel Duomo di Orvieto*. Bergamo: Instituto Italiano d'Arti Grafiche, 1946.

Carruthers, Mary J. "Time, Apocalypse, and the Plot of *Piers Plowman*." In *Acts of Interpretation*. Ed. Mary J. Carruthers and Elizabeth D. Kirk. Norman, OK: Pilgrim Books, 1982. Pp. 175–88.

Cassell, Anthony K. *Dante's Fearful Art of Justice*. Toronto: University of Toronto Press, 1984.

Chance, Jane. "'Disfigured is thy Face': Chaucer's Pardoner and the Protean Shape-Shifter Fals-Semblant." *Philological Quarterly* 67 (1988): 423–35.

Chastel, André. "L'Antéchrist à la Renaissance." In *L'Umanesimo e li demonico, Atti del II Congresso Internazionale di Studi Umanistici*. Ed. Enrico Castelli. Roma: Fratelli Bocca Editori, 1952. Pp. 177–86.

————. "L'Apocalypse en 1500: La fresque de l'Antéchrist à la Chapelle Saint-Brice d'Orvieto." *Bibliothèque d'humanisme et renaissance* 14 (1952): 124–40.

Chenu, M.-D. *Nature, Man, and Society in the Twelfth Century: Essays on New Theological Perspectives in the Latin West*. Trans. Jerome Taylor and Lester K. Little. Chicago: University of Chicago Press, 1968.

Cherniss, Michael D. *Boethian Apocalypse: Studies in Middle English Vision Poetry*. Norman, OK: Pilgrim Books, 1987.

Clasen, Sophronius. "Einteilung und Anliegen der Legenda maior s. Francisci Bonaventuras." *Franciscan Studies* 27 (1967): 115–62.

Cook, William R. "Tradition and Perfection: Monastic Typology in Bonaventure's *Life of St. Francis*." *American Benedictine Review* 33 (1982): 1–20.

Cooper, Helen. *The Structure of the Canterbury Tales*. Athens: University of Georgia Press, 1984.

Cousins, Ewert H. *Bonaventure and the Coincidence of Opposites*. Chicago: Franciscan Herald Press, 1978.

————. "The Coincidence of Opposites in the Christology of Saint Bonaventure." *Franciscan Studies* 28 (1968): 27–45.

Crocco, Antonio, ed. *L'età dello Spirito e la fine dei tempi in Gioacchino da Fiore e nel gioachimismo medievale*. Atti del II Congresso internazionale di Studi Gioachimiti (1984). San Giovanni in Fiore: Centro internazionale di Studi Gioachimiti, 1986.

Currie, Felicity. "Chaucer's Pardoner Again." *Leeds Studies in English* 4 (1971): 11–22.

Curry, Walter Clyde. *Chaucer and the Mediaeval Sciences*. Rev. ed. New York: Barnes & Noble, 1960.

Dahlberg, Charles. *The Literature of Unlikeness*. Hanover, NH: University Press of New England, 1988.

Damiata, Marino. *Pietà e Storia nell'Arbor Vitae di Ubertino da Casale*. Florence: Edizioni 'Studi Francescani,' 1988.

Daniel, E. Randolph. "Abbot Joachim of Fiore: The *De Ultimis Tribulationibus*." In *Prophecy and Millenarianism*. Ed. Williams. Pp. 165–89.

———. "Apocalyptic Conversion: The Joachite Alternative to the Crusades." *Traditio* 25 (1969): 127–54.

———. "The Double Procession of the Holy Spirit in Joachim of Fiore's Understanding of History." *Speculum* 55 (1980): 469–83.

———. "A Re-Examination of the Origins of Franciscan Joachitism." *Speculum* 43 (1968): 671–76.

———. "St. Bonaventure a Faithful Disciple of St. Francis? A Reexamination of the Question." In *S. Bonaventura 1274–1974*. Ed. Jacques Guy Bougerol. Grottaferrata: Collegio S. Bonaventura, 1974. 2:171–87.

———. "St. Bonaventure: Defender of Franciscan Eschatology." In *S.Bonaventura 1274–1974*. Ed. Jacques Guy Bougerol. Grottaferrata: Collegio S. Bonaventura, 1974. 4:793–806.

———. "St. Bonaventure's Debt to Joachim." *Medievalia et Humanistica* n.s. 11 (1982): 61–75.

Davis, Charles T. *Dante and the Idea of Rome*. Oxford: Oxford University Press, 1957.

———. *Dante's Italy and Other Essays*. Philadelphia: University of Pennsylvania Press, 1984.

de Fraja, Valeria. "Gioacchino da Fiore: bibliografia 1969–1988." *Florensia* 2 (1988): 7–59.

de Maio, R. "Savonarola, Alessandro VI e il mito dell'Anticristo." *Rivista storica italiana* 82 (1970): 533–59.

de Lubac, Henri. *Exégèse médiévale: les quatre sens de l'Écriture*. 2 vols. Paris: Aubier, 1961.

———. *La Postérité spirituelle de Joachim de Flore*. 2 vols. Paris: Editions Lethielleux, 1979–81.

Delasanta, Rodney. "Sacrament and Sacrifice in the Pardoner's Tale." *Annuale Mediaevale* 14 (1973): 43–52.

Denifle, H. "Das Evangelium aeternum und die Commission zu Anagni." *Archiv für Literatur und Kirchengeschichte des Mittelalters* 1 (1885): 49–142.

Dronke, Peter. *Dante and Medieval Latin Traditions*. Cambridge: Cambridge University Press, 1986.

Dufeil, Michel-Marie. *Guillaume de Saint-Amour et la polémique universitaire parisienne, 1250–1259*. Paris: Picard, 1972.

Dussler, Luitpold. *Signorelli des Meisters Gemälde*. Stuttgart: Deutsche Verlags-Anstalt, 1927.

Economou, George D. *The Goddess Natura in Medieval Literature*. Cambridge, MA: Harvard University Press, 1972.

————. "The Vision's Aftermath in *Piers Plowman*: The Poetics of the Middle English Dream-Vision." *Genre* 18 (1985): 313–21.

Edyvean, W. *Anselm of Havelberg and the Theology of History*. Rome: Catholic Book Agency, 1972.

Eleen, Luba. *The Illustration of the Pauline Epistles in French and English Bibles of the Twelfth and Thirteenth Centuries*. Oxford: Clarendon, 1982.

Emmerson, Richard Kenneth. "Antichrist as Anti-Saint: The Significance of Abbot Adso's *Libellus de Antichristo*." *American Benedictine Review* 30 (1979): 175–90.

————. *Antichrist in the Middle Ages: A Study of Medieval Apocalypticism, Art, and Literature*. Seattle: University of Washington Press, 1981.

————. "The Apocalypse in Medieval Culture: An Overview." In *The Apocalypse in the Middle Ages*. Ed. Emmerson and McGinn.

————. "Apocalypse Now and Then." *Modern Language Quarterly* 46 (1985): 429–39.

————. "'Coveitise to Konne,' 'Goddes Privetee,' and Will's Ambiguous Visionary Experience in *Piers Plowman*." In *Visions of Piers Plowman: Essays in Honor of David C. Fowler*. Ed. Míċeál F. Vaughan. East Lansing: Colleagues Press, 1992.

————. "'Nowe Ys Common This Daye': Enoch and Elias, Antichrist, and the Structure of the Chester Cycle." In *"Homo, Memento Finis": The Iconography of Just Judgment in Medieval Art and Drama*. Ed. David Bevington, et al. Early Drama, Art and Music Monograph Series 6. Kalamazoo, MI: Medieval Institute Publications, 1985. Pp. 89–120.

————. "The Prophetic, the Apocalyptic, and the Study of Medieval Literature." In *Poetic Prophecy in Western Literature*. Ed. Jan Wojcik and Raymond-Jean Frontain. Rutherford, NJ: Fairleigh-Dickinson University Press, 1984. Pp. 40–54.

————. Review of Kathryn Kerby-Fulton, *Reformist Apocalypticism and Piers Plowman*. *Modern Philology* 90 (Nov. 1992).

————. "Wynkyn de Worde's *Byrthe and Lyfe of Antechryst* and Popular Eschatology on the Eve of the English Reformation." *Medievalia* 14 (1991, for 1988): 281–311.

Emmerson, Richard Kenneth, and Ronald B. Herzman. "Antichrist, Simon Magus, and Dante's *Inferno XIX*." *Traditio* 36 (1980): 373–98.

————. "The Apocalyptic Age of Hypocrisy: Faus Semblant and Amant in the *Roman de la Rose*." *Speculum* 62 (1987): 612–34.

————. "*The Canterbury Tales* in Eschatological Perspective." In *The Use and Abuse of Eschatology in the Middle Ages*. Ed. Verbeke, Verhelst, and Welkenhuysen. Pp. 404–24.

————. Review of V. A. Kolve, *Chaucer and the Imagery of Narrative*. *Studies in the Age of Chaucer* 7 (1985): 212–18.

Emmerson, Richard Kenneth, and Suzanne Lewis. "Census and Bibliography of Medieval Manuscripts Containing Apocalypse Illustrations, 800–1500." *Traditio* 40 (1984): 337–79; 41 (1985): 367–409; 42 (1986): 443–72.

Emmerson, Richard Kenneth, and Bernard McGinn, eds. *The Apocalypse in the Middle Ages*. Ithaca, NY: Cornell University Press, 1992.

Fansler, Dean S. *Chaucer and the Roman de la Rose*. Columbia University Studies in English and Comparative Literature 7. New York: Columbia University Press, 1914; rpt. Gloucester, MA: Peter Smith, 1965.

Farrer, Austin. *A Rebirth of Images: The Making of St. John's Apocalypse*. 1949; rpt. Albany: State University of New York Press, 1986.

Fleming, John V. "Chaucer and Erasmus on the Pilgrimage to Canterbury: An Iconographical Speculation." In *The Popular Literature of Medieval England*. Ed. Thomas J. Heffernan. Tennessee Studies in Literature 28. Knoxville: University of Tennessee Press, 1985. Pp. 148–66.

———. "Chaucer and the Visual Arts of His Time." In *New Perspectives in Chaucer Criticism*. Ed. Donald M. Rose. Norman, OK: Pilgrim Books, 1981. Pp. 121–36.

———. *From Bonaventure to Bellini*. Princeton, NJ: Princeton University Press, 1982.

———. "The Iconographic Unity of the Blessing for Brother Leo." *Franziskanische Studien* 63 (1981): 203–20.

———. *An Introduction to the Franciscan Literature of the Middle Ages*. Chicago: Franciscan Herald Press, 1977.

———. *Reason and the Lover*. Princeton, NJ: Princeton University Press, 1984.

———. *The "Roman de la Rose": A Study in Allegory and Iconography*. Princeton, NJ: Princeton University Press, 1969.

———. "The Summoner's Prologue: An Iconographic Adjustment." *Chaucer Review* 2 (1967): 95–107.

Foster, Kenelm. "The Canto of the Damned Popes: *Inferno* XIX." *Dante Studies* 87 (1969): 47–68.

Friedman, John Block. "Antichrist and the Iconography of Dante's Geryon." *Journal of the Warburg and Courtauld Institutes* 35 (1972): 108–22.

Ganim, John M. *Chaucerian Theatricality*. Princeton, NJ: Princeton University Press, 1990.

Gardiner, F. S. *The Pilgrimage of Desire: A Study of Theme and Genre in Medieval Literature*. Leiden: Brill, 1971.

Gaster, M. "The Letter of Toledo." *Folk-Lore* 13 (1902): 126–29.

Gellrich, Jesse M. *The Idea of the Book in the Middle Ages: Language Theory, Mythology, and Fiction*. Ithaca, NY: Cornell University Press, 1985.

———. "The Parody of Medieval Music in the *Miller's Tale*." *Journal of English and Germanic Philology* 23 (1974): 176–88.

Gibson, Gail McMurray. "Resurrection as Dramatic Icon in *The Shipman's Tale*." In *Signs and Symbols in Chaucer's Poetry*. Ed. J. P. Hermann and J. J. Burke, Jr. University, AL: University of Alabama Press, 1981. Pp. 102–12.

Glasser, Marc. "The Pardoner and the Host: Chaucer's Analysis of the Canterbury Game." *CEA Critic* 46 (1983–84): 37–45.

Glorieux, P. "Le conflit de 1252–1257 à la lumière du mémoire de Guillaume de Saint-Amour." *Recherches de théologie ancienne et médiévale* 24 (1957), 354–72.

Gordon, James D. "Chaucer's Retraction: A Review of Opinion." In *Studies in Medieval Literature*. Ed. MacEdward Leach. Philadelphia: University of Pennsylvania Press, 1961. Pp. 81–96.

Green, Louis. *Chronicle Into History: An Essay on the Interpretation of History in*

Florentine Fourteenth-Century Chronicles. Cambridge: Cambridge University Press, 1972.

Grundmann, Herbert. "Dante und Joachim von Fiore zu Paradiso X-XI." *Deutsches Dante-Jahrbuch* 14 (1932): 210–56.

———. "Die Papstprophetien des Mittelalters." *Archiv für Kulturgeschichte* 19 (1929): 77–138. Rpt. *Joachim von Fiore.* Monumenta Germaniae Historica Schriften 25.2. Hanover, 1977. Pp. 1–57.

Hanning, Robert W. "'You Have Begun a Parlous Pleye': The Nature and Limits of Dramatic Mimesis as a Theme in Four Middle English 'Fall of Lucifer' Cycle Plays." *Comparative Drama* 7 (1973): 22–50.

Harder, Kelsie B. "Chaucer's Use of the Mystery Play Tradition in the *Miller's Tale.*" *Modern Language Notes* 17 (1956): 193–98.

Hartley, Marta Powell. "Narcissus, Hermaphroditus, and Attis: Ovidian Lovers at the Fontaine d'Amors in Guillaume de Lorris's *Roman de la Rose.*" *PMLA* 101 (1986): 324–35.

Henderson, George. "The Damnation of Nero and Related Themes." In *The Vanishing Past: Studies in Medieval Art, Liturgy and Metrology Presented to Christopher Hohler.* Ed. A. Borg and A. Martindale. Oxford: Oxford University Press, 1981. Pp. 39–51.

Herzman, Ronald B. "Dante and Francis." *Franciscan Studies* 42 (1982): 96–114.

———. "Dante and the Apocalypse." In *The Apocalypse in the Middle Ages.* Ed. Emmerson and McGinn.

———. "The *Friar's Tale*: Chaucer, Dante, and the *Translatio Studii.*" *ACTA* 9 (1985): 1–17.

———. "Millstones: An Approach to the *Miller's Tale* and the *Reeve's Tale.*" *English Record* 18 (1977): 18–21, 26.

———. "The *Reeve's Tale*, Symkyn, and Simon the Magician." *The American Benedictine Review* 33 (1982): 325–33.

———. Review of Peter Dronke, *Dante and Medieval Latin Traditions. Studies in the Age of Chaucer* 9 (1987): 209–12.

Herzman, Ronald B., and William R. Cook. "Simon the Magician and the Medieval Tradition." *Journal of Magic History* 2 (1980): 28–43.

Herzman, Ronald B., and William A. Stephany. "'O miseri seguaci': Sacramental Inversion in *Inferno* XIX." *Dante Studies* 96 (1978): 39–65.

Hill, Thomas. Review of John Fleming, *Reason and the Lover. Speculum* 60 (1985): 973–77.

Horn, Hans-Jurgen. "Giezie und Simonie." *Jahrbuch für Antike und Christentum* 8/9 (1965/66): 189–202.

Howard, Donald R. *The Idea of the Canterbury Tales.* Berkeley: University of California Press, 1976.

———. *Writers and Pilgrims: Medieval Pilgrimage Narratives and their Posterity.* Berkeley: University of California Press, 1980.

Hult, David F. *Self-fulfilling Prophecies: Readership and Authority in the First Roman de la Rose.* Cambridge: Cambridge University Press, 1986.

Jager, Eric. "Reading the *Roman* Inside Out: The Dream of Croesus as a *Caveat Lector.*" *Medium Aevum* 57 (1988): 67–74.

Jungman, Robert E. "The Pardoner's Quarrel with the Host." *Philological Quarterly* 55 (1976): 279–81.

Kamlah, Wilhelm. *Apokalypse und Geschichtstheologie: Die mittelalterliche Auslegung der Apokalypse vor Joachim von Fiore.* Historische Studien 285. Berlin: Emil Ebering, 1935.

Kaske, Robert E. "The *Canticum Canticorum* in the *Miller's Tale.*" *Studies in Philology* 59 (1962): 479–500.

———. "Dante's 'DXV' and 'Veltro.'" *Traditio* 17 (1961): 185–254.

———. "Dante's *Purgatorio* XXXII and XXXIII: A Survey of Christian History." *University of Toronto Quarterly* 43 (1974): 193–214.

———. "The Seven *Status Ecclesiae* in *Purgatorio* XXXII and XXXIII." In *Dante, Petrarch, Boccaccio: Studies in the Italian Trecento in Honor of Charles S. Singleton.* Ed. Aldo S. Bernardo and Anthony L. Pellegrini. Medieval and Renaissance Texts and Studies 22. Binghamton: State University of New York Press, 1983. Pp. 89–113.

Kean, P. M. *Chaucer and the Making of English Poetry.* 2 vols. London: Routledge and Kegan Paul, 1972.

Keller, Joseph R. "The Topoi of Virtue and Vice: A Study of Some Features of Social Complaint in the Middle Ages." Dissertation, Columbia University, 1958.

Kerby-Fulton, Kathryn. *Reformist Apocalypticism and Piers Plowman.* Cambridge: Cambridge University Press, 1990.

Khinoy, Stephen A. "Inside Chaucer's Pardoner?" *Chaucer Review* 6 (1972): 255–67.

Kirk, Elizabeth. *The Dream Thought of Piers Plowman.* New Haven, CN: Yale University Press, 1972.

Klein, Peter. *Endzeiterwartung und Ritterideologie: Die englischen Bilderapokalypsen der Fruhgotik und MS Douce 180.* Graz: Akademische Druck-u. Verlagsanstalt, 1983.

Knapp, Robert S. "Penance, Irony, and Chaucer's Retraction." *Assays* 2 (1983): 45–67.

Kolve, V. A. *Chaucer and the Imagery of Narrative: The First Five Canterbury Tales.* Stanford, CA: Stanford University Press, 1984.

Lagorio, Valerie M. "The Apocalyptic Mode in the Vulgate Cycle of Arthurian Romances." *Philological Quarterly* 57 (1978): 1–22.

Landes, Richard. "Lest the Millennium be Fulfilled: Apocalyptic Expectations and the Pattern of Western Chronography 100–800 CE." In *The Use and Abuse of Eschatology in the Middle Ages.* Ed. Verbeke, Verhelst, and Welkenhuysen. Pp. 137–211.

Lawton, David. "The Subject of *Piers Plowman.*" *The Yearbook of Langland Studies* 1 (1987): 1–30.

Lee, Harold. "The Anti-Lombard Figures of Joachim of Fiore: A Reinterpretation." In *Prophecy and Millenarianism.* Ed. Williams. Pp. 127–42.

Leicester, H. Marshall, Jr. *The Disenchanted Self: Representing the Subject in the Canterbury Tales.* Berkeley: University of California Press, 1990.

Lerner, Robert E. "Antichrists and Antichrist in Joachim of Fiore." *Speculum* 60 (1985): 553–70.

————. "The Black Death and Western European Eschatological Mentalities." *American Historical Review* 86 (1981): 533–52.

————. "Frederick II, Alive, Aloft and Allayed in Franciscan-Joachite Eschatology." In *The Use and Abuse of Eschatology in the Middle Ages*. Ed. Verbeke, Verhelst, and Welkenhuysen. Pp. 359–84.

————. *The Heresy of the Free Spirit in the Later Middle Ages*. Berkeley: University of California Press, 1972.

————. "Joachim of Fiore's Breakthrough to Chiliasm." *Cristianesimo nella storia* 6 (1985): 489–512.

————. "On the Origins of the Earliest Latin Pope Prophecies: A Reconsideration." *Fälschungen im Mittelalter*. Monumenta Germaniae Historica Schriften 33.5. Hanover: Hahnsche Buchhandlung, 1988. Pp. 611–35.

————. "Poverty, Preaching, and Eschatology in the Revelation Commentaries of 'Hugh of St. Cher.'" In *The Bible in the Medieval World: Essays in Memory of Beryl Smalley*. Ed. Katherine Walsh and Diana Wood. Oxford: Blackwells, 1985. Pp. 157–89.

————. *The Powers of Prophecy: The Cedar of Lebanon Vision from the Mongol Onslaught to the Dawn of the Enlightenment*. Berkeley: University of California Press, 1983.

————. "Refreshment of the Saints: The Time After Antichrist as a Station for Earthly Progress in Medieval Thought." *Traditio* 32 (1976): 97–144.

Levitan, Alan. "The Parody of Pentecost in Chaucer's *Summoner's Tale*." *University of Toronto Quarterly* 40 (1971): 236–46.

Lewis, C. S. *The Allegory of Love*. Oxford: Oxford University Press, 1936.

Lewis, Suzanne. "*Tractatus adversus Judaeos* in the Gulbenkian Apocalypse." *Art Bulletin* 68 (1986): 543–66.

Little, A. G. "Guide to Franciscan Studies." *Études franciscaines* 40 (1928): 517–33; 41 (1929): 64–78.

Lobrichon, Guy. "L'Ordre de ce temps et les désordres de la fin: Apocalypse et société, du IXᵉ à la fin du XIᵉ siècle." In *The Use and Abuse of Eschatology in the Middle Ages*. Ed. Verbeke, Verhelst, and Welkenhuysen. Pp. 221–41.

Louis, René. *Le roman de la Rose: Essai d'interprétation de l'allegorisme érotique*. Paris: Honoré Champion, 1974.

Lumiansky, R. M. *Of Sondry Folk: The Dramatic Principle of the Canterbury Tales*. Austin: University of Texas Press, 1955.

Luria, Maxwell. *A Reader's Guide to the Roman de la Rose*. Hamden, CN: Archon, 1982.

McAlpine, Monica E. "The Pardoner's Homosexuality and How It Matters." *PMLA* 95 (1980): 8–22.

McGinn, Bernard. "Angel Pope and Papal Antichrist." *Church History* 47 (1978): 155–73.

————. *The Calabrian Abbot: Joachim of Fiore in the History of Western Thought*. New York: Macmillan, 1985.

————. "Early Apocalypticism: The Ongoing Debate." In *The Apocalypse in English Renaissance Thought and Literature*. Ed. C. A. Patrides and Joseph Wittreich. Ithaca, NY: Cornell University Press, 1984. Pp. 23–31.

————. "Joachim and the Sibyl." *Cîteaux* 24 (1973): 97–138.

————. "Joachim of Fiore's *Tertius Status*: Some Theological Appraisals." In *L'età dello Spirito*. Ed. Crocco. Pp. 219–36.

————. "Portraying Antichrist in the Middle Ages." In *The Use and Abuse of Eschatology in the Middle Ages*. Ed. Verbeke, Verhelst, and Welkenhuysen. Pp. 1–48.

————. "Symbolism in the Thought of Joachim of Fiore." In *Prophecy and Millenarianism*. Ed. Williams. Pp. 143–64.

————. "'Teste David cum Sibylla': The Significance of the Sibylline Tradition in the Middle Ages." In *Women of the Medieval World*. Ed. J. Kirshner and S. Wemple. New York: Oxford University Press, 1985. Pp. 7–35.

McKean, Sister M. Faith, R.S.M. "The Role of Faux Semblant and Astenance Constrainte in the *Roman de la Rose*." In *Romance Studies in Memory of E. Ham*. Ed. U. T. Holmes. Hayward, CA, 1967. Pp. 103–7.

McKeon, Peter R. "The Status of the University of Paris as *Parens scientiarum*: An Episode in the Development of its Autonomy." *Speculum* 39 (1964): 651–75.

McVeigh, Terrence A. "Chaucer's Portraits of the Pardoner and Summoner and Wyclif's *Tractatus de Simonia*." *Classical Folia* 20 (1974): 54–58.

Mâle, Emile. *The Gothic Image: Religious Art in France of the Thirteenth Century*. Trans. D. Nussey. New York: Harper and Row, 1972.

————. *Les saints: compagnons du Christ*. Paris: Paul Hartmann, 1958.

Mann, Jill. *Chaucer and Medieval Estates Satire: The Literature of Social Classes and the General Prologue to the Canterbury Tales*. Cambridge: Cambridge University Press, 1973.

Manselli, Raoul. "A proposito del Cristianesimo di Dante: Gioacchino da Fiore, gioachimismo, Spiritualismo francescano." In *Letteratura e critica: Studi in onore di Natalino Sapegno*. Rome: Bulzoni, 1975. 2:163–92.

Marshall, David F. "Unmasking the Last Pilgrim: How and Why Chaucer Used the Retraction to Close *The Tales of Canterbury*." *Christianity and Literature* 31 (1982): 55–74.

Meiss, Millard. *Painting in Florence and Siena after the Black Death*. Princeton, NJ: Princeton University Press, 1951; rpt. in paperback, 1978.

Miller, Clarence H., and Roberta B. Bosse. "Chaucer's Pardoner and the Mass." *Chaucer Review* 6 (1972): 171–84.

Millichap, Joseph R. "Transubstantiation in the *Pardoner's Tale*." *Bulletin of the Rocky Mountain Modern Language Association* 28 (1974): 104–8.

Mockler, Anthony. *Francis of Assisi: The Wandering Years*. London: Phaidon Press, 1940.

Moorman, John. *A History of the Franciscan Order From Its Origins to the Year 1517*. Oxford: Clarendon, 1968.

Musa, Mark. *Advent at the Gates*. Bloomington: Indiana University Press, 1974.

Nolan, Barbara. *The Gothic Visionary Perspective*. Princeton, NJ: Princeton University Press, 1977.

O'Connor, John J. "The Astrological Background of the *Miller's Tale*." *Speculum* 31 (1956): 120–25.

Owen, Charles A. "The Crucial Passages in Five of *The Canterbury Tales*: A Study of Irony and Symbol." *Journal of English and Germanic Philology* 52 (1953): 294–311.

Phelan, John Leddy. *The Millennial Kingdom of the Franciscans in the New World: A Study of the Writings of Geronimo de Mendieta (1525–1604)*. University of California Publications in History 42. 2nd ed. Berkeley: University of California Press, 1970.

Piehler, Paul. *The Visionary Landscape: A Study in Medieval Allegory*. Montreal: McGill-Queen's University Press, 1971.

Pittock, Malcolm. "The Pardoner's Tale and the Quest of Death." *Essays in Criticism* 24 (1974): 107–23.

Poggioli, Renato. "Tragedy or Romance? A Reading of the Paolo and Francesca Episode in Dante's *Inferno*." *PMLA* 72 (1957): 313–58.

Pratt, Robert A. "The Order of the *Canterbury Tales*." *PMLA* 66 (1951): 1141–67.

Quilligan, Maureen. "Allegory, Allegoresis, and the Deallegorization of Language: The *Roman de la Rose*, the *De planctu Naturae*, and the *Parlement of Foules*." In *Allegory, Myth, and Symbol*. Ed. Morton W. Bloomfield. Harvard English Studies 9. Cambridge, MA: Harvard University Press, 1981. Pp. 163–86.

Ratzinger, Joseph. *The Theology of History in St. Bonaventure*. Trans. Zachary Hayes. Chicago: Franciscan Herald Press, 1971.

Rauh, Horst Dieter. *Das Bild des Antichrist im Mittelalter: von Tyconius zum deutschen Symbolismus*. Beiträge zur Geschichte der Philosophie und Theologie des Mittelalters, n.s. 9. Münster: Aschendorff, 1973.

Reeves, Marjorie. "Dante and the Prophetic View of History." In *The World of Dante: Essays on Dante and His Times*. Ed. Cecil Grayson. Oxford: Clarendon, 1980. Pp. 44–60.

———. *The Influence of Prophecy in the Later Middle Ages: A Study in Joachimism*. Oxford: Clarendon, 1969.

———. "The Originality and Influence of Joachim of Fiore." *Traditio* 36 (1980): 269–313.

———. "The Third Age: Dante's Debt to Gioacchino da Fiore." In *L'età dello Spirito*. Ed. Antonio Crocco. Pp. 125–39.

Reeves, Marjorie, and Beatrice Hirsch-Reich. *The Figurae of Joachim of Fiore*. Oxford-Warburg Studies. Oxford: Clarendon, 1972.

———. "The Seven Seals in the Writings of Joachim of Fiore." *Recherches de théologie ancienne et médiévale* 21 (1954): 211–47.

Reiss, Edmund. "The Pilgrimage Narrative and the *Canterbury Tales*." *Studies in Philology* 67 (1970): 295–305.

Riess, Jonathan B. "La genesi degli affreschi del Signorelli per la Cappella Nuova." In *Il duomo di Orvieto*. Ed. Lucio Riccetti. Rome: Laterza, 1988. Pp. 247–83.

———. "Luca Signorelli's Frescoes in the Chapel of San Brizio as Reflections of their Time and Place." In *Renaissance Studies in Honor of Craig Hugh Smyth*. Ed. Andrew Morrogh, et al. Florence: Giunti Barbera, 1985. 2:383–93.

———. "Republicanism and Tyranny in Signorelli's *Rule of the Antichrist*." In *Art and Politics in Late Medieval and Renaissance Italy*. Ed. Charles Rosenberg. Notre Dame, IN: University of Notre Dame Press, 1990. Pp. 157–86.

Robertson, D. W. *A Preface to Chaucer: Studies in Medieval Perspectives.* Princeton, NJ: Princeton University Press, 1962.

Rode, Herbert. *Die Mittelalterlichen Glasmalereien des Kölner Domes.* Corpus vitrearum medii aevi, Deutschland 4.1. Berlin: Deutscher Verlag für Kunstwissenschaft, 1974.

Rosenberg, Bruce A. "Swindling Alchemist, Antichrist." *Centennial Review* 6 (1962): 566–80.

Rossi, Albert L. "'A l'ultimo suo': *Paradiso* XXX and Its Vergilian Context." *Studies in Medieval and Renaissance History* n.s. 4 (1981): 39–88.

Rusconi, Roberto. "Apocalittica ed escatologia nella predicazione di Bernardino da Siena." *Studi Medievali* 3rd ser., 22 (1981): 85–128.

Ryan, Lawrence V. "*Stornei, Gru, Columbe*: The Bird Images in *Inferno* V." *Dante Studies* 94 (1976): 25–45.

Ryding, William W. "Faus Semblant: Hero or Hypocrite?" *Romanic Review* 60 (1969): 163–67.

Salmi, Mario. *Luca Signorelli.* Novara: Instituto Geografico de Agostini, 1953.

Sayce, Olive. "Chaucer's 'Retractions': The Conclusion of the *Canterbury Tales* and Its Place in Literary Tradition." *Medium Ævum* 40 (1971): 230–48.

Scarpellini, Pietro. *Luca Signorelli.* Collana d'Arte 10. Florence: G. Barbera Editore, 1964.

Schnapp, Jeffrey T. *The Transfiguration of History at the Center of Dante's Paradiso.* Princeton, NJ: Princeton University Press, 1986.

Selge, Kurt-Victor. *L'origine delle opere di Gioacchino da Fiore.* In *L'attesa della fine dei tempi nel Medioevo.* Ed. Ovidio Capitani and Jürgen Miethke. Bologna: Il Mulino, 1990. Pp. 87–131.

Serper, Arié. "L'influence de Guillaume de Saint-Amour sur Rutebeuf." *Romance Philology* 17 (1963–64): 391–402.

Singleton, Charles S. "Inferno XIX: 'O Simon Mago!' " *Modern Language Notes* 80 (1965): 92–99.

Smith, Forrest S. *Secular and Sacred Visionaries in the Late Middle Ages.* New York: Garland, 1986.

Spearing, A. C. *Medieval Dream-Poetry.* Cambridge: Cambridge University Press, 1976.

Stephany, William A. "Biblical Allusions to Conversion in *Purgatorio XXI*." *Stanford Italian Review* 3 (1983): 141–62.

Sumption, Jonathan. *Pilgrimage: An Image of Mediaeval Religion.* Totowa, NJ: Rowman and Littlefield, 1975.

Szittya, Penn R. *The Antifraternal Tradition in Medieval Literature.* Princeton, NJ: Princeton University Press, 1986.

Szoverffy, J. "The Legends of St. Peter in Medieval Latin Hymns." *Traditio* 10 (1954): 275–322.

Töpfer, Bernhard. "Eine Handschrift des Evangelium aeternum des Gerardino von Borgo San Donnino." *Zeitschrift für Geschichtswissenschaft* 7 (1960): 156–63.

Troncarelli, Fabio, and Elena B. di Gioia. "Scrittura, testo, immagine in un manoscritto gioachimita." *Scrittura e civiltà* 5 (1981): 149–85.

Tuve, Rosemond. *Allegorical Imagery: Some Mediaeval Books and Their Posterity.* Princeton, NJ: Princeton University Press, 1966.

Van Dyke, Carolynn. *The Fiction of Truth: Structures of Meaning in Narrative and Dramatic Allegory*. Ithaca, NY: Cornell University Press, 1985.

Vaughan, Míčeál F. "Chaucer's Imaginative One-Day Flood." *Philological Quarterly* 60 (1981): 117–23.

Verbeke, Werner, Daniel Verhelst, and Andries Welkenhuysen, eds. *The Use and Abuse of Eschatology in the Middle Ages*. Mediaevalia Lovaniensia 15. Leuven: Leuven University Press, 1988.

Wall, John. "Penance as Poetry in the Late Fourteenth Century." In *Medieval English Religious and Ethical Literature: Essays in Honour of G. H. Russell*. Ed. Gregory Kratzmann and James Simpson. Cambridge: D. S. Brewer, 1986. Pp. 179–91.

Watts, Pauline Moffitt. "Prophecy and Discovery: On the Spiritual Origins of Christopher Columbus's 'Enterprise of the Indies.'" *American Historical Review* 90 (1985): 73–102.

Weldon, James F. G. "The Structure of Dream Visions in *Piers Plowman*." *Mediaeval Studies* 49 (1987): 254–81.

Wessley, Stephen E. *Joachim of Fiore and Monastic Reform*. American University Studies 7.72. New York: Lang, 1990.

West, Delno C. and Sandra Zimdars-Swartz. *Joachim of Fiore: A Study in Spiritual Perception and History*. Bloomington: Indiana University Press, 1983.

Westlund, Joseph. "The *Knight's Tale* as an Impetus for Pilgrimage." *Philological Quarterly* 43 (1964): 526–37.

Wetherbee, Winthrop. *Platonism and Poetry in the Twelfth Century: The Literary Influence of the School of Chartres*. Princeton, NJ: Princeton University Press, 1972.

Whitaker, Muriel A. "Pearl and Some Illustrated Apocalypse Manuscripts." *Viator* 12 (1981): 183–96.

Williams, Ann, ed. *Prophecy and Millenarianism: Essays in Honour of Marjorie Reeves*. London: Longman, 1980.

Wilson, Adrian. *The Making of the Nuremberg Chronicle*. 2nd ed. Amsterdam: Nico Israel, 1978.

Wilson, Adrian, and Joyce Lancaster Wilson. *A Medieval Mirror: Speculum Humanae Salvationis, 1324–1500*. Berkeley: University of California Press, 1984.

Wittreich, Joseph Anthony, Jr. *Visionary Poetics: Milton's Tradition and His Legacy*. San Marino, CA: Huntington Library, 1979.

Wood, Chauncey. *Chaucer and the Country of the Stars: Poetic Uses of Astrological Imagery*. Princeton, NJ: Princeton University Press, 1970.

Ziegler, Philip. *The Black Death*. Harmondsworth: Pelican Books, 1970.

Index

University of Pennsylvania Press
MIDDLE AGES SERIES
Edward Peters, General Editor

F. R. P. Akehurst, trans. *The* Coutumes de Beauvaisis *of Philippe de Beaumanoir.*
    1992
David Anderson. *Before the Knight's Tale: Imitation of Classical Epic in Boccaccio's*
    Teseida. 1988
Benjamin Arnold. *Count and Bishop in Medieval Germany: A Study of Regional*
    Power, 1100–1350. 1991
Mark C. Bartusis. *The Late Byzantine Army: Arms and Society, 1204–1453.* 1992
J. M. W. Bean. *From Lord to Patron: Lordship in Late Medieval England.* 1990
Uta-Renate Blumenthal. *The Investiture Controversy: Church and Monarchy from the*
    Ninth to the Twelfth Century. 1988
Daniel Bornstein, trans. *Dino Compagni's* Chronicle *of Florence.* 1986
Betsy Bowden. *Chaucer Aloud: The Varieties of Textual Interpretation.* 1987
James William Brodman. *Ransoming Captives in Crusader Spain: The Order of Mer-*
    ced on the Christian-Islamic Frontier. 1986
Otto Brunner (Howard Kaminsky and James Van Horn Melton, eds. and trans.).
    Land *and Lordship: Structures of Governance in Medieval Austria.* 1992
Robert I. Burns, S.J., ed. *Emperor of Culture: Alfonso X the Learned of Castile and*
    His Thirteenth-Century Renaissance. 1990
David Burr. *Olivi and Franciscan Poverty: The Origins of the* Usus Pauper *Contro-*
    versy. 1989
Thomas Cable. *The English Alliterative Tradition.* 1991
Anthony K. Cassell and Victoria Kirkham, eds. and trans. *Diana's Hunt/Caccia di*
    Diana: Boccaccio's First Fiction. 1991
Brigitte Cazelles. *The Lady as Saint: A Collection of French Hagiographic Romances*
    of the Thirteenth Century. 1991
Anne L. Clark. *Elisabeth of Schönau: A Twelfth-Century Visionary.* 1992
Willene B. Clark and Meradith T. McMunn, eds. *Beasts and Birds of the Middle*
    Ages: The Bestiary and Its Legacy. 1989
Richard C. Dales. *The Scientific Achievement of the Middle Ages.* 1973
Charles T. Davis. *Dante's Italy and Other Essays.* 1984
Katherine Fischer Drew, trans. *The Burgundian Code.* 1972
Katherine Fischer Drew, trans. *The Laws of the Salian Franks.* 1991
Katherine Fischer Drew, trans. *The Lombard Laws.* 1973
Robert D. Fulk. *A History of Old English Meter.* 1992
Nancy Edwards. *The Archaeology of Early Medieval Ireland.* 1990
Margaret J. Ehrhart. *The Judgment of the Trojan Prince Paris in Medieval Literature.*
    1987

Richard K. Emmerson and Ronald B. Herzman. *The Apocalyptic Imagination in Medieval Literature.* 1992

Felipe Fernández-Armesto. *Before Columbus: Exploration and Colonization from the Mediterranean to the Atlantic, 1229–1492.* 1987

Patrick J. Geary. *Aristocracy in Provence: The Rhône Basin at the Dawn of the Carolingian Age.* 1985

Peter Heath. *Allegory and Philosophy in Avicenna (Ibn Sînâ), with a Translation of the* Mi'râj Nâma. 1992

J. N. Hillgarth, ed. *Christianity and Paganism, 350–750: The Conversion of Western Europe.* 1986

Richard C. Hoffmann. *Land, Liberties, and Lordship in a Late Medieval Countryside: Agrarian Structures and Change in the Duchy of Wrocław.* 1990

Robert Hollander. *Boccaccio's Last Fiction: Il Corbaccio.* 1988

Edward B. Irving, Jr. *Rereading* Beowulf. 1989

C. Stephen Jaeger. *The Origins of Courtliness: Civilizing Trends and the Formation of Courtly Ideals, 939–1210.* 1985

William Chester Jordan. *The French Monarchy and the Jews: From Philip Augustus to the Last Capetians.* 1989

William Chester Jordan. *From Servitude to Freedom: Manumission in the Sénonais in the Thirteenth Century.* 1986

Ellen E. Kittell. *From* Ad Hoc *to Routine: A Case Study in Medieval Bureaucracy.* 1991

Alan C. Kors and Edward Peters, eds. *Witchcraft in Europe, 1100–1700: A Documentary History.* 1972

Barbara M. Kreutz. *Before the Normans: Southern Italy in the Ninth and Tenth Centuries.* 1992

E. Ann Matter. *The Voice of My Beloved: The Song of Songs in Western Medieval Christianity.* 1990

María Rosa Menocal. *The Arabic Role in Medieval Literary History.* 1987

A. J. Minnis. *Medieval Theory of Authorship.* 1988

Lawrence Nees. *A Tainted Mantle: Hercules and the Classical Tradition at the Carolingian Court.* 1991

Lynn H. Nelson, trans. *The Chronicle of San Juan de la Peña: A Fourteenth-Century Official History of the Crown of Aragon.* 1991

Charlotte A. Newman. *The Anglo-Norman Nobility in the Reign of Henry I: The Second Generation.* 1988

Joseph F. O'Callaghan. *The Cortes of Castile-León, 1188–1350.* 1989

William D. Paden, ed. *The Voice of the Trobairitz: Perspectives on the Women Troubadours.* 1989

Edward Peters. *The Magician, the Witch, and the Law.* 1982

Edward Peters, ed. *Christian Society and the Crusades, 1198–1229:* Sources in Translation, including The Capture of Damietta by Oliver of Paderborn. 1971

Edward Peters, ed. *The First Crusade*: The Chronicle of Fulcher of Chartres *and Other Source Materials.* 1971

Edward Peters, ed. *Heresy and Authority in Medieval Europe.* 1980

James M. Powell. *Albertanus of Brescia: The Pursuit of Happiness in the Early Thirteenth Century.* 1992

James M. Powell. *Anatomy of a Crusade, 1213–1221*. 1986

Michael Resler, trans. Erec *by Hartmann von Aue*. 1987

Pierre Riché (Jo Ann McNamara, trans.). *Daily Life in the World of Charlemagne*. 1978

Jonathan Riley-Smith. *The First Crusade and the Idea of Crusading*. 1986

Joel T. Rosenthal. *Patriarchy and Families of Privilege in Fifteenth-Century England*. 1991

Steven D. Sargent, ed. and trans. *On the Threshold of Exact Science: Selected Writings of Anneliese Maier on Late Medieval Natural Philosophy*. 1982

Sarah Stanbury. *Seeing the* Gawain-*Poet: Description and the Act of Perception*. 1992

Thomas C. Stillinger. *The Song of Troilus: Lyric Authority in the Medieval Book*. 1992

Susan Mosher Stuard. *A State of Deference: Ragusa/Dubrovnik in the Medieval Centuries*. 1992

Susan Mosher Stuard, ed. *Women in Medieval History and Historiography*. 1987

Susan Mosher Stuard, ed. *Women in Medieval Society*. 1976

Jonathan Sumption. *The Hundred Years War: Trial by Battle*. 1992

Ronald E. Surtz. *The Guitar of God: Gender, Power, and Authority in the Visionary World of Mother Juana de la Cruz (1481–1534)*. 1990

Patricia Terry, trans. *Poems of the Elder Edda*. 1990

Frank Tobin. *Meister Eckhart: Thought and Language*. 1986

Ralph V. Turner. *Men Raised from the Dust: Administrative Service and Upward Mobility in Angevin England*. 1988

Harry Turtledove, trans. *The* Chronicle *of Theophanes: An English Translation of* Anni Mundi *6095–6305 (A.D. 602–813)*. 1982

Mary F. Wack. Lovesickness in the Middle Ages: *The* Viaticum *and Its Commentaries*. 1990

Benedicta Ward. *Miracles and the Medieval Mind: Theory, Record, and Event, 1000–1215*. 1982

Suzanne Fonay Wemple. *Women in Frankish Society: Marriage and the Cloister, 500–900*. 1981

This book has been set in Linotron Galliard. Galliard was designed for Mergenthaler in 1978 by Matthew Carter. Galliard retains many of the features of a sixteenth-century typeface cut by Robert Granjon but has some modifications that give it a more contemporary look.

Printed on acid-free paper.